AF701321

HISTORIES OF ECONOMIC THOUGHT

RESEARCH IN THE HISTORY OF ECONOMIC THOUGHT AND METHODOLOGY

Series Editors: Warren J. Samuels and Jeff E. Biddle

RESEARCH IN THE HISTORY OF ECONOMIC THOUGHT AND METHODOLOGY VOLUME 21-B

HISTORIES OF ECONOMIC THOUGHT

EDITED BY

WARREN J. SAMUELS

Department of Economics, Michigan State University, USA

2003

JAI

An Imprint of Elsevier Science

Amsterdam – Boston – London – New York – Oxford – Paris
San Diego – San Francisco – Singapore – Sydney – Tokyo

ELSEVIER SCIENCE Ltd
The Boulevard, Langford Lane
Kidlington, Oxford OX5 1GB, UK

© 2003 Elsevier Science Ltd. All rights reserved.

This work is protected under copyright by Elsevier Science, and the following terms and conditions apply to its use:

Photocopying
Single photocopies of single chapters may be made for personal use as allowed by national copyright laws. Permission of the Publisher and payment of a fee is required for all other photocopying, including multiple or systematic copying, copying for advertising or promotional purposes, resale, and all forms of document delivery. Special rates are available for educational institutions that wish to make photocopies for non-profit educational classroom use.

Permissions may be sought directly from Elsevier Science Global Rights Department, PO Box 800, Oxford OX5 1DX, UK; phone: (+44) 1865 843830, fax: (+44) 1865 853333, e-mail: permissions@elsevier.co.uk. You may also contact Global Rights directly through Elsevier's home page (http://www.elsevier.com), by selecting 'Obtaining Permissions'.

In the USA, users may clear permissions and make payments through the Copyright Clearance Center, Inc., 222 Rosewood Drive, Danvers, MA 01923, USA; phone: (+1) (978) 7508400, fax: (+1) (978) 7504744, and in the UK through the Copyright Licensing Agency Rapid Clearance Service (CLARCS), 90 Tottenham Court Road, London W1P 0LP, UK; phone: (+44) 207 631 5555; fax: (+44) 207 631 5500. Other countries may have a local reprographic rights agency for payments.

Derivative Works
Tables of contents may be reproduced for internal circulation, but permission of Elsevier Science is required for external resale or distribution of such material.
Permission of the Publisher is required for all other derivative works, including compilations and translations.

Electronic Storage or Usage
Permission of the Publisher is required to store or use electronically any material contained in this work, including any chapter or part of a chapter.

Except as outlined above, no part of this work may be reproduced, stored in a retrieval system or transmitted in any form or by any means, electronic, mechanical, photocopying, recording or otherwise, without prior written permission of the Publisher.
Address permissions requests to: Elsevier Science Global Rights Department, at the mail, fax and e-mail addresses noted above.

Notice
No responsibility is assumed by the Publisher for any injury and/or damage to persons or property as a matter of products liability, negligence or otherwise, or from any use or operation of any methods, products, instructions or ideas contained in the material herein. Because of rapid advances in the medical sciences, in particular, independent verification of diagnoses and drug dosages should be made.

First edition 2003

Library of Congress Cataloging in Publication Data
A catalog record from the Library of Congress has been applied for.

British Library Cataloguing in Publication Data
A catalogue record from the British Library has been applied for.

ISBN: 0-7623-0997-0
ISSN: 0743-4154 (Series)

∞ The paper used in this publication meets the requirements of ANSI/NISO Z39.48-1992 (Permanence of Paper).
Printed in The Netherlands.

CONTENTS

AN 1880 LIST OF REFERENCES IN ECONOMICS

Edited by Warren J. Samuels

The following is a list of references in economics dated Summer 1880. I am not sure of how the original document came into my possession. It is possible that the list is that of Richard T. Ely, but Ely was studying in Heidelberg in 1880. Because of the numerous errors and partial omissions, the list likely was recorded by a student in a class.

The original document generally presents last name, initial(s), and the title of the work – sometimes no title and often a short or descriptive title {noted, within braces, in cases of possible misapprehension}. I have tried to provide a complete reference (including author dates of birth and death) for each item, such as would have been available in 1880. In some cases more than one edition was available; I have generally given only one. In some cases, the firm is a printer, not a publisher as such. Where I have had a problem, I have indicated so by a question mark placed within braces: {?}. Braces are also used to indicate the original entry where this seems useful. Square brackets [ ] are as found in the original document. Whereas the items in the original document were not always in alphabetical order, they are placed so here – with the exception of "Truman," found in "F" and unidentified.

Despite its uncertain provenance, the list provides one insight into what seemed to count in either constituting or relevancy to economics, for some unknown reason, in 1880.

The list has several features or aspects: It reflects attention to economic history, currency questions, population, and the cultural and ethnographic conditions of economic life. Not surprisingly, the strong presence of Henry C.

Histories of Economic Thought, Volume 21-B, pages 1–8.
© 2003 Published by Elsevier Science Ltd.
ISBN: 0-7623-0997-0

Carey – his work, his circle and his publishing firm – are evident. The principal works of Adam Smith, Thomas Robert Malthus, David Ricardo, James and John Stuart Mill and William Stanley Jevons are included, though neither Karl Rodbertus nor Karl Marx nor Pierre Joseph Proudhon. The concentration seems to be on economic institutions and the factors and forces operative in economic life, and not, or not so much if at all, on the theories of value and price, the market and the price mechanism. The focus is on the actual economic system and its attendant array of policies, and, not at all surprisingly for 1880 (Jevons not withstanding), not on some pure abstract model of the economy.

I am indebted to Marianne Johnson for help in identifying and completing various entries.

SUMMER 1880

BOOKS OF REFERENCE

Atkinson, William. *Principles of Social and Political Economy*. London: Longman, Brown, Green, Longmans, and Roberts, 1858. {Principles of Political Economy}

Babbage, Charles. 1791–1871. *On the Economy of Machinery and Manufactures*. London: Knight, 1835.

Bagehot, Walter. 1826–1877. *Physics and Politics*. New York: D. Appleton, 1873.

Bastiat, Frédéric. 1801–1850. *Essays on Political Economy*. Chicago, IL: Western News Co., 1869. {Essays}

Bentham, Jeremy. 1748–1832. *The Theory of Legislation*. Boston, MA: Weeks, Jordan & Co., 1840.

Buckle, Henry Thomas. 1821–1862. *History of Civilization in England*. 2 vols. New York: D. Appleton, 1858–1862.

Blake, William P. 1826–1910. *The Production of the Precious Metals*. New York: G. P. Putnam & Sons, 1869. {Precious Metals}

Burton, John Hill. 1809–1881. *Political and Social Economy: Its Practical Application*. Edinburgh: Chambers, 1849. {Principles of Political Economy}

Byles, Sir John Barnard. 1801–1884. *Sophisms of Free-Trade and Popular Political Economy Examined*. London: Seeleys (4th ed.), 1850 (8th ed.), 1851 (9th ed.), Simpkin, Marshall & Co., 1870. (1st American ed.), from (9th English ed.), Philadelphia: H. C. Baird, 1872.

Carey, Henry Charles. 1793–1879. *Essay on the Rate of Wages*. Philadelphia, PA: Carey, Lea & Blanchard, 1835. {Essay on Wages}

Carey, Henry Charles. 1793–1879. *Principles of Political Economy*. Philadelphia, PA: Carey, Lea & Blanchard, 1837–1840.

Carey, Henry Charles. 1793–1879. *The Unity of Law; As Exhibited in the Relations of Physical, Social, Mental and Moral Science*. Philadelphia, PA: H. C. Baird, 1872. {H. S. Carey, Limits of Law}

Carey, Henry Charles. 1793–1879. *Miscellaneous Works of Henry C. Carey*. (2 Vols). Philadelphia, PA: B. C. Baird, 1865[?]. Or, *Miscellaneous Papers on the National Finances, the Currency, and Other Economic Subjects*. Philadelphia, PA: B. C. Baird, 1875. {Miscellaneous}

Champlin, James Tift. 1811–1882. Lessons on Political Economy. New York: A. S. Barnes & Co., 1868.

Cooper, Thomas. 1759–1839. *Lectures on the Elements of Political Economy* (2nd ed.) with additions. Columbia, SC: M'Morris & Wilson, 1829. {Lectures on Political Economy}

Cunningham, Timothy. –1789. *The History of Our Customs, Aids, Subsidies, National Debts, and Taxes: from William the Conqueror, to the Present Year*. London: W. Griffin, 1773. {History of Taxes}

Curtis, George Ticknor. 1812–1894. *Life of Daniel Webster*. New York: D. Appleton, 1872, c.1869.

De Quincey, Thomas. 1785–1859. *The Logic of Political Economy*. Boston: Ticknor and Fields, 1859.

De Quincey, Thomas. 1785–1859. *Politics and Political Economy*. New York: Houghton Mifflin [1877]. {Political Economy}

Dewey, Orville. 1794–1882. *Moral Views of Commerce, Society, and Politics*. New York, 1838.

Duncombe, Charles. 1819–1843. *Duncombe's Free Banking: An Essay on Banking, Currency, Finance, Exchanges, and Political Economy*. Cleveland, OH: Sanford, 1841. {Dunecrub [?], C. Free Banking}

Encyclopedia Brittanica (8th ed.), Boston, Little, Brown 1852–1868. (9th ed.), New York: Samuel L. Hall, 1875–1889. Political Economy

Elder, William. 1806–1885. *Questions of the Day: Economic and Social*. Philadelphia, PA: H. C. Baird, 1871.

Fawcett, Henry. 1833–1884. *Manual of Political Economy*. (5th ed.), revised and enlarged. London: Macmillan, 1876.

Ferguson, Adam. 1723–1816. *Principles of Moral and Political Science* (2 Vols). Edinburgh: W. Creech; London: A. Strahan and T. Cadell, 1792.

Fourier, Charles. 1772–1817. Oeuvres Complétes de Ch. Fourier. 6 vols. Paris: Librairie Sociétaire, 1841–1848.

Foster, Thomas Campbell. 1813–1882. *Letters on the Condition of the People of Ireland*. London: Chapman and Hall, 1846. {The Condition of Ireland}

Truman,. {Group Politics} {Out of alphabetical sequence? Freeman?

{Garvier, [ ] J. Principle of Population}. Possibly, Sir Archibald Alison [1792–1867], *The Principles of Population, and Their Connection with Human Happiness*. Edinburgh: W. Blackwood and Sons, 1840; or John Weyland, 1774–1854, *The Principles of Population and Production, as They are Affected by the Progress of Society; with a view to Moral and Political Consequences*. London: Baldwin, Cradock and Joy, 1816.

Godwin, William. 1756–1836. *An Enquiry Concerning Political Justice, and Its Influence on General Virtue and Happiness*. London: Longman, Hurst, Rees, Orme and Brown, 1820. 1st American edition, from 2nd London edition, Philadelphia, PA: Bioren and Madan, 1796.

Godwin, William. 1756–1836. Of Population: *An Enquiry Concerning the Power of Increase in the Numbers of Mankind, Being an Answer to Mr. Malthus's Essay on that Subject*. London: Longman, Hurst, Rees, Orme and Brown, 1820.

Greg, William R. 1809–1881. [Gray, W. R., in original] {?} *Essays on Political and Social Science, Contributed Chiefly to the Edinburgh Review* (2 Vols). London: Longman, Brown, Green and Longmans, 1853.

Gurvey [?] J. J. Colloquy with Dr. [ ]

Guyot, Arnold [Henry]. 1807–1884. *The Earth and Man*. London: J. W. Parker and Son, 1852.

Hamilton, Robert. 1743–1829. *The Progress of Society*. London: J. Murray, 1830.

Hayes, J. L. Possibly John L. Hayes. 1812–1887. *An Argument for a Protective Tariff*. Cambridge, MA: Wilson, 1880.

Howard, James. 1821–1889. *Continental Farming and Peasantry*. London: W. Ridgway, 1870.

Hume, David. 1711–1776. *Political Discourses*. Edinburgh: A. Kincaid and A. Donaldson, 1752. {Essays (Money)}

Hume, David. 1711–1776. *Philosophical Works*. Boston: Little, Brown, 1854. [Works]

Jacob, William. 1762?–1851. *An Historical Inquiry into the Production and Consumption of the Precious Metals*. Philadelphia, PA: Carey & Lea, 1832. {Precious Metals}

Jevons, William Stanley. 1835–1882. *The Theory of Political Economy*. London and New York: Macmillan, 1871.

Jevons, William Stanley. 1835–1882. *Money and the Mechanism of Exchange* (4th ed.), London: C. K. Paul & Co., 1878.

Kant, Immanuel. 1724–1804. *Physische Geographie*. Konigsberg: Gobbels und Unzer, 1802. {Kant, E. Physical Geography} Possibly John Lee Comstock [1789–1858], *A Treatise on Mathematical and Physical Geography*.

Hartford: Packard and Brown, 1837; or George Perkins Marsh [1801–1882], *Man and Nature; or, Physical Geography as Modified by Human Action*. New York: C. Scribner & Co., 1864.

Kidd, John. 1775–1851. *On the Adaptation of External Nature to the Physical Condition of Man, Principally with Reference to the Supply of his Wants, and the Exercise of his Intellectual Faculties*. New ed. Philadelphia, PA: Carey, Lea & Blanchard, 1836. {Adaptation of Nature to Man}

Levi, Leone. 1821–1888. *Commercial Law, Its Principles and Administration* (2 Vols). London: W. Benning & Co., 1850–1852.

Lieber, Francis. 1800–1872. *Essays on Property and Labor, as Connected with Natural Law and the Constitution of Society*. New York: Harper & Bros., 1842.

Leap [?], S [?] M. {English Money}

Linderman, Henry Richard. 1825–1879. *Money and Legal Tender in the United States*. New York: Putnam, 1878.

Locke, John. 1632–1704. *The Works of John Locke*. London: John Churchill, 1714. London: D. Browne, 1759. London: T. Longman, B. Law, 1794. {Works} {Two entries}

McCulloch, John Ramsey. 1789–1864. *The Principles of Political Economy, with a Sketch of the Rise and Progress of the Science*. Edinburgh: W. and C. Tait, 1825.

McCulloch, John Ramsey. 1789–1864. *A Dictionary, Practical, Theoretical, and Historical, of Commerce and Commercial Navigation*. New ed. London: Longmans, Green, 1875.

McKean, Kate. *Manual of Social Science; Being a Condensation of the "Principles of Social Science" of H. C. Carey*. Philadelphia, PA: H. C. Baird, 1864.

Maine, Henry Sumner. 1822–1888. *Ancient Law; Its Connection with the Early History of Society*. 3rd American ed., from 5th London ed. New York: Henry Holt and Co., 1871, 1880.

Maine, Henry Sumner. 1822–1888. Possibly *Lectures on the Early History of Institutions*. New York: H. Holt & Co., 1875, 1876, 1880; London: J. Murray, (1st ed.), 1875 (3rd ed.), 1880. Or, *Village-Communities in the East and West*, London: J. Murray (1st ed.), 1871 (3rd ed.), 1876. {Maine, H. S. [?] Tillage}

Malthus, Thomas Robert. 1766–1834. *An Essay on the Principle of Population; or, A View of its Past and Present Effects on Human Happiness*. 2 vols. London: J. Murray, 1817; 1st American ed., from 3rd London editition, Washington, D.C.: R. C. Weightman, 1809.

Malthus, Thomas Robert. 1766–1834. *Principles of Political Economy*. London: J. Murray, 1820.

Mill, James. 1773–1836. *Elements of Political Economy*. London: Baldwin, Cradock and Joy, 1821. {Principles of Political Economy}

Mill, John Stuart. 1806–1873. (3 Vols). *Dissertations and Discussions; Political, Philosophical, and Historical*. London: Longmans, Green, Reader and Dyer, 1867.

More, Sir Thomas. 1478–1535. *Utopia*. Boston, MA: Lincolnshire, R. Roberts, 1878.

Morris, William O'Connor. 1824–1904. Likely, *Letters on the Land Question of Ireland*. London: Longmans, Green and Co., 1870. [Irish Question}

Necker, Jacques. 1732–1804. *A Treatise on the Administration of the Finances of France*. London: J. Walter, 1785. [French Finance]

Parsons, William Franklin. (1834–). *Parsons' Hand-Book of Forms: A Compendium of Business and Social Rules*. 4th edition, revised and enlarged. Battle Creek, MI: J. E. White, 1882. {Parson, Laws for Business Men} {Unable to locate earlier edition}

Perry, Arthur Latham. 1830–1905. *An Introduction to Political Economy*. New York: Scribner, Armstrong & Co., 1877.

Plato. 427–327 B.C. *The Republic*. Benjamin Jowett, translator. First and second editions were included in his translation of *The Dialogues*, Oxford: Clarendon Press, 1st edition, 4 vols., 1871; 2nd edition, 5 vols., 1875. The 3rd edition of *The Republic* was published separately in 1888; the 3rd (and final) edition of *The Dialogues* was published in 1892.

Porter, George Richardson. 1792–1852. *The Progress of the Nation, in its Various Social and Economical Relations, from the Beginning of the Nineteenth Century*. London: J. Murray, 1851.

Potter, Alonzo. 1800–1865. *Political Economy; Its Objects, Uses, and Principles; Considered with Reference to the Condition of the American People*. New York: Harper (1841).

Prichard, James Cowles. 1786–1848. *The Natural History of Man: Comprising Inquiries into the Modifying Influence of Physical and Moral Agencies on the Different Tribes of the Human Family*. London: H. Baillièr, 1843. Or, *Researches into the Physical History of Man*. London: J. and A. Arch, 1813. {Physical [?] History of Mankind}

Raguet, Condy. 1784–1842. *The Principles of Free Trade*. Philadelphia, PA: Carey, Lee and Blanchard, 1835.

Raguet, Condy. 1784–1842. *A Treatise on Currency and Banking*. London: Ridgway and J. Miller, 1839, 2nd ed. 1840.

Ramsay, George. 1800–1871. *An Essay on the Distribution of Wealth.* Edinburgh: A. and C. Black, 1836.

Rau, Karl Heinrich. 1792–1870. *Grundsätze der Finanzwissenschaft* (2 Vols, 3rd ed.), Heidelberg: C. F. Winter, 1850–1851.

Rau, Karl Heinrich. 1792–1870. *Grundsätze der Volkswirthschaftslehre.* Heidelberg: C. F. Winder, 1860.

Ricardo, David. 1772–1823. *Principles of Political Economy and Taxation.* London: John Murray, 1821.

Rickards, Sir George Kettilby. 1812–1889. *Population and Capital.* London: Longman, Brown, Green and Longmans, 1854.

Roscher, Wilhelm. 1817–1894. *Die Grundlagen der Nationalökonomie.* Stuttgart: Cotta, 1864.

Sargant, William Lucas. 1809–1889. *Social Innovators and Their Schemes.* London: Smith, Elder and Co., 1858.

Sargant, William Lucas. 1809–1889. *Robert Owen and his Social Philosophy.* London: Smith, Elder and Co., 1860.

Say, Jean Baptiste. 1767–1832. *A Treatise on Political Economy.* Philadelphia, PA: J. B. Lippincott, 1867. {Principles of Political Economy}

Schuckers, Jacob W. 1822 or 1823–1901. *The Finances: Panics and Specie-Payments.* Philadelphia, PA: J. Campbell & Son, 1874. Philadelphia, PA: Henry Carey Baird, 1877. {Finance and Currency}

Schuckers, Jacob W. 1822 or 1823–1901. *A Brief Account of the Finances and Paper Money of the Revolutionary War.* Philadelphia, PA: J. Campbell, 1874. {Finance of Revolution}

Seaman, Ezra C. 1805–1880. *Essays on The Progress of Nations, in Civilization, Productive Industry, Wealth, and Population.* New York: Scribner, 1852.

Simpson, Stephen. 1789–1854. *The Working Man's Manual: A New Theory of political Economy, on the Principle of Production the Source of Wealth.* Philadelphia, PA: T. L. Bonsal, 1831. {The Workingman's Journal)

Sismondi, J.-C.-L. Simonde de Sismondi. 1773–1842. *Nouveaux Principes d'Economie Politique.* 2nd ed. Paris: Delaunay, 1827. {[Principles of Political Economy}

Sismondi, J.-C.-L. Simonde de Sismondi. 1773–1842. *Political Economy and the Philosophy of Government.* London: J. Chapman, 1847. {Political Economy}

Smith, Adam. 1723–1790. *An Inquiry into Nature and Causes of the Wealth of Nations* (2 Vols, 2nd ed.). Oxford: Clarendon Press, 1880. London and New York: T. Nelson and Sons, 1865.

Spencer, Herbert. 1820–1903. *Illustrations of Universal Progress.* New York: D. Appleton, 1865, 1880.

Spencer, Herbert. 1820–1903. *Social Statics*. New York: D. Appleton, 1873.

Sullivan, Sir Edward Robert. 1826–1899. *Protection to Native Industry*. London: E. Stanford, 1870.

Thompson, William. 1775–1833. *An Inquiry into the Principles of the Distribution of Wealth Most Conducive to Human Happiness*. London: W. S. Orr and Co., 1850.

Tucker, George. 1775–1861. *The Laws of Wages, Profit, and Rent, Investigated*. Philadelphia, PA: E. L. Carey & A. Hart, 1837. {Tupper [?], G.}

Wakefield, Edward Gibbon. 1796–1862. *A View of the Art of Colonization*. London: J. W. Parker, 1849. [Colonization]

Walker, Alexander. 1779–1852. *Intermarriage; or, The Mode in Which . . . Beauty, Health and Intellect Result from Certain Unions*. New York, 1843, from 6th London edition. Philadelphia, PA: Lindsay & Blakiston, 1866.

Walker, Amasa. 1799–1875. *The Science of Wealth; A Manual of Political Economy*. Boston: Little, Brown, 1869.

Webster, Noah. 1758–1843. *Miscellaneous Papers on Political and Commercial Subjects*. New York: E. Belden & Co., 1802. Or, *A Collection of Papers on Political, Literary, and Moral Subjects*. New York: Webster & Clark, 1843. {Papers}

Wollstonecraft, Mary. 1759–1797. *A Vindication of the Rights of Woman*. New York: C. Blanchard, 1856. {Woman's R[ole?]}

Wayland, Francis. 1796–1865. *The Elements of Moral Science*. Boston, MA: Gould and Lincoln, 1860.

Whittle, C. [?]

Whitney, Josiah Dwight. 1819–1896. *The Metallic Wealth of the United States, Described and Compared with that of Other Countries*. Philadelphia, PA: Lippincott, Grambo & Co., 1854.

Young, Arthur. 1741–1820. *A Six Month Tour Through the North of England*. London: W. Strahan, 1770, 1771.

Young, Arthur. 1741–1820. *A Tour in Ireland*. London: T. Cadell, 1780. {[Foreign] Tour}

Young, Edward. 1814–1909. *Labor in Europe and America*. Montreal: Dawson Bros., 1879.

CHARLES HENRY HULL'S SYLLABUS OF LECTURES ON THE HISTORY OF ECONOMIC THEORIES, CORNELL UNIVERSITY, 1895

Edited by Warren J. Samuels

The syllabus reproduced below, dated 1895, is a synopsis of lectures on the history of economic theories given by Charles Henry Hull at Cornell University supplemented by lists of references.

The document was located on the internet through FirstSearch and OCLC [http://firstsearch.oclc.org] on August 14, 1999. A copy was acquired from the John Hay Library of Brown University through Interlibrary Loan at Michigan State University in September 1999. It is published here with the permission of the John Hay Library of Brown University. Supplementary materials were provided by the Division of Rare and Manuscript Collections, Carl A. Kroch Library, Cornell University.

Charles Henry Hull lived almost his entire life in Ithaca, New York. He was born there on September 29, 1864. He graduated from Cornell University in 1889, when he was appointed assistant librarian, and after two years' study in Germany received his Ph.D. from the University of Halle in 1892. Returning to Cornell, Hull had a remarkable career in teaching, administration and public service. He was appointed Assistant Professor of Political Economy in 1893, Professor of American History in 1901, and Goldwin Smith Professor of

Histories of Economic Thought, Volume 21-B, pages 9–29.
© 2003 Published by Elsevier Science Ltd.
ISBN: 0-7623-0997-0

American History in 1912. He served as Secretary of the University Faculty, Dean of the College of Arts and Sciences, and Faculty representative to the Board of Trustees. He also served in a number of civic organizations, in many of them as president, including the local Community Chest, Hospital Association, Chamber of Commerce, Board of Education, and Cornell Library Association. He served as secretary and treasurer of the American Economic Association and editor of its Reports and Proceedings. He retired in September 1931, and died on July 15, 1936. His papers are in the Cornell University Library. Best known for his collection, *The Economic Writings of Sir William Petty* (two volumes, Cambridge University Press, 1899, reprinted by A. M. Kelley, 1963–1964, and Routledge/Thoemmes Press, 1997), he also published "Petty's Place in the History of Economic Theory," *Quarterly Journal of Economics*," Vol. 14 (May 1900), pp. 7–40; "The Service of Statistics to History," *Quarterly Publications of the American Statistical Association*, Vol. 14, n.s. No. 105, March 1914, pp. 30–39; Graunt or Petty? The Authorship of the Observations upon the Bills of Morality (Boston: Ginn, 1896, in part reprinted from *Political Science Quarterly*, Vol. 11 (March 1896), pp. 105–132; and *Debates on the Declaratory Act and the Repeal of the Stamp Act, 1776* (New York, 1912).

Historians of economic thought will be principally interested in the picture of the history of economic theory presented by Hull and in the references, both primary and secondary, which he chose to provide his students.

Hull presents the genesis of economic theory to have been the emergence of the modern commercial and industrial society. We read in the introduction that

> In modern times political economy begins as a theory of prosperity, to be achieved by governmental guidance of trade and industry. Transition, in latter half of eighteenth century, with industrial progress and with dissemination of political philosophy of "natural" liberty, to a conviction that prosperity must result from free industry and individual enterprise.

The genesis of economic theory encompasses the periods of both Mercantilist and Classical Economics and is tied to the new conditions of trade and production and their correlative phenomena:

> Transition from mediaeval industrial society, regulated by the relations of persons, to modern industrial society, based on the exchange of things. Phases of the transition which chiefly evoked and shaped early economic theories: the new gold (rise of prices), centralization of government (increased taxes, debased coinage), extension of commerce.

The synopsis continues:

> Elaborated in France by the physiocrats (ca. 1750 ff.) and in England by Adam Smith (1776) and his followers. Industrial changes of the 18th century made room for new economic theories. Economists regarded the new phenomena in the light of a new political doctrine:

> the Law of Nature – Stoicism, jus gentium of the Roman lawyers; Epicureanism, and the social compact; Grotius, Hobbes, Locke, Rousseau; the state of nature and natural rights. Fusion with theological notion of a divine harmony in creation. Resultant individualism. Timeliness of these negative theories.

The key is the sentence, "Industrial changes of the 18th century made room for new economic theories." That Hull considers the new theories both normatively statused and ontologically grounded is indicated in the ensuing discussion that concludes, "Timeliness of these negative theories."

Hull either is unaware of an internal tension in his treatment of the Physiocratic theory or, perhaps more likely, calls attention to it. I refer to the following lines:

> An objective theory, emphasizing, under the influence of natural science, the physical, neglecting the institutional limitations of industrial society. The three classes of society.

The crux of the interpretive problem resides in the status given to the clause, "neglecting the institutional limitations of industrial society" and the next sentence, "The three classes of society." The Physiocrats (like so many others) juxtaposed the state and rule of nature and of natural laws – as they always subjectively perceived, defined and applied them) – to the deleterious artifice of mankind. So the economy is transcendent to man. But the Physiocrats also specified a socioeconomic structure of three classes, roughly the landowners, the cultivators and industrial workers. Since – or to the extent that – the Physiocrats included class structure in their concept of the state of nature, then theirs was neither just a physicalist theory nor a pure conceptual abstract a-institutional theory. If one interprets them differently, however, in terms of the natural-artificial distinction and also includes class therein, the neglect is palpable.

One interesting interpretation relates to the impact of the American Revolution on English economic policy. Writing of the theoretical influence of Smith's *Wealth of Nations*, Hull says that

> Its practical influence in England increased by the Revolution in America, making the old navigation laws less effective, and by the overthrow of Napoleon, which suspended the rivalry with France.

Though the coverage and structure of the lectures seems fairly conventional, individual readers will find various interpretations and apparent emphases of particular interest. For example, significant emphasis seems to be placed on John Stuart Mill for his systematization (given as systemizing by Hull) of English Classical Economics and on the impact of Mill's abandonment of the wages-fund theory on the status of his system. The various criticisms of Classical economics, "the system of natural liberty," are said to be "not unjustified, but in themselves insufficient as the basis of a 'school.'" Hull denigrates List's stages analysis as "pseudo-history," inviting comparison with others' more sympathetic treatment of Adam Smith's (and others') stages analysis as conjectural history. Hull also denigrates "the patriotic exaggeration of his [List's] importance to the history of economics." Some attention is given to the problem of the relativity of economic doctrines. From the syllabus one would not sense the prospective importance of Alfred Marshall's *Principles of Economics*, though it is listed along with the textbooks of Henry Sidgwick and Joseph Shield Nicholson.

In Section III, "Reaction," Hull adopts the interpretive position that was to echo throughout the twentieth century. The criticisms of Classical economics, as indicated above, are said to be "not unjustified, but in themselves insufficient as the basis of a 'school.'" There are two problems with this: First, Classical economics had several common ideas but so much disagreement over all of them to warrant the question, if not the conclusion, that any such "school" has been an interpretive convention (as well serving as a basis for justification by appeal to authority, for both certain doctrines and economics as a scientific discipline). Second, no defense of the necessity of "schools" is given; in fact, it is largely a sociological phenomenon.

Finally, attention is called to the designation, in 1895, of "American Austrians."

As for the references, Hull includes both primary sources and leading, if selective, secondary sources, many of the latter in French and German. A sprinkling of sources in economic history is included. The superscripts in text material refer to corresponding items in the following reference list.

The original document – which was printed rather than typed – is reproduced below with only trivial stylistic changes and a few spelling corrections; the basic data is given as Hull provided. I have provided an updated and corrected list of writers mentioned, following Hull's original list. Left included are the library call numbers of references given to the student.

CORNELL UNIVERSITY

SYLLABUS OF LECTURES
ON THE HISTORY OF

ECONOMIC THEORIES

With References

By CHARLES HENRY HULL, PH.D.

ITHACA, N.Y.
1895

WRITERS MENTIONED,

With their Birth and Death Years.

Atkinson, 1827–
Bagehot, 1826–1877
Barbon, ? 1640–1698
Bastiat, 1801–1850
Bentham, 1748–1832
von Böhm-Bawerk, 1851–
Bowen, 1811–1890
Cairnes, 1823–1875
Calhoun, 1782–1850
Carey, 1793–1879
Carlyle, 1795–1881
Cauwès, 184–
Child, 1630–1699
Clay, 1777–1852
Cohn, 1840–
Comte, 1798–1857
Condorcet, 1743–1794
Conrad, 1839–
Cunningham, 184–
Dunoyer, 1786–1862
Dupont de Nemours, 1739–1817
Fawcett, 1833–1884
Fourier, 1772–1837
Frankenstein, 1861–
Franklin, 1706–1790
George, 1839–
Gide, 184–
Godwin, 1756–1836
Grotius, 1583–1645
Hales, ?–1571
Hamilton, 1757–1804
Hermann, 1795–1868
Hildebrand, 1812–1878
Hobbes, 1588–1679
Hume, 1711–1776
Jefferson, 1743–1826
Jevons, 1835–1882
Jones, 1790–1855
Kingsley, 1819–1875
Knies, 1821–
Laveleye, 1822–1893
Leroy-Beaulieu, 1843
Leslie, 1827–1882
List, 1789–1846
Locke, 1632–1704
Malthus, 1766–1834
Marshall, 1842–
Maurice, 1805–1872
Menger, 1840–
Mercier de la Riviére, 1720–? 1793
Mill, Jas., 1773–1836
Mill, J. S., 1806–1873
Molinari, 1819–
Müller, 1779–1829
Mun, f. 1630
Nicholson, 1850–
North, 1644–1691
Owen, 1771–1858
Perry, 1830–
Petty, 1623–1687
Proudhon, 1809–1865
Quesnay, 1694–1774
Rau, 1792–1870
Ricardo, 1772–1823
Rodbertus, 1805–
Rogers, 1823–1890
Roscher, 1817–1894
Rousseau, 1712–1778
Ruskin, 1819–
Saint Simon, 1760–1825
Sax, 1845–
Say, 1767–1832

Schaefelle, 1831–
Schmoller, 1838–
Schönberg, 1839–
Senior, 1790–1864
Sismondi, 1773–1842
Smith, 1723–1790
Stafford, fl. 1581
Sumner, 1840–
Thornton, 1813–1880
von Thünen, 1783–1850
Toynbee, 1852–1883
Tucker, 1711–1799
Turgot, 1727–1781
Wagner, 1835–
Walker, 1840–
Webster, 1782–1852
Wells, 1828–
West, 1783–1828
von Wieser, 1851–

WRITERS MENTIONED: COMPLETED AND CORRECTED LIST

Edward Atkinson, 1827–1905
Walter Bagehot, 1826–1877
Nichalas Barbon, ? 1640–1698
Frederic Bastiat, 1801–1850
Jeremy Bentham, 1748–1832
Eugen von Böhm-Bawerk, 1851–1914
Francis Bowen, 1811–1890
John Elliott Cairnes, 1823–1875
John C. Calhoun, 1782–1850
Henry Charles Carey, 1793–1879
Carlyle, 1795–1881
Paul Cauwès, 1843–1917
Sir Josiah Child, 1630–1699
Henry Clay, 1777–1852
Gustav Cohn, 1840–1919
Auguste Comte, 1798–1857
Marie Jean Antoine Nicholas Caritat, Marquis de Condorcet, 1743–1794
Johannes Conrad, 1839–1915
William Cunningham, 1849–1919
William Dunoyer, 1786–1862
Pierre Samuel Dupont de Nemours, 1739–1817
Henry Fawcett, 1833–1884
Charles Fourier, 1772–1837
Kuno Frankenstein, 1861–1897
Benjamin Franklin, 1706–1790
Henry George, 1839–1897
Charles Gide, 1847–1932
William Godwin, 1756–1836
Hugo Grotius, 1583–1645
John Hales, ?–1571
Alexander Hamilton, 1757–1804
Frederick Benedict Hermann, 1795–1868
Bruno Hildebrand, 1812–1878
Thomas Hobbes, 1588–1679
David Hume, 1711–1776
Thomas Jefferson, 1743–1826

William Stanley Jevons, 1835–1882
Richard Jones, 1790–1855
Charles Kingsley, 1819–1875
Karl Knies, 1821–1898
Emile Louis Victor de Laveleye, 1822–1893
Paul Leroy-Beaulieu, 1843–1916
Thomas Edward Cliff Leslie, 1827–1882
Friedrich List, 1789Ä1846
John Locke, 1632–1704
Thomas Robert Malthus, 1766–1834
Alfred Marshall, 1842–1924
Frederick Denison Maurice, 1805–1872
Carl Menger, 1840–1921
Pierre Paul Mercier de la Riviére, 1720–1793
James Mill, 1773–1836
John Stuart Mill, 1806–1873
Gustave de Molinari, 1819–1912
Adam Heinrich Müller, 1779–1829
Sir Thomas Mun, 1571–1641
Joseph Shield Nicholson, 1850–1927
Sir Dudley North, 1644–1691
Robert Owen, 1771–1858
Arthur Latham Perry, 1830–1905
Sir William Petty, 1623–1687
Pierre-Joseph Proudhon, 1809–1865
François Quesnay, 1694–1774
Karl HeinrichRau, 1792–1870
David Ricardo, 1772–1823
Johann Karl Rodbertus, 1805–1875
James Edwin Thorold Rogers, 1823–1890
Wilhelm Georg Frederich Roscher, 1817–1894
Jean-Jacques Rousseau, 1712–1778
John Ruskin, 1819–1900
Charles Henri de Rouvroy Saint Simon, 1760–1825
Emile Sax, 1845–1927
Jean-Baptiste Say, 1767–1832
Albert Eberhard Friedrich Schäffle, 1831–1904
Gustav Schmoller, 1838–1917
Gustav Friedrich von Schönberg, 1839–1908
Nassau William Senior, 1790–1864

Jean Charles Leonard Sismonde de Sismondi, 1773–1842
Adam Smith, 1723–1790
Sir Edward Stafford, 1552?–1605
William Graham Sumner, 1840–1910
William Thomas Thornton, 1813–1880
Johann Heinrich von Thünen, 1783–1850
Arnold Toynbee, 1852–1883
Josiah Tucker, 1712–1799
Anne Robert Jacques Turgot, 1727–1781
Adolph Heinrich Gotthelf Wagner, 1835–1917
Francis Amasa Walker, 1840–1897
Daniele Webster, 1782–1852
David Ames Wells, 1828–1898
Sir Edward West, 1782–1828
Friedrich von Wieser, 1851–1926

BIBLIOGRAPHICAL NOTE

Among the more important books about the history of political economy are:

BLOCK. *Les progrès de la science économique depuis A. Smith.* 1890. 2 v. [6455 B5–6]

BONAR. *Philosophy and political economy in some of their historical relations.* 1893. [6455 F72]

CANNAN. *Theories of production and distribution in English political economy from 1776 to 1848.* London: 1893. [6455 F69]

COHN. *History of political economy, tr. by J. A. Hill.* 1894. [6350 C]

CONRAD. *Handwõrterbuch der Staatswissenschaften.* 1890–1894. 6 v. [6156 G21Ä26]

COSSA. *Introduction to the study of political economy*, transl. by L. Dyer. 1893. [37 B21, also 6455 A36]

*CUNNINGHAM. *Growth of English industry and commerce.* 1890–92. 2 v. [4341 E66–67]

EISENHART. *Geschichte der Nationalökonomik.* 1891. [6455 F32]

ESPINAS. *Histoire des doctrines économiques.* 1892. [6455 F36]

HELD. *Zwei Bücher zur socialen Geschichte Englands.* 1881. [4342 F11]

*INGRAM. *History of political economy.* 1887. [6455 F6]

KAUTZ. *Die geschichtliche Entwickelung der National-Oekonomik und ihrer Literatur.* 1860. [6455 F29]

PALGRAVE. *Dictionary of political economy.* Vol. 1. 1894. [37 B31]

*PRICE. *Short history of political economy in England.* 1891. [6455 P66]

ROSCHER. *Geschichte der National-Oekonomik in Deutschland.* 1874. [6455 F14]

SAY. *Nouveau dictionnaire de l'économie politique.* 1891–1892. 2 v. [6455 G5Ä6]

*VON SCHEEL. *Geschichte der politischen Oekonomie*, (in I Schönberg, *Handbuch der politischen Oekonomie*, 74–106). 1885. [6455 G11]

**SELIGMAN. Changes in the tenets of political economy with time (in 7 "Science," 375–382). 1886. [12160]

Asterisks designate the books recommended for elementary reading, not necessarily the books in themselves most meritorious. For the titles of many other histories of economics, see Ingram, pp. xiv, xv, and Cossa, pp. 113–125; for references on specific authors and topics, see the body of the syllabus. The figures in brackets, e.g. [6455 G12], are the call numbers of the books in the University Library.

The use of books about the history of political economy may help to an understanding of the writings of economists; it can never serve as a substitute for the direct study of such writings. With two or three exceptions, the works of the economists mentioned in this syllabus, together with the works of many not mentioned, will be found in the Library.

INTRODUCTORY

Changes in the problems which economists have from time to time confronted, and in their attitude towards those problems. Consequent modification of the subjects and purposes of their speculations. In modern times political economy begins as a theory of prosperity, to be achieved by governmental guidance of trade and industry. Transition, in latter half of eighteenth century, with industrial progress and with dissemination of political philosophy of "natural" liberty, to a conviction that prosperity must result from free industry and individual enterprise. Transference of attention to the physical conditions determinative of production, and especially to the conditions determinative of distribution, under industrial freedom. Practical culmination, in England, in the repeal of the corn laws (1846), theoretical in J. S. Mill's Political Economy (1848). Stagnation of economics in England. Opposition to English economic theories by practical men in England, also by speculative writers among peoples whose industrial conditions or political ideas differed from those of Englishmen: in America, Carey, George, on the continent of Europe, the socialists, the "historical school." Opposition by the new deductive school Jevons, the Austrians, the Americans.

Periods in the history of political economy: Adam Smith's division; the usual division into mercantilist, physiocratic and industrial systems; Ingram's division.

I. THE MERCANTILE SYSTEM

Transition from mediaeval industrial society, regulated by the relations of persons, to modern industrial society, based on the exchange of things. Phases of the transition which chiefly evoked and shaped early economic theories: the new gold (rise of prices), centralization of government (increased taxes, debased coinage), extension of commerce.[1]

The mercantilist writers of the 16th and 17th centuries not properly a "school." But since they all seek, by legislation, to promote industrial and commercial supremacy as a means to national aggrandizement, they exhibit more or less generally certain common tendencies. Thus, moved by various reasons, political as well as economic, they for the most part hold gold and silver superior forms of wealth; they exalt foreign commerce, whose favorable balance[2] brings the precious metals into a country, above domestic trade, and encourage manufacturing industries and shipping, sometimes at the expense of agriculture, both because manufactures afford exports of greater value, and also because they give employment to more hands, a numerous population being desired.[3] These notions are expounded incidentally to the discussion of concrete questions, some writers emphasizing one, some another point

Prominent writers: Hales[4] (or Stafford? – "W.S."), price, money; Mun, balance of trade; Child, low interest; (the imitators of Holland); Petty,[5] taxation, political arithmetic; Locke, money; North, free trade; Barbon,[6] values, etc. Continental writers.

Practical mercantilism: Cromwell, Colbert, Frederic the Great. The exportation of money at first prohibited, customs duties, Act of Navigation, treaties of commercial reciprocity, external and internal colonization.[7] The "reaction against mercantilism."

References: General: – 2 Cunningham, 67–100, 227–255; R. Jones, Primitive political economy, in his Remains, 291–335 [6470 C31], and in 85 Edinburgh Rev., 426–452 [2761]; Hewins, English trade and finance, introduction [4342 E37]; *Roscher, Zur Geschichte d. engl. Volkswirthschaftslehre im, 16. u. 17. Jahrh. [1356o G3]; Smith, Wealth of Nations, bk. 1, ch. 1–8, especially Ch. 1, 2 and 8 (summarized by Nicholson, I Palgrave, 351–355) Ingram, 36–54; Cossa, 187–210; Eisenhart, 1–25; Kautz, 223–3351 Leser. Merkantilsystem, 4 Conrad, 1168–1173. *Special*. – [1]I Cunningham, 404–427. [2]*Bauer on Balance of trade, i Palgrave, 85–88. [3]Cannan, 124–130; Elster, in 2 Conrad, 476–484. [4]E. Lamond, The "Examination of Complaints" attributed to Stafford, 6 Engl. Hist. Rev., 284–305 [3003], also her ed. of the same, A discourse of the commonweal (6455 D11]. [5]Bevan. Petty, a study (6342 B]. [6]Bauer, in I Palgrave, 119–121. [7]Seeley, Expansion of England, 56–76 [47 F2].

II. THE SYSTEM OF NATURAL LIBERTY

Elaborated in France by the physiocrats (ca. 1750 ff.) and in England by Adam Smith (1779) and his followers. Industrial changes of the 18th century made room for new economic theories. Economists regarded the new phenomena in the light of a new political doctrine: the Law of Nature – Stoicism, *jus gentium* of the Roman lawyers; Epicureanism, and the social compact; Grotius, Hobbes, Locke, Rousseau; the state of nature and natural rights. Fusion with theological notion of a divine harmony in creation. Resultant individualism. Timeliness of these negative theories.

References. – **Leslie, The Political Rcouomy of Adam Smith, in his Essays, 148–166 [6495 E46], and in 14 Fortnightly Rev., 549–563 [2771]; Maine,

Ancient law, ch. 3 and 4 [40 A3]; Ritchie, Natural rights, 20–47 (6157 C21]; Bonar, 59–196; Windelband, History of philosophy, 425–436, 518–528 [7075 A28]; Hasbach, Die allgem. philos. Grundlagen der von Quesnay uud Smith begründeten politischen Oekonomie [6338 A10]; on industrial changes, 2 Cunningham, book viii.

1. THE PHYSIOCRATIC SCHOOL

Founded by Quesnay: Tableau économique; Maximes géneralés du gouvernement économique d'un royaume agricole (1758) – "pauvres 0aysans, pauvre royaume; pauvre royaume, pauvre roi." Mercier de la Riviére: L'ordre naturel et essentiel des sociétés politiques (1767). Turgot: Réflexions sur la formation et la distribution des richesses 1766). Dupont de Nemours: Physiocratie (1767). Meaning of the word. An objective theory, emphasizing, under the influence of natural science, the physical, neglecting the institutional limitations of inustrial society. The three classes of society. Theory of net product. L'impôt unique. Smith's treatment of the physiocrats. Their practical influence.

References: – Ingram, 60-70; von Scheel, 80–84; *Espinas, 214–240; Cohn, 21–29; Oncken, Quesnay, in 5 Conrad, 315–332; de Lavergne, Les économistes francais du 18e siecle, esp. 58–111, 167–278 [6455 D7]; Kautz, 336–371; *Schelle, Physiocrates, in 2 Say, 473–486; Patten, Dynamic economics, 12–13 [6341 K2).

2. ADAM SMITH

Predecessors of Smith in England: Hume, Tucker. Smith's life.[1] His plan of a social philosophy[2]: publication of the Theory of Moral Sentiments (1759) and of the Inquiry into the Nature and Causes of the Wealth of Nations (1776). Its five books. Outline of chief arguments: – National dividend increased by division of labor, which is limited by extent of market. Money; value in use, value in exchange. Price; market and natural. Cost-components of price: wages, profits, rent; their relations to fluctuations in price. Capital[3], or "stock," fixed and circulating; accumulated by parsimony. Productive and unproductive labor.[4] Historical parts of the book. Taxation and public expenditure.

Theoretical influence of the Wealth of Nations. Its optimistic character. (German criticisms of "Smithianismus."[5]) Its practical influence in England increased by the Revolution in America, making the old navigation laws less effective, and by the overthrow of Napoleon, which suspended the rivalry with France.[6]

References: General. – *Price, 1–34; Ingram, 87–110; *2 Cunningham, 416–441, and in I Economic Journal, 73–94 [6342 K]; Kautz, 405–471; Cossa, 285–298. *Special.* – [1]Rae, Life of Smith (6470 B45]; [2]Bonar, 146–152; *[3]Cannan, 55–89; *4Cannan, 18–31; Hildebrand, Die Nationalökonomie (der Gegenwart und Zukunft, 14–34 [6455 F4]; Knies, Die politische Oekonomie vom geschichtlichen Standpunkte, 223–293 [6455 A51]; Held, 154–175; Cohn, 30–40; [6]2 Cunningham, 256–262.

3. THE DEVELOPMENT OF ENGLISH ECONOMICS

A pessimistic tendency was given to economic speculation in England by two writers of controversial pamphlets,[1] Malthus and Ricardo, who discussed current questions suggested by the "industrial revolution", and especially by the wars with France in 1793–1815.

Malthus's life. Writings: Essay on the Principle of Population, pamphlets on the poor laws, and on the corn laws (Observations on the Effects of the Corn Laws, 1814; Grounds of an Opinion on the Policy of Restricting the Importation of Foreign Corn, 1815; Inquiry into the Nature and Progress of Rent, 18X5), unimportant later treatises, correspondence with Ricardo.

Ricardo's life and business experience. His theories first developed in various pamphlets, – value and money in his High Price of Bullion a Proof of the Depreciation of Bank Notes (1810), Reply to Bosanquet on the Bullion Committee (1811), and Proposals for an Economical and Secure Currency (1816); diminishing returns, rent, (wages) in his Essay on the Influence of a Low Price of Corn on the Profits of Stock (1815) – and subsequently embodied in his Principles of Political Economy and Taxation (1817). The more important of the modifications which Malthus and Ricardo affected in Smith's system relate to five matters (below *A-E*).

References. – Patten, Malthus and Ricardo, in 4 Publ. Am. Econ. Assoc., 333–358 [6342 B4], and *Interpretation of Ricardo, in 7 Quart. J. Of Econ., 322–352 [6342 D]; Eisenhart, 78–82; Toynbee, Industrial revolution, 1–26 [6495 B73]; Carman, Ricardo in Parliament, in 4 Economic J., 249–261, 4og-423 (6342 K]. *Special.* – Cannan, 384–388.

A. Population

English poor laws and allowance system. Condorcet and Godwin, perfectibility. Purpose of first ed. of Malthus's Essay on Population (1798). Arithmetical and geometrical ratios. Positive checks, resolvable into misery and vice. Second ed. (1803). Preventative checks: self-restraint, moral and prudential. Diminishing returns as an alleged historical fact made the centre of Malthusianism after 1815. Malthusianism and subsequent theories of distribution. Criticisms of the theory.

References: *General*. – **Bagehot, Malthus, in his Economic studies, 135–150 [37 D2x]; I Block, 529–557; Bonar, Malthus and his work [37 C4]; *Cannan, 130–147; 2 Cunningham, 557–564; Held, 204–222; Price, 35–6o; *Patten, A new statement of the law of population, 10 Pol. Sci. Qu., 44–61 [6341 1]; Toynbee, his Industrial revolution, 93–114 (6495 E73]; Wagner, Grundlegung, 3. Aufl. 451–463 [6475 E80]. 2 Cunningham, 494–505; I Palgrave, 33–34. Bonar, 199–205.

B. Diminishing Returns

Industrial and agricultural condition of England during the Napoleonic wars: foreign markets for manufactures, migration townward and northward, price of wheat, enclosures. Law of diminishing returns developed, 1815, by West, Malthus, and Ricardo. Confusion of diminishing returns under existing methods of cultivation with an historical tendency to diminishing returns.

References. – *Cannan, 147–182, and in 2 Econ. J., 53–69 [6342 K], (summarized in I Palgrave, 585–586); Patten, Dynamic economics, 144–147 [6341 K2].

C. Rent

The so-called Ricardian theory of rent (rent a differential, not an average) was promulgated in Malthus's "Inquiry," a protectionist pamphlet. Like the mercantilists, Malthus thought rent a "surplus." In his free trade "Essay," Ricardo, the city man, accepted the differential idea, but declared rent a "deduction." Profits fall because diminishing returns force cultivation to lower margins, thus raising the price of food, and consequently the wages of labor. The landlord placed in an unpleasant light

References – *Cannan, 216–228; Ingram, 125–133; Price, 61–86; 2 Block, 213–236; Held, 183–188; 2 Cunningham, 564–572.

D. Wages

Ricardo's subsistence theory of wages not new. Influence of Malthus's "Essay" on the theory. Ricardo emasculated it by introducing a reference to the standard of life; he assumed, however, that the standard would be low. Suggestions of a supply and demand theory in Smith and Ricardo; its development into the "wages fund."

References. – Cannan, 242–257; 2 Cunningham, 468–475; Held, 188–190; Walker, The wage-fund theory, in 120 North Am. Rev., 84–119 (2871].

E. Relation of Value to Cost

Ricardo's labor value theory refers to labor expended, Smith's (chiefly) to labor purchasable. Ricardo's exceptions: products of agriculture, of foreign countries, of industries employing fixed capital, money when seignorage is charged. Thus arise surpluses of value over cost, to trace whose distribution is the problem of later writers. Malthus, Ricardo and their immediate successors emphasized chiefly the surpluses due to land, and disputed as to the socially desirable distribution thereof (land nationalization). Later writers, living in more complicated and varied industrial surroundings, pointed out other differential – Mill (1848) of goods produced at a joint cost, Cairnes (1874) of labor skill, Walker (1886) of managing ability – and discussed the distribution of the resulting surpluses.

References. – Patten, The development of the classical theory of cost of production, in his Dynamic economics, 25–35 [6341 K2].

4. THE SYSTEMATIZING OF ENGLISH ECONOMICS

Formal character of the Wealth of Nations. J. B. Say's life and influence.[1] His Trité d'économie politique (1803, trans., 1821). Threefold division, production, distribution, consumption. Identification of the members of the productive triad with the three sharetakers. Lack of system in Malthus's larger works and of systematic formulation in Ricardo's Principles.[2]

The utilitarians – Bentham, the Westminister Review – and a general principle of social correlation. James Mill. Popular purpose of his Elements of Political Economy (1821). Finds in diminishing returns the central principle in distribution, and shoves it under theories previously elaborated. Production an introductory section. Interchange a theory of price, whereby distribution is effected.

The question of repudiation and the socialistic attacks on profits and on interest. Senior's Political Economy (1836) introduces the theory of abstinence.[3]

John Stuart Mill's life.[4] Instructed in Ricardo by his father. Writes Essays on Some Unsettled Questions of Political Economy in.1829–30. System of Logic (1843) a success. Publishes Essays (1844) and writes his Principles of Political Economy with Some of their Applications to Social Philosophy, published in 1848. Literary merit. Emphasizes physical determinants of production, institutional of distribution (Mill's later leaning toward socialism), and elaborates the theory of value, especially international values, and of international trade. Chief significance in the attempted correlation of economic theories with one another and with the sciences. Mill summarized the notions of laissez-faire economics. The prosperity following the repeal of the English corn laws set the seal of empirical approval upon the "classical" assumption of individual sufficiency. Fawcett a popularizer of Mill. In 1869, Mill, in a review of Thornton, On Labor, abandoned the wages-fund theory,[5] thus shattering the unique prestige his system had enjoyed. Cairnes tried without success to repair the damage, – Some Leading Principles of Political Uconomy Newly Expounded (1874).

Continental followers of the system of natural liberty: Dunoyer, Bastiat, Journal des économistes, Molinari, Leroy-Beaulieu; Rau, Hermann.

References: *General*. – Ingram, 138–141, 146–162; Sidgwick, Principles of political economy, p. 1–7 [37 C13]; Cossa, 326–351; Roscher, 1011–1012 [6455 F14]. *Special*. – [1]Dubois de L'Estang, J. B. Say in 2 Say, 783–790; Ingram, i163–165; Espinas, 301–304; [2]Gonner's ed., p. xxiii-xxvii (6470 B82]; [3]Böhm-Bowerk, Capital and interest, 269–287 [6515 B59]; Cannan, 213–216; [4]Mill's Autobiography [1866 F22 and 23]; Price, 87–114; [5]II Fortnightly Rev., 505–518 [2771].

III. REACTION

Protests against the conclusions of the system of natural liberty:

Sismondi, Adam Müller, von Thünen: Kingsley, Maurice, Ruskin, Carlyle; Saint Simon, Fourier, Proudhon, Owen, Rodbertus. Influence of these writers on popular opinion, and on later economists. Criticisms on the method of the "orthodox" economists, viz.: their separation of economics from sociology – Comte; their abstractness and neglect of history, resulting in cosmopolitanism and perpetualism; their assumption of individual sufficiency – "Kathedarsozialisten." These criticisms not unjustified, but in themselves insufficient as the basis of a "school." Nor have they led to the formation of a school, properly speaking. The so-called historical school in Germany and elsewhere too heterogeneous in opinion and in method for collective characterization.

List,[1] the agitator for a customs union and for state railways, and his Nationales System der politischen Oekonomie (1841); pseudo-historical theory of the necessary stages of industrial development, and its corollary of protection for Germany. List's merits, and the patriotic exaggeration of his importance to the history of economics.

The historical school of jurisprudence and its influence on academic economists. Roscher's' Grandriss zur Vorlesungen über die Stsatswirthschaft nach geschichtlicher Methode (1843); its projects incompletely realized in his System der Volkswirthschaft (1854–1894, 5 Vols); his Geschichte der National-Oekonomik in Deutschland (1874). Hildebrand's Die National-ökonomie der

Gegenwart und Zukunft (1848), and the Jahrbücher für Nationalökonomie (1863). Knies's Die politische Oekonomie vom Standpunkte der geschichtlichen Methode (1853), and his later monographs. Later German writers: the insufficiency of laissez-faire and the social reform movement – Verein für Sozialpolitik the socio-juridical tendency – Schaeffle, his monographs, his relation to Rau, his Lehrbuch (1874–1895); the historians out and out – Schmoller's writings, his Forschungen, his Jahrbuch. Attempts towards systemization: Schönnberg, Handbuch der politischen Oekonomie (1882, 2 Vols., 3rd ed., 1890, 3 Vols.), Cohn's System der Nationalökonomie (1885–1889), Conrad's Handwörterbuch der Stantswissenschaften (1894–), Frankenstein's Hand- und Lehr-Bach der Staatswissenschaften, (1894–).

Like tendencies in England[3]: Jones, Bagehot and the relativity of English political economy, Lombard Street (1873) and other writings. Cliffe Leslie. Toynbee. Thorold Rogers. Cunningham's Politics and Economics (1885), Growth of English Industry and Commerce (1882, 2d ed., 1890–1892). Recent text-books: Sidgwick's Principles of Political Economy (1883), Marshall's Principles of Economics (1890), Nicholson's Principles of Political Economy (1893), Palgrave's Dictionary of Political Economy (1894). The Economic Journal (1891).

Echo in France[4]: Laveleye; law faculties, Cauwès, Gide, Revue d'économie politique (1886) – and in Italy[5].

References: *General*. – *Ingram, 142–145, 196–215,221–231; Roscher, 1014–1020,1032–1048; Leslie, History of German political economy, in his Essays, 167–178 [6495 E46], and in 24 Fortnightly Rev., 93–101 [2771]; Meyer, Die neuere Nationalökonomie, 128–165 [6455 F49]; *Cossa, 410–425; v. Scheel, 98–106; Cohn, 100–135. *Special*. – Goldschmidt, Friedrich List, Deutschlands grosser Volkswirth (6475 E32]. [2]Schmoller, Roscher, in his Zur Literaturgeschichte der Staatswiss., 141–171. (6156 A5); Ashley, Roscher's programme of 1843, in 9 Qu. Jour. Econ., 99–105 (6342 D]. *3Foxwell, The economic movement in England, 2 Qu. jour. Econ., 84Äio3 (6342 D] ; Cohn, Die heutige Nationalökonomie in England and Amerika, 13 Schmoller's Jahrbuch, 1–46; *Price, 125–157, 183–186. [4]Gide, Political economy in France, 5 Pol. Sci. Qu, 603–635 [6341 I]; [5]Cossa, 501–513; Loria, in 2 Annals of the Amer. Acad., 203–224 [6350 C]; Rabbeno, in 6 Pol. Sci. Qu., 439–473 [6341 I]; Schullern-Schrattenhofen, Die theoretische Nationalökonomie Italiens [6455 F41].

IV. THE AUSTRIAN SCHOOL

Reason for appellation. Psychological basis, deductive method. Jevons's mnographs and Theory of Political Economy (1871). Mathematical method.

Concept of final utility. Similar ideas in Menger's Grundaätze der Volkswirthschaftalehre (1871). Elaborated and applied: by Sax, Theoretische Staatswirthschaft (1887), etc., also Die Verkehrsmittel (1878–79), by v. Wieser, Ursprung and Hauptgesetze des wirthschaftlichen Werthes (1884), Natural Value (1890, tr. 1893); by v. Böhm-Bawerk, Capital and interest (1884, tr. 1890), critical, and Positive theory of capital (1888, tr. 1891), constructive. American "Austrians."

References. – Cossa, 427–432; v. Böhm-Bawerk, The Austrian economists, in I Annals of the Amer. Acad., 361–384 [6350 C]; Bonar, The Austrian economists, in 3 Qu. J. Econ., 1–31 [6342 D]; Patten, Dynamic economics, 36–38 [6341 K2]; Price, 158–176; Böhmert, Jevons und seine Bedentung <u>für</u> die theoretische Nationalökonomie, in 15 Schmoller's Jahrbuch, III, 76–124.

V. POLITICAL ECONOMY IN THE UNITED STATES

Rapid industrial progress 1776–186o largely prevented emergence of the problems which stimulated English economic thinkers. Attention chiefly absorbed by questions of constitutional law and by the aspects of slavery. Economic notions of Franklin, Hamilton, Jefferson, Calhoun, Clay, Webster. Economic study before the civil war the avocation of academic teachers, chiefly clergymen, who accepted English conclusions with qualifications, *e.g.*, rejection of Malthusian theory, recognition of differences in wages and in profits, advocacy of protection. Bowen's American Political Economy (1856) perhaps the ablest of their books.

Carey's life. Principles of Political Economy (1837–1840), Past, Present and Future, (1848), Principles of Social Science (1858–1859), The Unity of Law (1872). Value, rent, exhaustion of the soil, protection. Carey's followers.

Civil war. Elimination of slavery and of many constitutional questions. Development of transportation; taking up of public domain. Older writers: Perry, Sumner, Wells, Atkinson. F. A. Walker: census, Wages Question (1876), Money (1879), Political Economy (1883), Source of Business Profits (1886). Henry George, Progress and Poverty (1879). Influence of foreign studies; the American Economic Association, 1885; "Science" Economic Discussion (1886); younger writers: economic journals.

References. – Dunbar, Economic science in America, 122 No. Am. Rev., 124–154 [2871]; Leslie, Political economy in the U. S., 34 Fortnightly Rev., 488–509 [2771]; Cossa, 460–483; Godkin, Why political economy has not been cultivated in America, 5 Nation, 255–256 [51 F3): Cohn, Die heutige Nationalökonomie in England and Amerika, 13 Schmoller's Jahrbuch, 947–982; Furber, Studien zur Entwicklung der ökonomischen Theorien in Amerika [6455

F81]; Livermore, Carey and his social system, in 5 Pol. Sci. Qu., 553–582; Ingram, 170–175; Jenks, Carey als Nationalökonom [6470 E71].

WALTON H. HAMILTON'S OUTLINES FOR THE PRINCIPLES OF ECONOMICS, UNIVERSITY OF MICHIGAN, 1911

Edited by Warren J. Samuels

The document published below was given to Luca Fiorito by Sarah Dorfman. It came from the collection of her late husband, Joseph Dorfman. Fiorito kindly gave it to me. The original document will be donated to the Bentley Historical Library at the University of Michigan, which has a small Walton H. Hamilton collection of reprints.

Walton H. Hamilton had several distinguished careers. Born October 30, 1881 in Tennessee, he received the B.A. from the University of Texas and the Ph.D. from the University of Michigan in 1913. He was an instructor at Michigan, 1910–1913, the period from which this document dates; thereafter a professor of political economy, 1913–1914. He taught political economy/economics at the University of Chicago, 1914–1915, Amherst College, 1915–1923, and the Robert Brookings Graduate School, 1923–1928. Never having formally studied law, he was professor of law at Yale University from 1928 to 1948, where he was a leader of the Yale approach to Legal Realism (the jurisprudential correlative to institutional economics), and also a member of the famous law firm of Arnold, Fortas, and Porter in Washington, D.C., 1948–1958. He held a number of governmental positions during the 1930s and 1940s, including U.S. delegate to the International Labor Conference in Geneva in 1935 and special assistant to the U.S. attorney general, 1938–1945. He was a prolific contributor to, first, economics and, later, law journals and the author of numerous books. He was a specialist in the legal control of business and as such a prominent

Histories of Economic Thought, Volume 21-B, pages 31–87.
© 2003 Published by Elsevier Science Ltd.
ISBN: 0-7623-0997-0

figure in the field of law and economics. He is increasingly being recognized as a major founder of institutional economics, alongside Thorstein Veblen, Wesley C. Mitchell, John R. Commons, and John Maurice Clark; indeed, Hamilton may well have been responsible for the term institutional economics. He had one of the most brilliant and incisive minds of the twentieth century, able to discern and work at the level of fundamentals and to approach and deconstruct a problem from several angles – all of which is evident in the document published below. He died in Washington, D.C., on October 27, 1958.

The document is a bound typescript of 38 onionskin pages of text plus a title page. The paper is quite fragile. The typing is poor and the print is uneven in darkness. The text has almost no right margins, is typed with uneven strength, and is laden with typographical errors. The latter have been corrected. (My word processor identified many uses of "which" that should be "that." No such corrections have been made.)

In post-World War II courses in Principles of Economics it was commonplace to consider the definition of the national income accounts, especially what was and was not included in Gross National, or Domestic, Product. Definitions embody and give effect to conceptions of the world and theories thereof. GNP and GDP do not have an independent existence. They are terms of economic art, and give effect to methodological and substantive judgments. The typical operating assumption is that the definition uniquely and importantly identifies the object or concept being named. But definitions are socially constructed; they do not, or not necessarily, bear any direct relationship to some transcendent, given category. The meaning of a definition derives from the use to which it is put; definitions are instrumental, even when they give effect to preconceptions and theories about the object or concept being defined – in fact, that is one way in which they are instrumental.

During the period when Hamilton's outlines were used, economists engaged in several controversies over definitions and these controversies form the basis for much of the document published below. The subjects, in the order found below, include: the scope of economics; the nature of economic laws; the nature of production; the identity of the factors of production – land, labor, and capital – and their interrelations; the definitions of capital and of the productivity of capital – hence of productivity itself; the meaning of value, cost, and utility; the nature – and source and justification – of interest; and so on. The aggregate of definitions served to identify, and in a way define, the economy as such, e.g. the conceptual relations between capital and labor.

The literature of the period was rampant with articles claiming to provide *the* correct definition, and *the* correct ground or theory on which the correct definition rested (typically it was only implicit that a theory was involved).

Legendary disputes took place over the meaning (definition) of value, cost, productivity, and capital. Almost no attention was given to the functional or instrumental nature of definitions, or to how it might be possible – if not actually the case (itself, of course, a theory) – to adopt different definitions for different purposes, e.g. to concentrate on different facets of the object being defined.

Some of the controversies remain active, though more or less subdued, in the professional literature of economics. Many of these terms, such as capital (and its correlative, investment) are given definitions that, paradoxically, on the one hand, have become standardized, and, on the other, vary both within and between schools of economic thought.

Definitions of such terms as value, capital, profit, interest, and productivity were not just technical matters. As some of the materials indicate, also at issue is the justification of present distributional arrangements. Economics has long been involved in the working out of normative theories to justify profits and interest in relation to wages. Accordingly, definitions of those terms and analysis of productivity in connection therewith, took on larger ramifications.

In any event, Hamilton's materials indicate the identity and complexity of the controversies then rampant, including the array of positions taken in each.

From the standpoint of the year 2000, some of the discussion, in part that pertaining to alternative economic systems, appears rather quaint.

A central topic is the relation of utility and cost of production in the formation of value, or price. Some twenty years after Alfred Marshall's scissors analogy, the foundations of what became price theory were being explored. Central to the account presented here to students, evident largely through questions on readings, is a composite of the principles of imputation and marginal productivity. The flavor is more Austrian than Marshallian. In particular, the various aspects of "cost" are underscored. The idea of value as transcendent to, and ultimately governing, price is also present. Classical ideas are mixed up with more modern, and therefore more relativist, ideas. The conflict between unilinear lines of causation and general simultaneous determination of all prices is evident. One cannot be certain where Hamilton was leading his students. It is clear that he expected them to work through very complex ideas and a variety of theoretical formulations; how much he succeeded is another matter. But also clear, and important, is that the document is not in itself a theoretical treatise; it is a pedagogical tool.

Hamilton's procedure is generally, for each topic, to commence with Preliminary Questions and to move on to Readings, Questions on the Readings, and Problems. Malcolm Rutherford has pointed out that notes for Hamilton's courses at Amherst c.1915 were highly unusual in that they consisted of lists of questions (Malcolm Rutherford, "Morris A. Copeland: A Case Study in the History of Institutional Economics," manuscript, 2000, p. 45, n. 1.

I am indebted to my wife, Sylvia Samuels, for scanning both this and other documents onto her computer. Alas, because of the poor quality of the typing, the initial scanned product was also poor.

THE PRINCIPLES OF ECONOMICS
POLITICAL ECONOMY 7
OUTLINES

Prepared for the use of the class

by

Walton H. Hamilton

Instructor in Economics

THE UNIVERSITY OF MICHIGAN,

Ann Arbor, Michigan, 1911

The Principles of Economics

I
The Nature and Boundaries of Political Economy

A. Preliminary Questions:

(1) Should a piece of coal be studied in geology, chemistry, botany, physics, or industry? Should a piece of coal be studied in economics?

(2) Is the organization, the mechanism, and the processes of industry a subject that falls within the province of political economy? Does political economy take any account of these things?

(3) Has political economy anything to do with woman's suffrage? prohibition? reciprocity with Canada? the popular election of United States senators? an income tax?

(4) What questions raised in the discussion of the English budget are economic? What questions raised are not economic?

(5) When you studied physics or chemistry did you pass judgments upon the laws you formulated? Why? Should you in economics?

(6) What do you conceive to be the purpose of economic study?

B. Readings

(1) General:

Taylor, *Outlines*, pp. 4–5;
Seligman, *Principles of Economics*, pp. 27–33.

(2) Other elementary readings:

Pierson, *Principles of Economics*, pp. 1–9;
Fetter, *Principles of Economics*, pp. 3–6;
Ely, *Outlines of Economics*, pp. 11–14;
Walker, *Political Economy*, pp. 24–29;
Senior, *Political Economy*, pp. 1–5.

(3) More advanced readings:

Keynes, *The Scope and Method of Political Economy*, Chapters ii–iv, vii–viii;
Cairnes, *Political Economy: Its Character and Logical Method*, Lectures 3 and 4;
Marshall, *Principles of Economies*, Bk. i, Chapters v and vi.

C. Questions on the Reading:

(1) What is the aim of economic study?

(2) What is the point of view from which economics should be studied?

(3) What, in general, is the subject-matter of political economy?
(4) Draw, as accurately as you can, the boundary line between economics and the study of industry.
(5) Is the economic view-point an ethical view-point?
(6) Is the purpose of economics primarily to furnish material and tools to the social reformer?
(7) What is the relationship of economics to politics? To psychology? To the natural sciences?

D. Problems

(1) Discuss from your present outlook the correctness of the following definitions of political economy:
  (a) Reflections upon the formation and distribution of wealth.
  (b) Researches upon the nature and causes of the wealth of nations.
  (c) The study of the production and distribution of wealth.
  (d) A study of man's actions in the ordinary business of life.
  (e) The science of wealth.
  (f) A study of the extent to which society is making the best use of its resources and the methods by which society can got more from its potential productive powers.
  g. A study of man's attempts to make a living in its social aspects.
(2) Name laws recently passed by Congress, or by state legislatures, which have economic consequences. Name laws passed by the same bodies which do not have economic consequences.
(3) Select some law recently enacted. Name several economic consequences which are likely to follow from the law. Name several non-economic consequences which are likely to follow.
(4) Read a national or state platform which has recently been drawn by some political party. Make a list of all the promises and demands which contain industrial and economic questions. Under each, point out the features which are purely industrial; the features which are purely economic.
(5) Make a list of all the arguments you have heard advanced for or against the protective tariff. Which of these are industrial? Which are economic? Which are neither?
(6) Is economics concerned with Pass race suicide? Immigration? The negro problem? old-age pension? the creation of a powerful navy? Socialism.
(7) Did the discovery of America make political economy more important? (Fetter).

(8) "The purpose of political economy, as is evident from the pages of any economic treatise, is to teach the individual how to acquire wealth. It has absolutely nothing to do with the notion of self-sacrifice." Is the author of the above correct in his judgment of the purpose of political economy? Is the truth of the last statement a valid criticism of political economy?

(9) Solve problems 12, 13, 14, 15, 16, and 17 in the Outlines.

II
The Nature of Economic Law

A. Preliminary questions:

(1) What do you mean by a moral law? Give an example.
(2) What do you mean by a civil law? Give an example.
(3) What do you mean by a natural law? Give an example.
(4) State the characteristics of each of these three kinds of laws. Differentiate them very carefully.
(5) Is a natural law in any sense an active force or a cause of things? (Davenport).
(6) What do you mean when you speak of a body falling in obedience to law?
(7) What do you mean when you speak of a law of motion?
(8) Just what, then, is a natural law?
(9) In what sense are natural laws true?
(10) Does a natural law always work?

B. Reading: Note under I. The following references are elementary:

Taylor, *Outlines*, pp. 7–8;
Seligman, pp. 23–27;
Marshall, *Economics of Industry*, Bk. I, Chapter iv;
Gide, *Political Economy*, pp. 9–15;
Seager, *Introduction to Economics*, pp. 58–59.

C. Questions on the Readings:

(1) What are happenings? Phenomena?
(2) What is meant by sequence? Coexistence?
(3) Just what does the expression "cause and effect" mean?
(4) What hypotheses underlie the attempt to formulate natural laws?
(5) How are natural laws discovered and formulated?
(6) Give an exact definition of a natural law?

(7) What is meant by the expression, "All natural laws are hypothetical in character"?
(8) Why is it harder to discover and formulate natural laws in economics than in the natural sciences?
(9) Do the phenomena of economics lend themselves to formulation into laws in the sense that the phenomena of the natural sciences do?
(10) What hypotheses underlie the attempt of economists to discover the natural laws in economics?
(11) Can there be natural laws in economics? What of temporal and local considerations and conditions?
(12) Are economic laws temporary and local in character?
(13) Is the method of political economy deductive or inductive?
(14) Should economics make use of the a priori or the a posteriori method?

D. Problems:
(1) "It is absurd to speak of natural laws in the economic world. Industrial life is in a state of constant flux; so how can there be any statements of invariable sequence?" (a) Show that the author of the above does not possess a sufficiently comprehensive idea of the character of natural law. (b) Admitting that society is changing, does it follow that society is changing in all respects? Can you still make out a clear case for the existence of natural law in the economic realm? Show that some economic principles hold good for any industrial society; e.g. show that there in a sense in which Robinson Crusoe could be said to exchange one article for another or show that the small boy who carries fifty cents in his pocket in anticipation of spending it for a circus ticket really draws interest on his money.
(2) "Natural laws do not hold in the economic realm. Everyone knows that everyone who is in business is free to do as he pleases. So long as he obeys the law there is no force compelling him to do this thing or that thing. Further, it is perfectly absurd to say that his actions are governed by natural law for the business man always acts for his own individual profit." Criticize.
(3) "To the extent that the city regulates its municipal monopolies and the nation its railroads, industry may be said to move in obedience to law; but, aside from governmental control, there is no law in the industrial world." What conception of natural law is held by the writer quoted above? Point out his mistakes.
(4) "Ever since Adam Smith, the economists have been attempting to formulate a body of economic principles. Thus far they have satisfied

no one, not even themselves. Their trouble is that they are looking for law where, in the very nature of things, there can be no law. Anyone with reasonable intelligence can see that in the Industrial world there is anarchy. Cut-throat competition still rules among the smaller traders. Higher up, the trust are still engaged in sapping the life from the bodies of industrial rivals and squeezing dividend out of the pockets of unprotected consumers. There can be no law where there is no order." Is the above a fair picture of the industrial world? Even it were, would the writer be justified in his statement that there is no economic law to discover?

(5) "In the sense in which the expression "natural law" is used in the sciences, there can be no natural law in economics. Imagine a discussion of economic subjects written by an American Indian of the fifteenth century for his own people. His discussion of production would be a discussion of the best methods of warfare. Agriculture would be relegated by him to the province of domestic economy. Scalping would by him be made the source of the value of the most prized articles in use. Or imagine a treatise on economics by a Greek philosopher. It would dwell at length upon the management of slaves, and upon the principles governing their value. No space would be given to capital or interest. Even exchange would receive very slight attention. Even the very important question of wages would be treated merely as the question of the most economical method of feeding slaves. Or imagine a treatise written by one on a feudal estate or in a Saxon village or in a Chinese hamlet. The laws of economics which are valid today will be worthless two hundred years from now, except as a mere intellectual curiosity. Economics cannot be thought of as a body of natural laws." Discuss and criticize.

(6) In what sense is the word law used or implied in each of the following: "The divine law is that you should love one another"? "The laws of Moses have I kept from my youth up"? "The soul that sinneth it shall die"?

(7) "There are no laws in political economy, only assumptions." What do you suppose led to this statement? Is it true?

(8) "Economic action grows out of individual volition. Hence it is subject to all the chance caprice, and fancy to which the human mind is subject. Nothing is so fickle as the human mind. Then how can there be economic law?" Criticize.

(9) "It is impossible to arrive at the statement of a natural law without careful and painstaking experimentation. The economist cannot

construct in his laboratory an industrial world of his own. He cannot at will repeat an experiment in industrial activity. There is, of course, law in the industrial world as there is law everywhere. But because of inability to perform experiments, the laws of the industrial world will never be discovered and formulated." Criticize.

(10) Solve problems 1, 2, 4, and 7 in the Outlines.

III
The Nature of Production

A. Preliminary Questions:

(1) Is the raising of cattle production? The conversion of hides into leather?

(2) Is the making of footballs out of leather and other materials production? Their transportation? Their sale?

(3) Is the playing of a baseball game by professionals productive, if a charge for admission is made?

(4) Is the playing of a baseball game by amateurs production, if no charge for admission is made? If a charge is made?

(5) Is the throwing of a baseball by two boys for their own amusement productive?

(6) A section of the country gives up fishing. A man continues to make nets. Is he a producer?

(7) In a section of the country there is a greater demand than ever before for fishing nets. No more men go into the business, and each man turns out just as many as before. Has the effort put forth by the laborer engaged in the business become more productive?

(8) What is production? Does the economic idea conflict with the physical impossibility of creating matter?

B. Reading:

(1) The following readings, if done in proper order, will give a fair idea of the gradual enlargement of the concept of production in the course of economic theory:

Ingram, *History of Political Economy*, pp. 62–63;

Adam Smith, *Wealth of Nations*, Bk. ii, Chapter 3, the first eight paragraphs;

Mill, *Principles of Political Economy*, Bk. 1, Chapter 3, Sections 1–4;

Gunton, *Principles of Social Economics*, pp. 68–72.

(2) Advanced readings:

Taylor, pp. 29–32;
Fetter, pp. 257–269, 419;
Seligman, pp. 257–278;
Nicholson, *Principles of Political Economy*, pp. 32–47;
Gide, pp. 113–118;
Smart, *Distribution of Income*, pp. 23–33;
Taylor, *Readings in Economics*, pp. 22–27.

C. Questions on the Readings:

(1) What labor was considered productive by the physiocrats? What was their underlying conception of production?
(2) To what extent did Adam Smith enlarge this concept of production?
(3) To what extent is Mill's conception of production an enlargement of Adam Smith's?
(4) What things, not included by Mill, does Gunton include in production?
(5) Draw a line, if you can, between direct and indirect acts of production. Give examples.
(6) Distinguish, if you can, between utilization and production. Should economics make the distinction? What is its importance?
(7) So far as economics are concerned, how do services embodied in material objects differ from services which are not this embodied?
(8) Should the concept of production be limited to the act of producing goods for market?
(9) Do you consider Mill's concept too narrow? Gunton's too broad? How much truth is there in each?
(10) Does production properly fall within the realm of economics? What phases must be studied in other sciences? In what other sciences?

D. Problems:

(1) In the light of your knowledge of economic theory, discuss the following definitions of production:
(a) The creation of material objects.
(b) The creation of objects of life-giving powers.
(c) The means by which wealth is produced.
(d) The creation of utilities.
(e) Efforts directly or indirectly applied which tend to impart to matter any of the attributes which make it available for human wants.
(f) The creation of values.

(g) The creation of economic utilities by the application of man's mental and physical powers to the materials of nature.

(2) "It is the height of absurdity to call the maker of musical instruments a producer, and the man who plays upon that instrument a non-producer." Upon what grounds do you suppose that the author of the above arrives at his conclusion? Is he right?

(3) "One has a right to form categories arbitrarily, provided his line of cleavage does not pass through a homogeneous class. But into this very logical error the classical economists fell when they limited productive labor to efforts which embody themselves in a material form." Explain and criticize.

(4) "Services which do not embody themselves in a material form are not susceptible of accumulation; for that reason they are not wealth, and those who render them are not producers." By illustrations, show the impossibility of drawing a hard and fast line between services which do and services which do not embody themselves in a material form. Is the point relative to accumulation well taken?

(5) "The selling of whiskey, the running of gambling halls, the sale of lottery tickets, and other enterprises of similar nature are not productive; for none of these things conduce to the ultimate betterment of society." Criticize.

(6) Is the mining of copper and tin productive? Is the manufacture of brass from these articles productive? Is the conversion of brass into musical instruments productive? Is the playing upon a musical instrument by a professional musician at a concert to which a charge for admission has been made productive? By an amateur at a concert to which a charge for admission has been made? By an amateur at a concert to which no charge for admission has been made? By an amateur in his own family circle? By an amateur for his own amusement?

(7) "Transportation and sale do not result in any change in the quality, the quantity, or the character of goods. They bring about purely no physical change in goods. So how can they be thought of as productive." Criticize.

(8) "All of the services performed by the retail merchants today could be performed by one-fourth of their number. Here there is a tremendous waste of social productive powers. In short, it is not too much to say that the class as a class is not productive." Does economics consider wholes or classes? Is the merchant productive? Are all merchants productive?

(9) "Economics has no business concerning itself, except incidentally, with production. Production is purely an industrial process, and, as such, its proper place is the science of industry. The function of economics is to explain value problems. Economists are beginning to recognize this, as is evidenced by the fact that two recent and popular text-books do not discuss production as a separate division of economics." Discuss and criticize.

(10) Solve problems 7, 8, and 9 in the Outlines, p. 33.

IV
The Factors of Production

A. Preliminary Questions:

(1) Make a list of the principal things you would need if you were starting a furniture factory.

(2) Trace each back to its ultimate source. Arrive in this way at the factors of production.

(3) Does capital wear out? Can flow capital be produced? How?

(4) Does land wear out? Can It be increased?

(5) Is a fertile prairie land? A "new ground" after the forest has been cut off? The same field ditched and fenced? A tract of desert land made fertile by irrigation?

(6) Except for drying fish and for the use of boats and other fishing tackle do sea fishers make any use of land?

(7) By means of citing several concrete cases, name several natural agents which are of importance in the productive process. Show the connection of each with the process.

(8) What natural agents are free goods?

(9) Is a horse and buggy owned by a live man capital? A horse and buggy owned by a sewing-machine agent and used by him in his business? A horse and buggy owned by a manker [sic] and used by him for recreation?

(10) Does land exist apart from capital? Capital apart from land?

B. Readings:

(1) General references:

Taylor, pp. 33–40;
Fetter, pp. 114–117, 173–177;
Seager, paragraphs 61, 69, 70, 71, 74;
Seligman, pp. 319–321, 285–286.

(2) References on the concept of capital
Fisher, *Capital and Income*, pp. 51–60;
Fisher, Precedents for Defining Capital, in the *Quarterly Journal of Economics*, May 1904, pp. 386–408;
Fetter, Recent Discussion of the Capital Concept, *Quarterly Journal of Economics*, November 1903, pp. 54–96;
Tuttle, The Real Capital Concept, in *Quarterly Journal of Economics*, November 1903, pp. 54–96;
Tuttle, The Fundamental Notion of Capital Once More, in *Quarterly Journal of Economics*, November 1904, pp. 811–110;

(3) References on the separation of land and capital:
Johnson, Rent in Modern Economic Theory, in *Publications of The American Economic Association*, 3rd Series, No. 2, pp. 21–43;
Carver, *The Distribution Wealth*, pp. 107–122;
Fetter, pp. 152–158;
Seligman, pp. 300–303;
Commons, *The Distribution of Wealth*, pp. 27–41.

C. Questions on the Readings:

(1) What has economics gained by arriving at the conclusion that there are three or four economic factors?
(2) What does the economist include under labor? What commonly termed labor is excluded?
(3) Are all contributions by nature to production contributions that need to be taken account of in economics?
(4) Give examples, if you can, of contributions of nature to the wealth of nations which do not have to be taken into account in a study of the individualistic economic system.
(5) Just what does the term land include? What things commonly denominated land does the economist exclude from the category? What things not usually called land does the economist include?
(6) Name several definitions of capital. What elements do they have in common? In what respects do they disagree?
(7) What seems to you to be the most acceptable definition of capital?
(8) What is the basis for the separation of the contributions to production into the three categories of land, labor and capital?
(9) What differences exist between labor and capital? Why not call labor capital?
(10) Make a list of the reasons advanced for the separation of labor and capital as productive factors.

(11) Make a similar list of the reasons advanced for the inclusion of land within the category capital.
(12) Strike out reasons which are not valid, and draw your own conclusions.
(13) Is the question of the separation of land and capital a question of practical moment?
(14) Certain economists try to distinguish between physical land and economic land. What do they make the basis of the distinction? Are they right?

D. Problems:

(1) In the light of your present knowledge, criticize the following definitions of capital:
   (a) Mere congealed labor.
   (b) A stock of wealth existing at an instant of time.
   (c) The result of past industry devoted to further production.
   (d) Material wealth in the hands of the productive classes.
   (e) Wealth which yields income.
   (f) Durable goods devoted to production.
   (g) Any wealth which serves more than one use.
   (h) Tools of production.
   (i) Material and material goods which bring in profit.

(2) A dog has been trained to guard sheep. Has there been an increase in any of the productive factors? In which one? How was the increase effected?

(3) "I admit that in the eighteenth century and in the first half of the nineteenth century abstinence was necessary to the accumulation of capital. But this does not prove that abstinence is always necessary to the accumulation of capital. A primitive pastoral society accumulates capital without abstinence; it simply allows the cattle, in which form its wealth is invested, to multiply. At the present day the railroads and other corporations practice no abstinence; they merely allow their capital to increase by investing in improvements a part of their earnings. Under socialism abstinence would be necessary; for the state would add to its fund of capital from time to time by setting aside part of the earnings which accrue to it as sole entrepreneur." Show that, in each of these cases, abstinence plays a part in the accumulation of capital.

(4) If a country were possessed of natural resources which were not subject to the law of diminishing returns, and if the country possessed only a limited amount of capital and labor, subject to diminishing returns,

with an indefinite number of wants to satisfy, would there be any land on that country? Answer both yes and no, and justify your answer.

(5) A railroad has just been constructed through a rich but undeveloped section of the country. The railroad is being financed and operated by a joint stock company. No dividends are to be paid during the four years subsequent to the organization of the company; but a dividend of six and one-fourth percent is guaranteed for each year after the first four. The amount actually invested is $800,000. The prevailing rate of interest is six and one-fourth. Does $800,000 represent the total cost of the road? If you invest $80 in a share of stock what does justice, as commonly understood, require the face value of that share to be?

(6) "To include land and capital under the general head 'factors of production' is to give to each concept a teleological implication. Land, then, must denote, not superficial extension and position, but these natural powers and factors which are or can be devoted to the production of those peculiar commodities demanded by society. Consequently a change in the wants of society, or a discovery of a new means of utilizing the power of nature increases the amount of land. Land, in this sense, is as easy to increase as capital." Explain, and defend or criticize.

(7) In Sparta we are told, that all human effort directed towards production was put forth by slaves. Make a classification of factors of production which will fit the industrial conditions of the Spartan state? Make a list of the elements which go into each of these divisions.

(8) "Building a skyscraper utilizing a waterfall, discovering new powers of the soil, improving a highway, running a railroad through a new section of the country are means by which the potentialities of land are utilized. But none of these means adds to the quantity of land?" In what sense is the word land used? Justify or criticize the above statement.

(9) Let us suppose that in the days before the Reformation, the beds from which came the herring, which were the chief subsistence of all good Catholics on Fridays and during Lent, were owned by private individuals. In the case of the production of the fish, what was the contribution of land to production? After the Reformation, when there were no longer so many good Catholics, and when herring were not greatly in demand, the whole industry declined., The beds at sea could be used for nothing else. After this decline was there as much land as when the demand for fish was at its height? Suppose that the beds were not privately owned, what was the contribution of land to production? In this case would the amount of land have decreased

after the Reformation? Suppose that the demand for herring had disappeared altogether, and the beds could not be used for any other purpose, would there have been a decrease in the amount of land?

(10) Is money capital? Is the credit system?

(11) Is the work of the banker labor? Of the college football player? Of the professional baseball player? Of the promoter? Of the opera singer? Of the hod-carrier? Of the preacher? Of the settlement worker?

(12) Solve problems 6, 14, 23, 26, 28, in the Outlines, 47–50.

V
The Productivity of Capital

A. Preliminary Questions:

(1) Can production be carried on without the use of labor? Land? Capital?

(2) How is labor brought into existence? Land? Capital?

(3) Can any factor of production be thought of as containing elements of some other or others?

(4) What is meant by the statement: "The real factors of production are the primary elements out of which the factors, land, labor, and capital, as we know them, are made?"

(5) What is the theoretical difference in the two statements following: "The capital produced a net return of five bushels of wheat per acre"; and "the capital produced a net return of five dollars per acre."?

(6) In two hours a man can crush a certain stone without previously fashioning any instruments; in one hour he can construct a rude hammer out of materials which are at hand, and with this in another hour he can crush the stone. Which method will he use? Why? Under what circumstances would he have been certain to have used the first? Under what, the second?

(7) Under the first hypothesis in the example above, is any part of the return to be attributed to a factor other than labor? Suppose that with the hammer he could have crushed the rock in one-half an hour, would any part of the product have been attributed to a factor other than labor?

(8) Suppose that the difference of one half hour's time were due entirely to the fact that the man began his work at one end of the stone rather than at the other, to what factor would you attribute the increased product?

(9) In question 6, change the word hours to days. Answer the questions given in 6; Answer the questions given in 7; in 8.

(10) In question 6, change the word hours to months. Answer questions given in 6; in 7; in 8.
(11) In question 6 change the word hours to years. Answer the questions given in 6, in 7, in 8.
(12) Do you find that the time interval has anything to do with the answers which you give to these questions? If so, in just what way?
(13) Has the ability of the laborer to support himself, or the existence of a separate capitalistic class anything to do with your answers to the above questions?
(14) What bearing have the facts brought out in your answers to the above question upon the question whether there is a separate product of capital or not?
(15) What bearing have the facts brought out in your answers to the above questions upon the question whether or not capital is productive!

B. Reading:
(1) Capital as an independent factor of production:
Taussig, *Outlines of a Theory of Wages*, p. 388;
Boehm-Bawerk, *Positive Theory of Capital*, pp. 92–99;
Carver, pp. 215–219.
(2) Interest as the product of capital:
Boehm-Bawerk, *Capital and Interest*, pp. 114–119;
Boehm-Bawerk, pp. 214–215, 263–265.
(3) The productivity of capital services:
Taylor, pp. 236–240.

C. Questions on the Readings:
(1) What are the grounds for concluding that labor and land are the original factors of production?
(2) What position in the productive process is assigned by Boehm-Bawerk to capital?
(3) What position in the productive process is assigned to capital by Carver? By Taussig? What are their reasons?
(4) What criticism can Boehm-Bawerk and Taussig make of Carver's position?
(5) What are the characteristics of the "capitalistic" method of production?
(6) In answer to the conclusion reached in 5, can it be urged that, even where labor works alone, the time element is involved? What would be the force of such an argument? Can all labor be thought of as involving waiting?

(7) Just where should the line be drawn between capitalistic, and non-capitalistic methods of production?
(8) State the use theory of interest; the exchange theory.
(9) Can Taussig reconcile the use theory with his conclusions that there is no separate product of capital?
(10) Will Taussig have to give up the productivity theory of wages?
(11) What criticism of the use theory is made by advocates of the exchange theory? Illustrate by an example involving explicit interest.
(12) Illustrate the exchange theory, if you can, by an example involving implicit interest.
(13) What is there in common between the exchange theory of interest and the socialistic theory of interest?
(14) In what respects do the two theories differ from each other?
(15) How does Prof. Taylor prove the productivity of capital services? How does his view differ from that of the productivity theorists? From that of Taussig? From that of Boehm-Bawark?

D. Problems:
(1) How would a sudden increase in the efficiency of industry affect the supply of capital? (Chicago)
(2) How would a sudden increase in the efficiency of industry affect the demand for capital?
(3) "Money is barren, and coal and iron cannot breed. Were all capital of this non-increasing kind, being non-productive, it would not yield interest. But a flock of sheep, herd of cattle, or group of Belgian hares will, from its own natural powers of production, increase and multiply. In like manner a forest will grow and crops will spring up. Interest exists because crops and animals grow, and because the seed becomes the crop." What view of productivity is implicit in the above quotation? Discuss and criticize the theory.
(4) "A man who puts one thousand dollars in a savings bank can demand that it receive interest, for the reason that he might invest it in a flock of sheep and let it accumulate naturally." Discuss and criticize.
(5) "Land yields interest, because it yields a perpetual series of crops. But interest must likewise be attainable from other capital else everyone would invest in land." How far does this argument go? What would be your principal criticism of it?
(6) "Land, furniture, and other perishable goods should yield a rent because of the wear and tear which is involved in their use. But there is not the same wear and tear in the case of money that there is in

the case of land and furniture. For that reason capital does not really earn an income." Show that the writer has mistaken the very nature of interest.

(7) "I admit that in a sense capital is productive. One may invest borrowed capital in agriculture in which form it yields a return. But, even in this case, the borrower must suffer; for one does not know how much agriculture will yield, and the risk must always be taken by the borrower." Point out the confusion present in the mind of the author of the quotation.

(8) "Capital, only when it is invested in land or livestock, is productive. Even in these cases capital is not always productive. There is ever present a great element of chance. In fact it is not too much to say that in the long run the total gains in agriculture exactly equal the total losses."

(9) "What," says Turgot, "that someone should be able to pay me or to make me pay for the petty use of a piece of furniture or a trinket, and that it should be a crime to charge me anything for the immense advantage I get for the use of a sum of money for the same things; and all because the subtle intellect of a lawyer can separate in one case the use of the thing from the thing itself, and in the other case cannot!" On what ground does the author of the above justify interest?

(10) "If two owners of real capital wish to exchange their products, each of them is disposed to demand for the labor of storing and as profit, as much over the intrinsic value of the product as the other will grant him; necessity, however, makes them meet each other half-way. But money represents real capital; with real capital a profit can be made; and hence, interest." Explain, point out the confusion in the author's mind, and criticize his real proposition.

(11) "In themselves all capitals are dead; there is no truth in the assertion of their independent productivity. From the return to labor, and from the amount of goods produced by it, the capitalist receives his share; but he has no claim to anything more than the expense that furnishing the capital has cost him." What theory of interest is implicit in the above? Criticize it.

(12) "If capital had not itself a productive power, independent of the labor which has created it, how could it be that a capital, to all eternity, produces an income independent of the industrial activity which employs it?" Can you answer the question?

(13) "In every instant where capital is so employed as to produce a profit, it manifestly arises either from its supplanting a portion of labor, which

would otherwise be performed by man, or from its performance of labor beyond the reach of the personal exertions of man to accomplish." Explain and criticize.

(14) "If the capitalistic, or roundabout, process of production required no time, then capital would not be productive, and there would be no interest." Discuss.

(15) "If, in this country, all men had equal possessions and there were no separate capitalistic and proletarian classes, there would be no interest." Do you agree? Why?

Appendix

Is Capital Productive?

By F. M. Taylor

I. Analysis of the question:
   A. Does the function credited to the capitalist make any economic contribution to human welfare?
      (1) In consumptive borrowing.
      (2) In productive borrowing.
   B. If said contribution is made, is it properly to be credited to the capitalist?
   C. Is said contribution properly described by the word "Production"?

II. Discussion:
   A. (1) Does the function credited to the capitalist make any economic contribution to human welfare in the sense of consumptional borrowing?
      Surely yes. To this case, the Exchange Theory as to the real nature of the capitalistic transaction applies. (Explain that theory.) {If} exchange is of advantage to the borrower: (a) different provision for the present and the future; (b) underestimate of the future. Read Boehm-Bawerk, Positive Theory, 249–259.
   (2) Does the capitalist function make any contribution in productive borrowing? Are capitalistic processes more efficient than non-capitalistic, or are more-capitalistic processes more efficient than less-capitalistic?
      (i) Interpretation of the question:
         (a) No, not merely gross productivity, must be established. (Explain).
         (b) If labor is homogeneous, case 1, what does the question mean? (Give an illustration of net productivity.)

(c) If labor is heterogeneous, case 2, what does the question mean? (Usually in the present order, we could know directly only that more value results from the capitalistic method. Explain. What would the question mean to a communistic society, supposing such society to take utility, rather than value, as its economic guide? Explain what this means. If a communistic society were using just the same amount of human factors, {it} would find the results larger from the capitalistic than from the non-capitalistic methods.)

(ii) Argument for the affirmative in case 1. In such cases, the proof is a matter of mere arithmetic. The actual adoption of the capitalistic method proves its superior efficiency.

(iii) Argument for the affirmative answer in case 2. Is not the existence of a surplus value significant and sufficient proof of a product surplus? (The value of product actually proves sufficient to cover: (1) the value of the intermediate product, i.e. of the concealed past labor involved; and (2) the value of the current labor and, then, leave a surplus. Since the labor spent on the intermediate product would not have been more costly if used directly, its actual use in the former way proves a greater product return.) (Another line of argument: The existence of a value element infallibly indicates a utility, advantage, product element; though the converse is not true. Utility alone is not sufficient to make value; but, without utility, value cannot arise. The absence of a value surplus proves that there was a product surplus.) (Another line of argument: According to "automatic imputation" theory, one in production inevitably gets credited with what is substantially its contribution; hence the existence of productive interest proves a contribution of capital. Read Taylor, pp. 154–159.)

B. Is the said contribution properly chargeable to the capitalist?

(1) Is it properly credited to the legitimate owner of the capital? Non-debatable.

(2) Can private persons be legitimate owners of capital?

(i) From the standpoint of socialistic ethics, only the negative answer is possible.

(ii) Utilitarian economics, utilitarian ethics, might give an affirmative answer. Discuss briefly. Read Taylor, pp. 295–297.

C. Is the contribution of capital properly described by the word "production"?

(1) Objection: the capitalistic and non-capitalistic methods of production are merely two different methods of laboring; – labor more distributed in time vs. labor less distributed-in-time. Answer: even so, the capitalist furnishes one element in that more-distributed procedure, – viz. waiting. Say that he does part of the work if you please.

(2) Second objection: the product is no greater in the capitalistic than in the non-capitalistic procedure, provided the two products are measured in the same unit, i.e. provided both are measured from the point of view of the present. Answer: This confuses our problem with the interest problem. The entrepreneur is concerned, not with present vs. future, but with little vs. much. He wants a stock of present goods, not because they are present in the sense of being able to satisfy present wants, but because they are the promise of mainly future goods.

(3) Third objection: The capitalistic office is to bear the burden of accepting a reward which has an element of inferiority, viz. futurity. The productive operations are affected by labor, but the return is inferior in being of future date. The capitalist accepts this disadvantage, and so merits his reward, but he does not thereby produce. Answer: again a confusion with the interest problem. Accepting the exchange theory as the immediate origin of interest, we would still find that one reason why entrepreneurs came to the market wishing to buy present goods with future is that with these goods they can increase productivity. See Fisher, *The Rate of Interest*, p. 186.

(4) Even if we concede that in a strictly proper sense of "produce" we cannot apply the term to the function of the capitalist, there seems, after all no alternative. It is responsible for the existence of a considerable share of the product. How else can you describe the fact than to say that capital produces?

VI
The Law of Diminishing Returns

A. Preliminary Questions:

(1) Why is extensive agriculture characteristic of new countries? Intensive agriculture of old countries?

(2) Under what conditions would greater economy be used in relation to land than to the other factors? In relation to capital? Labor?
(3) Why are buildings of brick and stone not erected in small vil1ages? Why do large cities build skyscrapers? Why not build one-hundred-story buildings?
(4) Why should the nation give attention to the conservation of its natural resources?
(5) How does the farmer come into contact with the law of diminishing returns?
(6) "The most important of the applications of the law of diminishing returns is in relation to land." Is this statement true? Why?
(7) Relate the law of diminishing returns directly to several great movements in history.
(8) By means of illustrations, distinguish between technical diminishing returns and value diminishing returns.

B. Reading:
(1) Cautions to the student:
(a) Avoid confusing the law of diminishing returns, which is the statement of a sequence, with statements about the condition of a particular industry at a particular time and place.
(b) Do not confuse diminishing returns with the exhaustion of the soil, or with changes in population or industries in definitely named regions.
(c) Distinguish carefully both in nature and formulation, between the instrumental law and the industrial law, and be sure that you knew which the author has in mind.
(d) Do not confuse technical returns with value returns; nor the productive factors, cosidered as quantities, with those factors considered as values.
(e) Do not impute returns, first to the changing factor and then to the constant factor,
(2) Required readings:
(a) Required:
Taylor, *Outlines*, 1909 ed., pp. 63–72.
(b) Highly recommended:
Carver, pp. 71–82, 94–101;
Seligman paragraphs 83, 106, 133, 160, 168, and 175;
Fetter pp. 61–72.
(c) Other elementary readings:

Seager, paragraphs 64 and 72;
Johnson, *Introductory Economics*, pp. 79–96.

(d) More advanced readings:
Commons, pp. 116–159;
Carver, pp. 83–101;
Cannan, *Production and Distribution*, pp. 147–182;
Senior, *Political Economy*, pp. 81–86.

C. Questions on the Reading:

(1) Clear up the fundamental concepts used in the discussion: a constant factor, changing factor, productivity, efficiency, maximum, etc.
(2) By means of a series of propositions adduce the proof of the instrumental law of diminishing returns. State the law and give illustrations.
(3) In what stage can instruments be worked? In what stage of efficiency will they be worked? In what stage of productivity?
(4) By means of a series of propositions adduce the proof of the industrial law of diminishing returns. State the law and give illustrations.
(5) In what respects are the two laws unlike in nature? In formulation?
(6) Is it possible to lay down a law of increasing returns for certain industries? If so, is this law parallel to the law of diminishing returns as laid down for other industries?
(7) Is it possible to use the law in a broader sense, say in relation to national industry as a whole?
(8) Is there a possibility of capital accumulating to such an extent that industry will be unable to make use of it at all?
(9) Relate the law of diminishing returns to the general principles of value.
(10) Relate it to the Ricardian law of rent.
(11) Relate it to the law of wages.
(12) Relate it to the law of interest.
(13) In what other ways does the law play a part in economic theory?
(14) Of what practical consequence is it?

D. Problems:

(1) Show how the law of diminishing returns has to be taken account of by those who would perform the following undertakings: building a mill dam, erecting a skyscraper, sinking oil wells in a definite region, setting out strawberry plants, erecting a number of barns on a very large estate.
(2) A recent book on mediaeval history contains the theory that in the second and third centuries the barbarians, restricted to a definite region by the Roman frontier, were, to save themselves from starvation,

forced to adopt intensive methods of agriculture, and that the adoption of the intensive methods was the economic force which resulted in the formation of tribes and of the union of these tribes into confederacies. Accepting the theory as true, what role in the process would be attributed to the law of diminishing returns?

(3) Relate the law of diminishing returns to the so-called migration of the nation in the fourth and fifth centuries, to the settlement of America, to the Western movement of population in the United States, to the colonial policies of some of the great nations of today.

(4) Relate the law of diminishing returns to the problem of immigration, to the movement for scientific farming, to the question of industrial efficiency, to the movement for reclamation of arid lands and irrigation, to the high cost of living, to the emigration of American citizens to Canada, and to other practical questions of the day.

(5) "The law of diminishing conditions was formulated in England, and, without doubt, applies to conditions existing there. But the law has only local validity as is evident from its inapplicability to American conditions. In America we have not found it necessary to resort to poorer and poorer land as population has increased. On the contrary, since our first settlements were along the seaboard, which is the most infertile part of the country, as population has moved westward, we have taken under cultivation better and better lands. Further in each community the poorer lands are usually first cultivated because those lands do not have to be drained or cleared. Then, as capital has accumulated, we have drained swamps and cleared 'new lands', thus taking under cultivation the best lands of all. This experience of America is sufficient to disprove the universality of the law of diminishing returns." Show that the author of the above has an erroneous conception of the character of natural law. Show that his implied statement of the law is incorrect. Even if the experience of America has been as he represents it to have been, does this disprove the law?

(6) "The law of diminishing returns applies to agriculture, but not to manufacture. As one applied 'dose' after 'dose' of labor to any field of definite area, a point is finally reached after which each succeeding 'dose' will yield a smaller return than the one which preceded it. But a manufacturing establishment can double its output and at the same time reduce the cost of production per unit of product." Show that the two cases mentioned above are not really parallel.

(7) A lot in a large city has cost $500,000. A building is to be erected upon it. A building of one story will cost $100,000. If additional

stories are to be built, each will entail an expense of $50,000 more than the cost entailed by the story under it. If the owner desires to secure the largest amount of floor space at the least cost per floor, how many stories will be built?

(8) Suppose that in the problem above it is possible to rent the first floor of the proposed building for $36,,000 and each floor above it for $22,000. How many stories will be built if the owner desires to realize the highest rate percent upon the capital invested in the building?

(9) A tenant rents a farm of several acres, and agrees to pay as rent ten bushels of wheat per acre. One day's work on each acre will produce 5 bushels of wheat. A second day's work will produce 6; a third, 5; a fourth, 4; a fifth 3; a sixth, 2 1/2; a seventh, 2; an eighth, 1 1/2 and a ninth, 1. If the tenant desires to receive for each day's work the maximum quantity of wheat, how many days' work will he put on each acre? If the working season is limited to 90 days, how many acres can he rent?

(10) Suppose that the rent, in the above problem, were only 5 bushels of wheat per acre, how many days would he put on each acre? How many acres will he rent? Suppose that there were no rent to be paid, how many days would he put on each acre? How many acres would he cultivate? What would his wages be in each of the three cases?

(11) "In many industries, e.g. the meat-packing industry, the law of diminish returns does not hold. Every increase in the size of the business has made it possible to reduce the cost per unit of product. In fact the law really applies only to a very few industries." Criticize.

(12) "In manufacturing a day's labor produces more than it did thirty years ago; in agriculture, it produces much less. This proves that agriculture is subject to the law of diminishing returns while manufacture is not." Point out the confusion in the mind of the author of the above.

VII
The Theory of Value

A. Preliminary Questions:

(1) Is there any sense in which Crusoe would be said to buy one thing with another, or to exchange things? (Davenport)

(2) Point out by very definite and concrete examples how the housewife applies to her domestic work principles of political economy. Show how she is guided by the principle of marginal utility and marginal cost. Reconcile the two principles as they apply to her work.

(3) Why does silk sell for more than calico? Cake than beer, steel than iron?
(4) What is the value of season's work to a primitive man living in isolation in a fertile river valley? Would the value be the same if he were living in a mountainous region?
(5) What is the value of a season's work to an English farmer? Were the Gulf Stream non-existent, would the value remain the same? Had America not been discovered, would the value remain the same?
(6) A farm and an apartment house are bringing in the same income. Will they be valued at the same figure?
(7) Is there anything in common between "cost," "the onerous exertion necessary to get goods," and cost as the necessary expenses of production?
(8) "The value of a single commodity, or of several commodities, may rise or fall, but a general rise or fall of values is an economic impossibility." Is this statement true?
(9) x, y, and z are used in making a. If the value of a decreases, what effect will it have upon the values of x, y, and z? If x decreases in value, what affect will it have upon the value of a? Upon the value of y and z?
(10) The marginal utility of a surgeon's knife is far higher than another knife made out of the same elements and devoted to another use. Will its price be determined by its cost of production?
(11) A toothbrush and a razor have practically the same marginal utility yet the cost of the labor is practically the same as the cost of the toothbrush. Are the prices of these two articles determined by marginal utility or by marginal cost?
(12) What part is played by value in economic conduct?

B. Reading;
  (1) Market price, Taylor, pp. 110–120.
  (2) Normal price of concrete goods:
    (A) Fixed-supply goods, Taylor, pp. 128–130.
    (B) Variable-supply goods:
      (a) Constant-cost goods, Taylor, pp. 132–136;
      (b) Increasing-cost goods, Taylor, pp. 140–142;
    (C) Diminishing-cost goods, Taylor, pp. 144–145.

C. The heart of value theory is to be found in the problem of the price of ultimate cost goods. Because of its importance and difficulty, this part of the discussion is outlined below with considerable fullness. Where the point could be made with clearness in that way, questions may have been used; where the question method has presented difficulties, an attempt has been made to make clear the points or importance by means of a series of propositions.

(1) A statement of the problem:

(a) Preliminary questions:

(i) In the discussion of the normal price of producible commodities what assumptions are made as to entrepreneurs' costs? Are these assumptions true? (Taylor, p. 153).

(ii) From whatever source it gets it, is it true that a machine that is new has a certain value? As a machine is used up what becomes of its value?

(iii) A machine is a produced good. Can its value be resolved into the values of more primary elements?

(iv) Explain the statement, "Consumption goods and intermediate goods are only media through which society is evaluating more primary elements."

(v) Technically, a product is the result of many elements, e.g. labor, waiting, iron ore, limestone, water, air. In writing an equation to represent the economic situation, should all of these technical elements be included? Explain fully.

(b) The problem may be thus stated in formal propositions:

(i) Any consumption good, say A, technically is made up of elements, say a, b, c, d, e, f, g, ...

(ii) Some of these elements exist in superabundance and do not have to be economized by man? Let's say that f and g belong to that class. Such elements do not have to be taken into consideration economically.

(iii) Some of these elements, say b, d, and h, . . . are made up of still more primary elements, say b′, b″, . . . d′, d″ . . . etc.

(iv) Some of these, say d′, d′″, . . ., are made up of still more primary elements, etc.

(v) The process outlined above resolves all goods into their original elements. These elements, final and indivisible, are called ultimate cost goods.

(vi) The number of these ultimate cost goods is immaterial.

(vii) Our problem is to find principles which determine the value of these ultimate cost goods.

(viii) It is proposed to show: (1) the existence of the utility of the ultimate cost goods only in consumption goods; and

(2) that each of these goods which is producible has a price which also expresses its marginal disutility or cost.

(ix) The difficulty of the task lies in: (1) the existence of the utility of the ultimate cost only in some consumption good; (2) the existence of the utility of the ultimate cost good only in the marginal produce of the cost good; and (3) the existence of this utility as a part only of the marginal utility of the product (on the statement of the problem, see Taylor, pp. 153–154).

(2) The argument for the proposition contained in b above:

(a) "That the prices of ultimate cost goods must express the marginal utilities imputable to them." Answer the following questions:

(i) To what use will the last unit be put? Express in economic terms how n units will be used.

(ii) To what use will the last unit be put? Express in economic terms how n units will be used.

(iii) The same state has m units of y, and p units of z. In what order, logically not chronologically, will the units of these two goods be used? To what points will the two goods be used?

(iv) The units x, y, and z . . . are used in r different combinations to produce r different products. Will the value of any unit of x, or y, or z, always be the same irrespective of the good in whose production it is used? Answer very clearly.

(v) A is a consumption good. It is made up of the four elements w, x, y, and z, but uses a different number of units of each of the four elements. Express the economic composition of A by means of an algebraic equation.

(vi) If our problem were a technical one, we would have to add two other elements, say air and water, represented by the symbols u and v. Why do we not put, say, 3u and 5v, into the above equation?

(vii) B, C and D are consumption goods. Each is composed of the elements w, x, y, and z, but in different proportions. Express the economic composition of each of these goods by means of an equation.

(viii) Substitute in place of the symbols A, B, C, and D, in the equations you have written, prices. Should these prices be market prices or normal prices?

(ix) Solve the equations and determine the value of each ultimate element.

(x) In actual life is it usually possible by means of one series of equations to get back to ultimate goods, or will a solution of the first series of equations give as the values of commodities more elementary than those with which we started, but themselves composites of primary elements?

(xi) Suppose that A, B, C, and D retain the prices which you have given them above, and suppose that the prices of the ultimate cost goods change, say two become dearer and two become cheaper. How will the prices of the producers of the four articles be affected? What influence will this have upon the actions of the entrepreneurs? How long will this influence continue? When equilibrium is restored, what will be the final result?

(xii) Suppose that the ultimate good is not fixed in output, and that the output increases, will price still express a marginal utility? What if the output decreases? (Taylor, pp. 154–159).

(b) "That, if ultimate cost goods depend for their existence upon human choice, their price tends to be the one which expresses not only their marginal utility, but also the marginal utility involved in supplying them." Answer the following questions:

(i) By means of schedules show the difference between the statements that price will be fixed at a point which will tend to express marginal disutility, and that marginal disutility has a real share in the fixing of price.

(ii) To prove that waiting power lends itself to the disutility principle, what would one have to prove? Illustrate, by means of schedules, the rate of interest as partly determined by the disutility principle.

(iii) Does labor of the higher grades lend itself to the disutility principle? Does labor of the lower grades? If either does, illustrate by means of schedules the determination of wages (Taylor, pp. 159–162).

D. The relation of utility to cost in the theory of value may be expressed in the form of a series of propositions:

(1) In the last analysis, ultimate goods are composites of simpler elements, and have their values determined by their costs of production.

(2) Consumption goods and most production goods are composites of simpler elements, and have their values determined by their cost of production.

(3) The value or cost of any such good is equal to, and is measured by, the sum of the marginal utilities (or disutilities, in the case of producible goods) of the elements composing the good, each being taken as many times as units of it have gone into the production of the concrete good whose value is being determined (Taylor, pp. 162–164). Point out the reconciliation between costs and utility, and show how the former is a means to the end which the latter attempts to accomplish. By means of illustrations make clear the principle in 3.

E. Problems:

(1) By means of the principle of marginal utility explain the mysteries of the so-called paradoxes of value. They are as follows:

(a) A more useful article, like . . ., is less valuable than a less useful article, like . . ..

(b) The most useful articles, like . . . and . . ., have no value at all.

(c) The part is sometimes more valuable than the whole; for, by destroying a part, the remainder is often sold for more than the whole would fetch.

(2) By means of the principles which you have learned, explain the values mentioned in the two equations which follow:

(a) "And there was famine in Samaria, and they besieged it, until an ass's head was sold for fourscore pieces of silver . . .," II Kings, vi, 25 (Upon the morrow) ". . . two measures of barley for a shekel and a measure of fine flour for a shekel," II Kings, vii, 18.

(b) "Then Peleus' son ordained straightway the prizes for a third contest, offering them to Danaana, for the grievous, wrestling match: for the university a great tripod for standing on the fire, prized by the Achaians among them at twelve oxen's worth; and for the loser he brought a woman into their midst, skilled in manifold work, and they prized her at four oxen," Homer, Iliad, Bk. xxiii.

(3) Five consumption goods, whose prices are known, are made out of three intermediate products, but in different proportions. One of the intermediate products is composed of two elements which may be used separately. In one of the five consumption goods, the first of these two elements is used alone, and in another the second of the two elements is used alone. In producing the other three consumption goods, the intermediate good which is divisible is used in its indivisible form. Indicate, by a series of equations, how the values of the ultimate cost goods are to be determined. In the actual world how are they determined?

(4) Draw up a series of equations showing the economic composition of four consumption goods. Change the price of one of the products. What changes must occur in the prices of the ultimate cost goods? Do your results invalidate the principles laid down in the discussion above?

(5) "There is no inconsistency between marginal utility as the force which fixes prices and costs as determinants of prices. Ultimately marginal utility does determine all values, but cost of production immediately determines value, and is the means by which marginal utility works itself out." Explain fully. Does this statement require any qualification?

(6) "It is a petitio principii to say that the cost of production is the cause of the value of things. For, as the cost of production is, . . . nothing but the value of the wealth consumed in the course of production, such a train of argument would merely explain value by value" Gide, *Political Economy*, p. 66. Criticize.

(7) "Certain economists have made an attempt to explain value by cost of production; yet these same economists have admitted that the value of the cost good is derived from the value of the product of that good, which, in turn, depends upon the utility of the product. Such economists are reasoning in a circle. Their task is futile, for it is perfectly evident that cost, being a derivative, cannot explain value." Analyze and criticize.

(8) "Since man's productive powers are limited, and since his wants are practically infinite, labor is and ever must be a fixed supply good. As such its value is determined by the marginal utility of its produce. Under no circumstances has marginal disutility any role to play in the matter." Discuss.

(9) "There has long been controversy as to whether 'cost of production' or 'utility' govern value. It might as reasonably be disputed whether it is the upper or the lower blade of a pair of scissors that cuts the piece of paper," Marshall, *Economics of Industry*, p. 221. Discuss.

(10) "Utility is the primary cause of value; sacrifice, merely a condition . . . Prices rise whenever demand tends to raise them, unless counteracting tendencies in the volume of supply are thereby set up. The physical sciences excellently illustrate social forces in this respect. Water flowing from one receptacle to another sets its own limit to the process. Freezing brings an end to the solidifying process through a self-manufactured protection against the frost . . . The larger part of social phenomena are of this self-limiting type, where forces set in action counteracting tendencies," Davenport, *Outlines of Economic Theory*, pp. 58–59. Discuss. Can you reconcile this with the quotation in 9?

(11) "That Tokay was not valuable because there were Tokay vineyards, but that the Tokay vineyards were valuable because Tokay has a high value, no one will be inclined to deny . . . As the moon reflects the sun's rays on to the earth, so the many-sided costs reflect the value which they receive from their marginal product on to other products. The principle of value is never in them, but outside them in the marginal value of the products." Boehm-Bawerk, Positive Theory of Capital, 189. Discuss. Can this be reconciled with the quotation from Marshall? With the quotation from Davenport?

(12) "I hold labor to be essentially variable, so that its value must be determined by the value of the product, not the value of the product by that of labor," Jevons, *Theory of Political Economy*, p. 165. Do you agree with this statement?

VIII
Cost, Utility, and Value

A. Preliminary Questions

(1) What does cost mean to a farmer, who has plenty of land, who had few and simple wants, and who raises, not for the market, but for his own consumption?

(2) What will cost mean if he has many wants and his working days are limited?

(3) In what sense do we imply the word "cost," when we ask whether a nation is increasing its material means of satisfaction by the means in which it consumes its resources?

(4) What does a business man mean by his costs of production?

(5) In what sense of the word "cost" can we make it rank with utility as a co-determinant of value? Give an illustration.

(6) In what sense do we use the word "cost" when we say it is a means through which utility determines the price of an article?

(7) In a Crusoe economy does the equivalence between cost and utility hold generally, or only at the margin? (Davenport)

(8) Is value the result or the cause of cost? Where is the ultimate causation?

B. Reading:

Gide, pp. 65–66, 54–60;
Smart, *Introduction to the Theory of Value*, pp. 71–80;

Marshall, *Economics of Industry*, pp. 200–201;
Von Wieser, *Natural Value*, pp. 195–198;
Carver, pp. 31–37, 50–51; 1–57;
Boehm-Bawerk, *The Positive Theory of Capital*, pp. 179–189;
Seligman, pp. 189–201;
Commons, pp. 14–20;
Jevons, pp. 155–161;
Fisher, *Capital and Income*, pp. 173–174, 188–190.

C. Questions on the Reading

(1) In a community, composed of people who had only one want, which could be satisfied by natural products, but only after time spent in search, what would determine the value of an article? What would determine the cost of production? When would effort stop?

(2) In a community, composed of people possessed of two wants, which could be satisfied in the same way, what would determine the value of a unit of each commodity? What would be the cost of production of each? When would the individual turn from one article to the other?

(3) In the same community, if it required twice as much effort to produce one article as the other, would a unit of the first exchange for two units of the second? If necessary, add qualifying conditions.

(4) Suppose that a community has wants for five articles, and that each article is made from a single ultimate good, what will determine the value of one of these articles? What will determine the value of one of the more ultimate goods? What will be the cost of production of one of the articles? Cost in what sense?

(5) Suppose that in the case above, each of the more ultimate goods is produced from two separate and independent goods, what will determine the value of the two goods taken together? What will determine the value of one of them?

(6) Suppose that in the case above, one productive good is used in three different ways: as a consumption good, as a productive element in good A, and as a productive element in good B. What will determine its value? Whence gets its cost? In what sense are using the word cost?

(7) Suppose a community which consumes n different goods made up of m different elements, and suppose that the m elements are made up of p different factors, etc. Suppose that singly, by two's, by three's etc., but in different proportions, these productive elements enter into final goods, and that they are themselves, in the same way, composite products. Tell how the values of the consumption goods, of the goods

of the second rank, and the ultimate cost goods are determined. In this explanation use the word cost in two senses, but keep clearly the distinction between the two.

(8) Suppose a community like the above, composed of persons possessed of an infinite number of wants which are subject to the law of diminishing utility, and suppose all goods produced to be subject to the law of increasing costs. Suppose that marginal utility fixes the value of ultimate cost goods, and that the values of finished goods are fixed by the laws of costs. Under these conditions what determines how much of any good will be produced? Does the value of the finished product correspond to the marginal utility of that product? To the cost? In what sense are you using the word cost?

(9) Formulate, as carefully and as accurately as you can, the laws for value, making the theory of the value of ultimate cost goods your starting point, and ending with the law of market price.

D. Problems:

(1) In what sense is the word cost used in each of the following quotations?

(a) "I cannot sell this for less; if I did, I would be selling below cost."

(b) "This bale of cotton cost many a hard day's work."

(c) "This machine cost many tons of iron, much labor, and many feet of lumber."

(d) "I would like to study Hebrew; but the cost is too great."

(e) "To study economics has cost me a course in physics."

(f) "A man can get what he wants in college, if he is willing to stand the cost."

(g) "The good is not produced, because the cost of production is too high."

(h) "In economics our interest is in relative rather than in absolute cost."

(2) "Value is determined by demand and supply." "Value is determined by cost of production." "Value is determined by cost of reproduction." "Value is determined by marginal utility." Can these propositions be reconciled? (Chicago)

(3) "In the present economic system, the value of any good is determined by the cost of production, which is a composite item, made up of and equal to the sum of the marginal utilities of the ultimate cost goods which have gone into its production, the marginal utility of each

costgood being taken as many times as units of that good have gone into the production of the consumption good in question." Explain the above question. What role does it assign to utility in the determination of value? To cost? How does it reconcile the two? Does it take account Of real costs? What would be the affect of adding the words "or disutility" after the words "marginal utilities" on their first appearance above?

(4) "But 'costs' are nothing else than the complex of those productive goods which have value – the labour, concrete capital, uses of wealth, and so on which must be expended in making the product" Boehm-Bawerk, *Positive Theory*, p. 183. Explain and illustrate. Prove or disprove.

(5) "It is characteristic of productive goods that they admit of infinitely more various uses than consumption goods. The value of the productive unit adjusts itself to the marginal and value of that product that possesses the least marginal utility of all products for whose production the unit might economically have been employed," Boehm-Bawerk, p. 186. Explain and illustrate. How will the value of supermarginal products be determined?

(6) "Here the conduction of value describes, as it were, a broken line. First it goes from the marginal product to the means of production and fixes their value; then it goes in the opposite direction, from the means of production to the other products which may be made by them. In the end, therefore, products of higher immediate marginal utility get their value from the side of their means of production," Boehm-Bawerk, p. 188. Illustrate. What problem above contains virtually the same statement? In what sense is the word costs used? Is there a place here for disutility costs?

(7) "As a fact people are right when they say that costs regulate value . . . It holds only so far as it is possible to obtain, at will and at the right time, substitutes through production . . . Even where the law of costs holds, costs are not the final, but only the intermediate cause of value. They do not give it to their products, but receive it from them," Boehm-Bawark, p. 188. Explain and criticize.

(8) "The real determinant of value is utility, cost is a mere guide to rational economic conduct." "The real determinant of value is cost; utility is a mere guide to rational economic conduct." Explain fully the theory of value contained in these two quotations. Illustrate each with schedules.

(9) "The price of a commodity is determined by the expenses of production of the most expensive part of the customary supply. This supply

is determined by the relative power possessed by the different cooperating factors of limiting their share of the total product relatively to the wants and resources of society. Cost of production coincides with, and partly determines, expenses in the case of the marginal savings of capitalists, marginal monopoly laborers, and all freely competing laborers." Commons. To reach these conclusions from what premises must Commons start? By what steps doe he probably come to his conclusions? Are they valid? Does he have in mind the prices paid for finished commodities or the prices paid for ultimate cost goods? Does he go far enough in his analysis?

(10) "In a comprehensive view of production there is no cost of production in the objective sense at all. All of what is called cost is cost only with respect to certain accounts, it is also income with respect to certain other accounts," Fisher, *Capital and Income*, p. 171. Does Fisher here contribute anything new?

(11) "We found that the so-called cost of production has no existence as an element of the objective income stream, and that, therefore, the only costs of production which are not also elements of income are the subjective labor and trouble of these engaged in that production," Fisher, p. 184. Explain this statement. How does Fisher reach the conclusion? Do you agree?

(12) "Normally the value of capital will vary with the past cost of production. But, however determined, it is the estimated future cost alone which enters into the calculation of present value. All of these principles are well illustrated in the case of the (Panama) canal," Fisher, pp. 188–189. What is Fisher's proposition? He holds it to be true of what class or classes of goods?

(13) "The same principle holds all the way back in the productive processes. The labor expended is staked (either by the laborer or the entrepreneur) in anticipation of the prices which the buyer will be willing to pay. If the anticipated prices are not expected to cover the value of the labor and the other costs plus the interest upon them, the result will be that the labor and other costs will not be expended. Hence, by trial and error the labor and other costs will, under normal conditions, gradually be fitted to the prices," Fisher, p. 189. What role is here assigned to costs in the determination of price? Does Fisher prove his case?

(14) "When prices find this normal level at which costs plus interest are covered, it is not because in the past costs of production have determined prices in advance, but because the sellers have been good

speculators as to what prices would be" Fisher, pp. 189–190. In what sense is the word costs used? What argument is Fisher evidently trying to answer? Does he succeed?

(15) "We see, then, that although prices have a normal relation to past costs, this relation does not always hold true; and that, whether it holds true or not, the costs do not predetermine the prices except in the sense that the producers have skillfully adapted the stocks available now, and those to be available at succeeding points of time, to the demand for them," Fisher, p. 190. Criticize.

(16) "I must absolutely deny that wages can in any sense be taken to represent the labor element in the cost of production. Wages, as Mr. Mill observed, may be regarded as cost to the capitalist who advances them; though perhaps it would be more correct to say that, so far as they go, they measure his cost, which really consists in the deprivation of immediate enjoyment implied in the fact of the advance. But to the laborer wages are reward, not cost; nor can it be said that they stand in any constant relation to that which really constitutes cost to him. If they did, wages in all occupations in all countries, and in all times, would be in proportion to the severity of the toil which they recompensed," Cairnes, *Leading Principles*, p. 53. Explain the above statement. What are the views held by Cairnes on the relation of cost and utility to value?

(17) "The failure to realize that value is a social conception has led to much pointless controversy. Utility is not sufficient to give value. For anything to have value, its supply must be limited. But if the supply is limited, it will cost some sacrifice to secure it or to reproduce it. Hence either utility or cost may be declared the measure of value. Regarded from this point of view the discussion as to which is the real measure of value is as futile as to ask how to measure the sound or quality of a hammer's blow on a bell. Without the particular kind of bell there would be a different quality of sound; without this particular kind of hammer there would likewise be a different quality of sound. So in economic life we deal with the demand for anything as compared with its supply. To affirm that either utility or cost exclusively measures value is as incomplete as to say that either demand or supply exclusively fixes value," Seligman, 199. What theory of value is here expressed? Is this consistent with the rest of his discussion?

(18) "We may thus roughly say that individual labor or cost of production fixes value; but what it really does is not to fix value, but to express

the value that is fixed by social forces as a whole. The value is not due to the labor of the individual who has made it, but to the social service which it is going to render, – that is to the social sacrifice which it is going to save. If it does not render that service, it will not possess that value no matter how such individual labor has been spent on it. On the other hand, if less individual labor be spent on it, it will have less value, not because less individual labor has been spent, but because the marginal service to society is now less. Utility, and not cost, is the ultimate cause of value," Seligman, pp. 200–201. What conception has Seligman of cost? Define clearly his terms, and state just what he means. Is he consistent in the two quotations above? Do you agree with him?

IX
Early Theories of Interest

A. Preliminary Questions:

(1) Show how the phenomenon of interest is concealed in each of the following: the value of an orchard, retail prices, wages for labor on productive goods, the value of a share of stock, the saving of ice until summer time.

(2) A small boy, instead of spending his pennies, saves them and with them purchases a ticket to a circus. Show how this involves the phenomenon of interest.

(3) Etymologically which better describes the phenomenon in question, usury or interest? Which is the older word? What is indicated by the fact that one of these has given way to the other?

(4) Point out in Crusoe economy as many examples of interest as you can. What kind of interest do you find here?

(5) What social, economic and religious institutions and conditions determined the attitude of the people of the Middle Ages toward interest? In what ways? Was their attitude a natural one?

(6) Is there any logical connection between the ethical theory of value held in the Middle Ages and the prohibition of interest?

(7) What concept of the interest bearer was present in the minds of the church authorities who opposed interest?

(8) Was the church really opposed to the taking of explicit interest? Of implicit interest?

(9) Consult several friends who have not had the course in economic theory as to their explanation of why interest exists. If in answering

they merely shift ground, follow up their arguments until you get their views as to the ultimate cause of interest.

(10) Give some examples of the neglect of repairs through lack of resources, and show how it involved time value. (Fetter)

(11) "The phenomenon of interest as a whole presents the remarkable picture of a lifeless thing producing an everlasting and inexhaustible supply of goods," Boehm-Bawerk. Explain.

(12) Distinguish between the theoretical and the social problem of interest.

(13) Distinguish net interest and gross interest. Which does economics consider?

(14) Generally speaking in what ages, in what conditions of economic development, and among what classes in society will you find hostility to the taking of interest?

(15) State the conditions under which there might be a negative explicit interest. Could there ever be a negative implicit interest?

B. Reading:

Boehm~Bawerk, *Capital and Interest*, pp. 1–50;
Fisher, *The Rate of Interest*, pp. 3–9.

C. Below are given, in the briefest possible form, the arguments for and against interest advanced in antiquity and in the Middle Ages. In two or three cases the exact words of the author are given; but in most cases the arguments are much too long to be reproduced; and, therefore, the substance is given, reduced to the minimum of space. Since the thought of the Middle Ages really predominated up to the time of Turgot and Adam Smith, the quotations extend to this period.

(1) "Thou shall not lend upon interest to thy brother; interest of money, interest of victuals, interest upon anything that is lent upon interest. Unto a foreigner thou mayest lend upon interest; but unto thy brother thou shall not lend upon interest, that Jehovah thy God may bless thee in all that thou puttest thy hand unto, in the land whither thou goest in to possess it," Deuteronomy, pp. xxiii, 19–20. Upon what ground was interest probably forbidden to the Hebrews? Does this passage make any contribution to the theory of interest?

(2) "Of the two sorts of money, getting one, as I have just said, is a part of household management, the other is retail trade: the former necessary and honorable, a kind exchange which is justly censured; for it is unnatural and a mode by which men gain from one another. The most hated sort, and with the greatest reason, is usury, which

makes a gain out of money itself, and not from the natural use of it. For money was intended to be used in exchange, but not to increase at interest. And this term usury (tokos), which means the birth of money from money, is applied to the breeding of money, because the offspring resembles the parent. Therefore, of all modes of making money this is the most unnatural," Aristotle, *The Politics* (Jowett's translation), p. 19. To what extent does Aristotle's conclusion depend upon the fact that the word for usury (tokos) also means offspring? Can money bear fruit? Whence comes the lender's gain? The borrower's gain?

(3) "But love your enemies and do them good, and lend, never despairing; and your reward shall be great, and ye shall be sons of the Most High: for he is kind towards the unthankful and evil." Luke, vi, 35. From the context, what command is given about taking interest? What reasons were back of the command? Acting from the same motive, would the debtor insist upon paying interest? Is there given any theoretical argument for the prohibition? How was this passage likely to be used in the Middle Ages?

(4) "The fourth ground is that money brings forth no fruit from itself, nor gives birth to anything. On this ground it is inadmissible or unfair to take anything over and above the lent sum for the use of the same, since this is not so much taken from money which brings forth no fruit, as from the industry of another," Covarruvias. From whom has the author acquired his views? Do you expect to find the ideas of Greek and Hebrew authors combined and used by the scholar of the Middle Ages?

(5) "Inasmuch as there are articles the use of which consists in their consumption and is inseparable therefrom, it is unjust to ask for replacement of one of these articles and usury besides. In so doing one would be charging two prices for the same article. Money is an article of this kind," Thomas Aquinas. Determine, if you can, the theory of value held by Aquinas. What is his capital concept? What is his theory of interest?

(6) "When one lands the good lent becomes the property of the debtor. Therefore interest is paid by the debtor for the use of goods which he himself owns," Gonzalez Tellez. Refute the argument.

(7) "It is claimed by creditors that they charge interest for time. That their argument has no show of plausibility is evidenced by the fact that the interest charge varies with the time. But time is a common good, bestowed upon all alike by our heavenly Father. The creditor, by

charging interest, defrauds God, for whose free gift he asks a price," Thomas Aquinas. Discuss.

(8) "Although a loan should be nominally without interest, yet, if the debtor delays payments he should be fined for his delay (mora) and the creditor should receive compensation in the form of interest." Delay how long? Should the fine be proportional to the length of the delay? Why should the creditor receive compensation? What is the matter with this argument?

(9) "Unemployed money is certainly barren; but the borrower does not let it lie unemployed. He invests it, and pays interest out of the gain which he makes on his money," Calvin. Show that, instead of explaining interest, this merely shifts the ground.

(10) "Since of necessity men must give and take money on loans, and since they are so hard of heart that they will not lend it otherwise, there is nothing for it but that interest should be permitted," Bacon. Does Bacon touch the question of the theoretical basis of interest? If so, how?

(11) "Interest is the payment for the use of sums of money lent. In lending the use of the thing is made over by its owner to another person. In the case of durable goods, where the uses of a thing can be easily separated from the thing itself, if use is not to be paid for, transaction is a Commodatum; if paid for, a Locatio. In the case of perishable goods, if the use is not to be paid for, it is a loan without interest; otherwise, a loan with interest. Since in the case of durable commodities a thing can be separated from its use, interest can rightfully be charged for its use. Then interest should be allowed on perishable commodities, for there is at bottom no difference. I know that it may be objected that in the case of perishable commodities there is a real difference insomuch as the use consists in one act of consumption. But such an argument would lead to an abolition of the loan bearing no interest, since, in the case of the perishable thing, it is impossible to transfer a 'use' whose existence is denied, even if no interest is asked. Further, in the case of perishable goods, because property is destroyed in consumption, the lender may suffer delays, anxieties, and losses. To recompense him for these, interest should be allowed," Salmasius. State the theory in your own words. How sound is the first argument used? Does the argument in the last two sentences really touch the interest problem? Here we find germs of what theories of interest?

(12) "The cause for interest, like the cause for rent, is to be found in unequal distribution. One has more money than he uses and another

has less, and so the former finds a tenant for his money for the very reason that a landlord finds a tenant for his land. For money, when employed in trade, is able to produce more than the borrower is able to pay as interest, just as the land is able to pay more than the tenant has to pay as rent. To receive a profit from the loan of m money is as equitable and lawful as to receive money or produce for the rent of land," Locke. How does Locke try to justify interest? Instead of a justification of interest, his argument may be made to lead to what alternative conclusion? As a theorist where would you place Locke? What would Locke say as to the cause of value"

(13) "It is needless to inquire which of the circumstances, to wit, low interest or low profits, is the cause and which is the effect. They both arise from an intensive commerce, and mutually favor each other. No man will accept low profits where he can have high interest, and no man will accept low interest where he can have high profits," Hume. In what sense does Hume use the word interest? Profits? So far as you can determine from Hume's words, where does he find the ultimate source of interest?

(14) "Since value is the relation in which things stand to our needs, we need no equivalence in weight or number of pieces. What is required is simply an equality in use. Present and future sums of money of equal amount are not of equal value. An addition to the future sum is not necessary to establish real equality between the two. Interest is paid because present sums of money are more valuable than future sums. This is due to the greater security of present sums. Interest is paid to balance the dangers of loss, accident, and the like," Galiani. Can the first part of this argument be supported by a different reason for the inequality of present and future sums of money? Can you find in the first part of his argument a real contribution to the interest problem? In the last part of his argument is he really referring to interest?

(15) "Since every sum of money represents, or may represent, a given piece of land, definite in amount, it follows that the interesse of the money is represented by the annual return of the land. Consequently it varies with the amount of the return, and the average rate of money interesse is equalized with the average return of the land," Beccaria. This theory explains loan interest in what terms? How does it account for natural interest? If you were called on to give a name to this theory what would you call it? Is it like any modern theory with which you are familiar?

(16) "Money has no natural use; it merely represents. But to obtain a profit from this representative character is to seek in a glass for the figure it represents. Owners of money can not rightfully argue that they must live from the produce of their money; for they could change their money to other goods, and live by hiring out those goods. In the case of money, unlike houses and furniture, there is no wear and tear to serve as the basis of an interest charge. Even the borrower may invest money where it will bring in a profit, unforeseen accidents happen, and on that account the borrower will always lose. Money interest gives income to hornets who live by robbing the hoards of the bees of society," Mirabeau. State and criticize carefully each argument advanced by Mirabeau.

(17) "Money is not barren, so long as, by proper employment, the lender might make a profit with it, and by lending give up the possibility of this profit to the borrower. Interest is further justified because there is a use of capital that is separable from capital itself, and may be sold separately." How much does this contribute to the solution of the interest problem? What arguments in the above quotation are not included here?

(18) "As something can everywhere be made by the use of money, something ought everywhere to be paid for the use of it," Adam Smith. How does this argument differ from the argument in question 15? In what relation does Adam Smith stand to the Physiocrats? Why should the question be asked in this connection? In what terms does Adam Smith explain loan interest? Does this solve the interest problem?

X
Interest Theories of Early Political Economy

A. Preliminary Questions:

(1) Why was there no opposition to natural interest before the Industrial Revolution?

(2) To what extent was the real interest problem considered before the Industrial Revolution?

(3) In what ways, and for what reasons, would you expect the Industrial Revolution to cause attention to be given to the interest problem?

(4) "In valuing a piece of land we make a discount calculation," Explain.

(5) "The capital value of land is nothing more than one of the many forms in which the phenomenon of interest meets us in economic life," Boehm-Bawek. Explain.

(6) "To trace the profit of capital to the possibility of acquiring land in exchange for definite sums of capital is nothing else than to refer from one phenomenal form of interest to another," Boehm-Bawerk. Explain.
(7) Starting with the premises underlying Physiocratic doctrine, construct a theory of interest consistent with the general body of Physiocratic doctrine.
(8) In early political economy, with what other share, or shares, in distribution would you expect to find interest confused?
(9) What concept of capital was held by the writers of the early classical school? How did this affect the theories of interest developed by them?
(10) In an agricultural community, depending upon slave labor, how would the value of a slave be determined? What part would be played by the cost of production? What would you understand by cost of production? How would interest come in?
(11) Historically which problem is first taken up, the theoretical basis for interest, or the justice of the interest charge? Account for this.
(12) Would, or would you not, expect to find the early writers on political economy closely connecting their interest theories with their theories of value? Would you expect to find that there was, at bottom, a close connection between the two?

B. Reading:
Boehm-Bawerk, *Capital and Interest*, pp. 61–107;
Turgot, *Reflection upon the Formation and the Distribution of Wealth*;
Adam Smith, *The Wealth of Nations*;
Ricardo, *Principles of Political Economy and Taxation*;
Torrens, *Production of Wealth*;
McCulloch, *Principles of Political Economy*;
Canard, *Principles d'Economie Politique*.

C. In most cases the quotations given below are abstracts of the theories of the writers and not their exact words. To induce the student to consult some of the works for himself, a few questions are asked which can be answered only from the works themselves.
(1) "There must be a net profit upon the capital employed in agriculture, otherwise agriculture would be abandoned for other pursuits," Mercier de la Riviere. This quotation reproduces what old argument in a new form?
(2) "The possession of land guarantees a permanent income without work, namely rent. We may price land in movable goods and exchange it

for them. The exchange price depends upon the relation of supply and demand, forming a multiple of the yearly income that may be drawn from the land. Every capital is the equivalent of a piece of land, yielding an income equal to a certain percentage of capital. Since the owner of the capital can, by buying land, obtain a permanent yearly income, he will not put his capital in an industrial, agricultural, or commercial undertaking, if he cannot expect just as large a profit from the capital so employed as he could obtain through the purchase of land. For that reason, capital, in all branches of industry, must yield a profit," Turgot. Can you, by carrying this argument one step further, prove that Turgot is reasoning in a circle? What does Turgot attempt to make the foundation of his interest theory? How does his use of this foundation differ from Calvin's?

(3) The following is a more concrete statement of the theory given in 2. "A capital of $100,000 must yield $5,000, because with $100,000 a man can buy a piece of land yielding such a rent." Why may one with $100,000 buy a piece of land yielding such a rent? Under what conditions would a piece of land yielding an income of $5,000 be worth $50,000? $100,000? $200,000? What of the rate of interest?

(4) A piece of land will yield to its owner and his heirs altogether an income of not 10, or 20, or 30 times its annual rent, but of many hundred times its annual rent. Why does it sell for only a fraction of this sum?

(5) "There must be a profit from capital. Otherwise the capitalist would have no interest in spending his capital in the productive employment of laborers. The profit of capital arises because buyers have to pay something more for the goods than the value which the goods would get from the labor expended upon them. Interest is a deduction made by the capitalist in his own favor from the returns to labor," Adam Smith. Is the inconsistency in the last two sentences real or merely seeming? In the next to last sentence what question naturally arises? In the last sentence you find the germ of what theory?

(6) Is Adam Smith's explanation of interest a risk cost? Abstinence pain cost? Productive service? Alternative effectiveness for gain? Mere entrepreneur outlay in creating the capital? A labor pain cost in the creation of capital? Is interest a cost because capital originally cost labor or because the instruments are substitutes for labor? (Davenport).

(7) "When capital is productively employed, there regularly remains over in the hands of the entrepreneur a surplus proportional to the amount of the capital. The value of the goods produced by the assistance of the capital is regularly greater than the value of the goods consumed.

The question is, Why is there this constant surplus-value," Boehm-Bawerk. Is this a correct statement of the interest problem? State it in your own words.

(8) "Everyone knows that money bears interest. But why does it? If two owners of real capital wish to exchange their products, each of them is disposed to demand, for to labor of storing and as profit, as much over the intrinsic value of the product as the other will grant him; necessity, however, makes then meet each other half way. But money represents real capital; with real capital a profit can be made; and hence interest," Count Cancrin. What words are meant to explain the existence of natural interest? Of loan interest?

(9) "The small number of capitalists, as compared with the great number of wage-earners, make it possible for the capitalist to buy wage-labor at a price which leaves him a rent. This furnishes the basis of interest," Count Soden. This furnishes a basis for what theory of interest? Show the author's confusion of small numbers with monopoly.

(10) "In themselves all capitals are dead, and there is no truth in the assertion of their independent labor. A capitalist is entitled to the exact equivalent of all that he contributes to production; but to no surplus. The surplus is either produced by the laborer, and should go to him, or it is produced by nature and should go to the whole industrial mass of mankind. But, if the capitalist receives no surplus, he would refrain from accumulation. To get the use of capital, the laborer must submit to give up to the capitalist something of the return of his labor," Lotz. Except for the last two sentences, Lotz makes a very close approach to what theory of interest? His argument in the last two sentences is like that of what other writer? What theory of interest is contained in the last two sentences?

(11) "If he (the capitalist) is to resolve to save his wealth, accumulate it, and make it into capital, he must get an advantage of another sort, viz., a yearly income lasting as long as his capital lasts. In this way the possession of a capital becomes to individuals . . . the source of an income which is called rent of capital, rent of stock, or interest," Rau. Rau merely follows what author? At what time did Rau live? What theory of interest would you have expected him to adopt?

(12) "The value of a good is determined by the cost of its cultivation on marginal land. The cost of production included two items, the share of the laborer and the share of the capitalist. The laborer receives as a wage enough for his subsistence; the capitalist gets the residuum. Value is regulated by the quantity of labor expended in production. As

cultivation is extended to inferior lands, the value of the product per unit will rise. Consequently a higher wage must be paid to the laborer and there remains a small amount for the capitalist. Profits cannot fall to zero, because the expectation of profit is the motive to accumulation. The competition of capitalists can only temporarily lower the profits of capital, when (wage-fund theory) the increased quantity of capital at first raises wages. Gradually, because of increase in population, wages will sink to the old level. The forcing of production to less productive lands alone will permanently lower profits," Ricardo. From what source, and how does Ricardo explain the rate of profits? Upon what theory does this interest theory depend? What other theories underlying it are also open to attack? Can you show that Ricardo, somewhere in the argument given above, has confused accompanying circumstances with causes? Has Ricardo to any extent been influenced by the Physiocrats? Show that, according to Ricardo, profits may be said to rest upon independent determining grounds.

(13) In Ricardo's theory is the value of the capital or the capital use greater by the mere fact of time? In what sense is it true that neither labor nor profits can increase except at the expense of the other? How can changes in wages and profits affect relative costs, and so affect values? Why these changes? Have they real cost changes behind them? (Dav[enport]).

(14) "There exists a distinction between natural price and market price. Natural price, identical with cost of production, is that which we must give in order to obtain the article we want from the great warehouse of nature. Market price must always include the customary rate of profit for the time being, otherwise industry would be suspended. Market price will exceed natural price by the customary rate of profit," Torrens. What is the peculiarity of this statement? What modern writer makes practically the same statement? Why does the actual price of goods leave over a profit to capital?

(15) "Labor is the only source of wealth. Value is determined by the quantity of labor required in production. Profits are only another name for the wages of accumulated labor. If a cask of wine stored in a cellar acquires additional value, the addendum must be imputed, not to time, but to the additional labor laid out on the wine; for the additional value accrues only in the case of the immature wine, on which, therefore, a change of effect is produced. Time cannot produce any effect; it merely affords space for really efficient causes to operate, and can, therefore, have nothing to do with value," McCulloch. Has he shown that the change in

wine is due to an addition to labor? What has he shown? State his argument in words that lay bare the fallacy contained.

(16) "An individual has two capitals, one consisting of $1,000 of new wine; the other of $900 of leather and $100 in money. The wine is put in the cellar; the $100 is paid to a shoemaker to convert the leather into shoes. At the end of a year, the capitalist will have two equivalent values – perhaps $1,100 of wine and $1,100 of shoes. The two cases are parallel. Both wine and shoes are the results of equal quantities of labor," McCulloch. In what respects are the two cases parallel? Whence comes the surplus value?

(17) "One portion of human labor, necessary labor, must be spent in the support of man; another, superfluous labor, may be employed in the production of goods that go beyond immediate necessity, and create a claim for as much labor as the production of these goods have cost. Labor is thus the source of all exchange value. It is the possibility of accumulating surplus labor that society has to thank for all progress. This labor may yield rents by being employed in three ways: first, in improving land, yielding land rent; second, in the acquisition of personal skill, yielding a surplus above the natural wage; and third, in institutions of commerce, yielding a market interest, a monetary surplus. Land rent and the surplus accruing to skilled labor are so obvious as to need no explanation. Commerce, accordingly like the other two sources of rent, presupposes an accumulation of superfluous labor which must, in consequence, have a rent," Canard. What is there in the argument to justify the word "accordingly"? How would Canard have justified it? Can you make this argument agree in general with Turgot's theory of interest?

XI
Theories of Imputation

A. Preliminary Questions:

(1) "Production is a synthesis, distribution an analysis," Clark. Define production; distribution. Do the two statements constitute a true parallel?

(2) What do writers on economics mean when they use such expressions as "the social income," "the social dividend," etc.

(3) What do you suppose that Clark means when he says that the problem of distribution is functional rather than personal? (*Essentials of Economic Theory*, p. 89).

(4) Into how many shares would you expect the income of society to be divided? By what principles have you been taught that the income of each share is to be determined? The forces determining each share come to a head at what point?
(5) How does the question of distribution link itself with question of value? Is it only a question of value?
(6) "The question of distribution is nothing more than the question of the determination of the value of the marginal unit of separate product goods which is offered for sale on the market." Do you agree?
(7) "If the last, or marginal, unit of a good can be once isolated, then its value can be determined, and thereby the rate of income to that good." With this as a basis, construct a scheme for determining the value of a unit of a productive good.
(8) "All units of the same commodity have the same value. But a commodity which is bought on the market is a composite product, made up of a number of simple commodities, each of which has its own value per unit. If we know the prices of the several commodities, we may, by knowing the composition of these commodities, determine the prices of the more elementary commodities out of which they are constituted." Explain and illustrate.
(9) Given the value of a building and lot in a popular street; how can the value of the lot be determined?
(10) How can the intangible assets of a furniture company be determined?
(11) Is the determination of a unit of a cost good an automatic act, or a matter of conscious determination?
(12) State in your own words at least two theories of imputation. Is there any conflict between them? Upon what theory of distribution is each one based?

B. Reading:

Clark, *Essentials*, pp. 74–158;
Seager, 3rd ed., pp. 158–162, 206–209, 225–226, 244–245, 186–187, 218–219, 269–270, 255–256, 270–272, 273–274;
Von Wieser, pp. 72–78, 81–92;
Taylor, *Principles*, 1910 ed., pp. 153–164.

C. Questions and Problems:

(a) Clark's theory of imputation
(1) What assumptions relative to society, industry, and industrial factors underlie Clark's theory of distribution? (*Essentials*, p. 75).

(2) What is meant by an equilibrium of industrial groups? What are the characteristics of Clark's static society? (pp. 128–132).

(3) What is Clark's general statement of the law which determines the share which each factor of production is to receive in the distributive process? (pp. 77–82).

(4) Does Clark assume capital to be a factor of production, independent of and coordinate with labor? (pp. 115–118, 125) Does he attribute to capital a "specific" productivity? Just what do you mean by specific productivity?

(5) With how many separate and distinct shares would you expect Clark to begin? With what shares?

(6) How does he manage to eliminate profits from the problem? (pp. 87–88).

(7) By what means does Clark eliminate the share going to land from the problem?

(8) What shares are now left? What is now his problem? State it in your own words.

(9) In Clark's system, what function is performed by the entrepreneur? What is his distinctive place in the distributive scheme? (pp. 121–122).

(10) What is Clark's means for determining the "final" productivity of labor? (p. 183).

(11) In his discussion of the determination of final productivity, Clark says, "We may set men to works, a few at a time, until they are all employed, and we may measure the product of each of the detachments. We should make the different sections of the labor force as similar to each other as it is possible to make them, and call each section a unit of labor" (p. 133). By what means, then, would Clark determine the productivity of labor? Does this method succeed in solving the real question at issue?

(12) Why does Clark take a detachment of men as a unit? Note particularly what is meant by the word *unit*. Since here one man supplies three with work, and yonder two men supply one, since industries feed to many other industries, and are themselves fed by many other industries, what must be the size of Clark's unit? Is it possible in present society to select such a symmetrical unit?

(13) "In its last analysis the law applies to the industry of all society. The final unit in the case consists of shoemakers, cotton spinners, builders, foundrymen, miners, cultivators, etc., and of men of all sub-trades included in the general callings. As the component

detachments come into the field, they apportion themselves among the occupations that are represented, and that too in nicely adjusted proportions" (p. 141). For what then has Clark determined, the rate of wages? Show that this unit is a hopeless affair so far as solving the problems of distribution goes. Why may it not include all labor?

(14) Suppose that Clark had taken as a unit twice his present unit, would the product of a unit of labor be just twice what it is? What if he had taken as a unit half of his present unit? Of what concern is the size of the unit? Has the symmetry of his unit anything to do with the size of the unit which may be taken?

(15) In discussing the application of labor by doses, Clark says, "The whole equipment of *capital goods* will have to undergo a complete transformation; but the essential thing is that the amount of capital shall not be changed" (p. 135). In what unit is capital measured? What is Clark's capital concept? Clark is here trying to solve a static problem; is he using dynamic methods? If so, is he justified in so doing? What objections do you see to his changing the forms of the capital after each increase in the laboring force?

(16) As the forms of capital change with an increase in the laboring force, do the modes in which labor is utilized in production necessarily change? After the form of the capital is changed, can we use men possessed of just the skill and just the kinds of labor power which were used before? Or, must we conceive of the *amount* of labor as unchanged, and of the *forms* in which we find it as alone changing? If so, in what unit is the quantity of labor to be measured?

(17) After an addition has been made to the laboring force, and a change has occurred in the forms of the capital goods, are we to presume that technical methods and organization are as they were before the change? Is he now using the same raw materials, or is he using different raw materials? Is he producing exactly the same product which was being produced before the change? In short, has Clark solved his problem, or has he merely created a new problem by shifting his ground?

(18) "We will make the buildings larger, and therefore, of necessity cheaper in their forms and materials. We will make the tools and machines more numerous and simple," etc. What are the implications here relative to the character of the workmen?

Technical methods? Materials used? Etc.? Does this introduce into the problem dynamic factors? Does this change this whole situation, and result in the production of a different product with a different kind of labor force, different capital instruments, different technical methods, etc.?

(19) Does Clark's plan result in changing the number or the character of laborers in other industries, the amount of capital or the forms of capital employed in other industries, the demand for the products of other industries, or the demand on the part of the consumers for articles in general? In answering this question try to obtain as definite a notion of the labor unit which he employs as possible. If it results in any of the above changes, how does the fact affect the solution of Clark's problem?

(20) What technical assumptions underlie this theory of imputation? By how many methods may a product be turned out? Are Clark's assumptions empirically true?

(21) Why does Clark finally determine upon the withdrawal, rather than the addition, of one unit as the test of final productivity? Is this method free from the objections which may be charged against the method of adding a unit?

(22) "The interest on capital is fixed exactly as are the wages of labor" (p. 147). By what process does Clark determine the rate of interest?

(23) "Wages, and interest may, in one sense, be said to be residually determined; in another, independently determined." Explain, according to Clark.

(24) In one of Clark's figures the total amount of wages is represented by a rectangle, and the total amount of interest by a triangle. In another the total amount of interest is represented by a rectangle and the total amount of wages by a triangle. Prove, according to Clark, that the triangle in each figure must equal the rectangle in the other figure.

(b) Seager's theory of imputation

(1) What assumptions about industrial society underlie Seager's theory of distribution? (Introduction, 3rd ed., pp. 158–162).

(2) For what reasons does Seager lay down the proposition of the mobility of land? (pp. 206–209). Capital? (pp. 244–245). Is the assumption of such mobility necessary to his scheme of distribution?

(3) How does Seager eliminate profits from his scheme of distribution? (pp. 158–162, 186–187).

(4) How does Seager eliminate rent from his problem of distribution? (pp. 218–219, 267–270).

(5) What does Seager's problem then become? State it in your own words. How does the entrepreneur come into his problem? What is the margin of indifference? (pp. 255–256).

(6) Develop, as clearly and as fully as you can, Seager's theory of wages and interest (pp. 270–272, 273–274).

(7) What determines the action of the entrepreneur in fixing the margin between the employment of capital and the employment of labor? Is Seager's explanation consistent with the actions of the entrepreneur?

(8) Does, or does not, Seager succeed in solving the economic question as to how wages and interest are actually determined?

(c) Von Wieser's theory of imputation

(1) Why, in an exchange society, is it difficult to isolate the marginal unit of a productive good and determine its value? (*Natural Value*, p. 72).

(2) What is von Wieser's statement of the problem of imputation? (pp. 74–77).

(3) What is Menger's solution of the problem of imputation? What, in general, is von Wieser's criticism of Menger's solution? Why does von Wieser make the addition to the product by the addition of the final unit rather than the subtraction from the product by the taking away of the last unit, the real test of the value of the unit? (pp. 81–85).

(4) "Suppose that a hunter's life depends upon his last cartridge killing the tiger about to spring upon him . . . Rifle and cartridge have here an exact calculable value" (p. 86). In this case how is the value of each to be determined? Is this a typical and usual case, or is it exceptional?

(5) "Suppose an artist were to fashion a pewter vessel . . . Suppose . . . this were the only artist who could really do artistic work . . . And suppose that, besides the pieces of pewter which he had employed, no other material of similar suitability were to be had" (p. 86). In this case how could the value of the artist's work and the value of the pewter be determined? But, suppose that gold were used for the same work, and that gold were also used for

other purposes, then how could the value of each of the productive goods be determined?

(6) By what method does von Wieser succeed in isolating the contribution of e productive factor? According to this theory how many factors of production may there be? In solving the problem of imputation, how many equations must we take? Suppose that there are more equations than unknown quantities, one of what two things must be true? Must the prices used in the equations be market prices or normal prices?

(7) Does von Wieser try to find how the value of productive factors is determined, or does he merely try to find how a price which is already in existence, hidden in some combination or combinations of productive elements, can be ascertained? (pp. 86–89).

(8) Does von Wieser give us a real solution of the problem?

(d) Taylor's theory of imputation

(1) Turn to the topic discussing the theory of value, read it carefully, and answer the questions given there relative to Taylor's theory of imputation.

(2) Show that the determination of the rate of wages, the rate of interest, etc., is an automatic process (*Principles*, 1910 ed., pp. 153–164)

(3) Suppose that with three unknown quantities and three equations a solution is impossible, i.e. that one or more of the factors has a value which is not imputable to it, so long as prices of the finished commodities remain as they are, what process is in operation?

(4) Show that the prices of consumers' goods, the prices of intermediate products, and the prices of ultimate cost goods are all being determined at the same time.

(5) State Taylor's theory in a series of logically connected propositions, using your own words.

LECTURES BY JAMES S. EARLEY ON THE DEVELOPMENT OF ECONOMICS, UNIVERSITY OF WISCONSIN, 1954–1955

Notes Taken by Warren J. Samuels

The document presented below is based on notes taken in Economics 201, Development of Economics, given by James S. Earley during the academic year 1954–1955. Included are notes from guest lectures by Eugene Rotwein on David Hume, by Paul Sweezy on Marxian economics, by Martin Bronfenbrenner on mathematical economics, and by H. M. Robertson on Marshall. Also published below is the syllabus for the course.

James S. Earley, along with Martin Bronfenbrenner and Eugene Rotwein, taught the courses in economic theory in the Department of Economics at the University of Wisconsin during the period of my residence as a doctoral student, 1954–1957. Earley taught graduate courses in microeconomic theory and the combination of macroeconomic and monetary theory; Bronfenbrenner, distribution theory, business cycle theory and econometrics; and Rotwein, imperfect competition theory. All of the theory courses were taught with great attention to the relevant history of economic thought. The three professors combined interests in theory and in history of economic thought more common by far in their day than in ours. Their courses were taught among the specialized courses that remained from the period of Institutionalist dominance, still taught by professors trained by John R. Commons – but not for much longer, as they were on the verge of retirement. Neoclassical economic theory was strongly

Histories of Economic Thought, Volume 21-B, pages 89–271.
© 2003 Published by Elsevier Science Ltd.
ISBN: 0-7623-0997-0

and effectively taught by Earley, Bronfenbrenner, and Rotwein, though neither as exclusively as elsewhere nor as was to be the case at Wisconsin starting in the early 1960s. The three theorists held their own, pretty much with aplomb and dignity, sometimes showing the leavening, if not incipient eclecticism, seemingly consequent to, or at least reinforced by, their exposure to Wisconsin Institutionalism.

James Stainforth Earley was born in North Dakota on October 16, 1908 and was educated at Antioch (B.A., 1932), the University of London, and Wisconsin, where he received his M.A. in 1934 and Ph.D. in 1939. He was a member of the Wisconsin economics faculty from 1937 until 1967, serving as chairman from 1962 to 1965. During World War Two he served as a Senior Economist with the Office of Price Administration and as Chief Economist in the Department of State, advising on British Commonwealth foreign affairs. In the latter capacity he worked with John Maynard Keynes. His principal fields of specialization were economic theory, history of economic thought, money and banking, and business organization and decision making. From 1960–1970 Earley was Director of the Quality of Credit Program of the National Bureau of Economic Research. In 1967 he moved to the University of California-Riverside, working principally in the field of financial macroeconomics and emphasizing the importance of a full employment policy. There he served as department chair during 1967–1970 and Dean of the College of Social and Behavioral Sciences during 1970–1973, retiring in 1979. He died on July 6, 1997 at the age of eighty-nine. He published four books and some two-dozen journal articles and book chapters. He was an early exponent of Keynesian economics; later on, he was much impressed with Joseph Schumpeter's work.

I found Earley to be relatively diffident about his attitude toward John R. Commons and Institutionalism; such, at any rate, is my memory. I thought of him as neither a friend nor a foe of Institutionalism. Given both his doctorate from Wisconsin and his teaching of mainstream economic theory at Wisconsin, I thought he had made his peace with it, if such needed to be made. Earley had published an article relating to the Richard Lester-Fritz Machlup post-war controversy over marginalism, in which he used resources of the American Management Association to research managerial decision making. This was in the Commons "look and see" empirical tradition.

I note the foregoing in part because of remarks made by Paul A. Samuelson on January 9, 2000, as recipient of the John R. Commons Award given by Omicron Delta Epsilon. Samuelson included Earley in a list of "illustrious alumni from Wisconsin" who "decorate the honor roll of political economy, alongside of and undistinguishable from John R. Commons's co-workers and their intellectual grandchildren" ("The Goldern Virtue of Eclecticism in

Economics," American Economist, Vol. 44 (Spring 2000), p. 4). The list included names such as Selig Perlman, Edwin Emil Witte, Harold Groves and Walter Heller. But it also included, in addition to Earley, Arthur Goldberger and Guy Orcutt. I was surprised to find Earley included in this pantheon. I surmised that his inclusion was because Earley both had his doctorate from and had taught at Wisconsin; perhaps because of his managerialism article.

I posed the problem of Earley as a disciple of Commons' to Eugene Rotwein, his colleague at Wisconsin, and to Samuelson. Rotwein first noted that Earley used Marshall's *Principles* in his graduate course in price theory and went on to say,

> Plainly, Jim's thinking reflected a neo-classical perspective and he was interested in questions that arose within the context of mainstream economics. Jim was skeptical of the value of high level abstraction if not appropriately modified when used in the analysis of actual experience, and perhaps to some significant degree this may reflect the influence of his exposure to institutionalism at Wisconsin.
>
> In any case I do not see a basis for regarding him as a "disciple of Commons." In fact I cannot recall a single discussion with Jim in which he referred to any substantive aspect of Commons' work. I wonder how Samuelson arrived at his odd characterization (Rotwein to Samuels, March 9, 2000).

Samuelson wrote that

> The Jim Earley I knew was not representative of the early Ely-Common-Witte Wisconsin School. But his interest in Schumpeter's works and other interests were also not representative of the more recent *analytical* trends in mainstream economics. "Our Lord's House has many mansions" but that is true also of political economy (Samuelson to Samuels, March 13, 2000).

The answer, then, is that Samuelson included Earley (alongside Commons et al.) in *political economy* but not in the Wisconsin school of Institutionalism. It is a sensible view, and literally what Samuelson's ODE remarks say – especially if one emphasizes "alongside of" and not "indistinguishable from" – notably his emphasis on Schumpeter rather than Commons.

In the notes published below some evidence of the influence of Commons' point of view on a fundamental issue, blended with that of Schumpeter, is to be found, in particular: Marx misconceived the relations between the state and economic groups, that in effect the dominant economic groups would control the state, as their handmaiden; whereas a more realistic view is that: (1) the state has become bureaucratic and tries to reconcile rather than decide in favor of one or the opposing interests; and (2) groups gain political power not only on the basis of property but also on votes, prestige, and indeed the politician himself is something of a businessman engaged in a highly competitive business (Schumpeter).

In editing these notes, I was struck by the following, which I did not consciously appreciate before. Earley seems to juxtapose the emergence of an abstract pure a-institutional conceptual economy to the view that institutions matter in working with actual economies. In retrospect, I think Earley admired both positions but was bothered by their limitations. I also think he was uncomfortable with the practice of drawing policy conclusions about institutional change based on the pure conceptual model and the practice of doing likewise by institutionalists, without adequate justification in either case. This may be a matter of my own projection, and not Earley's position, but it is at least roughly consistent, for example, with Samuelson's emphasis on Earley's political economy.

Earley's course on the history of economic thought provided a careful, perceptive, deep and sensible account and critique of the subject, starting (after some attention to historiographical matters) with the Mercantilists. He was a dedicated and open-minded scholar in the field. These qualities are evident in the notes (with due regard to the points made in the next paragraph). He gave an impressive course.

The document is the product of: (1) the original notes, taken in class in more or less stenographic and outline form; (2) the notes, somewhat enhanced by memory, written up later each day as sentences and paragraphs, still in elaborate outline form; and (3) the notes, presented below, resulting from recently checking (2) against (1) and making emendations and corrections, with due regard to the passage of time. (The only exception is the notes from H. M. Robertson's lecture. These were not written up immediately afterward. The material presented below was written up in March 2000, with much caution.) The sole objective has been to use both sets of notes from 1954–1955 to indicate what was presented in the course. The amplifying language of the typed notes (2) was generally retained. The notes are a mixture of statements with both complete and incomplete sentences, and outlines. Typographical and minor stylistic corrections have also been made. The document is a set of notes and not a finished text. It was not written for publication; nor has it been transformed by serious editing. No attempt has been made to correct factual details. Some self-embarrassing warts remain.

The notes, therefore, are *not* a verbatim record of the lectures. They provide an indication of topics covered and points made and recorded. The intention at the time was not to make a note of everything, only what seemed important, interesting and/or useful to a student both exceptionally interested in the materials and subject to examination.

These notes are the product of lectures, presented to graduate students, not the text of an advanced treatise laden with subtle and nuanced distinctions – however much it may be the case that the basic ideas would be similar. Any errors or ambiguities in note taking or in preparation of text should not be attributed to Earley.

The tone and syntax of the notes is clearly not Earley's, quite aside from matters of content. I have resisted the temptation to rewrite the notes, however little or much would be necessary, in order to make them read more eloquently, and less like the notes they in fact are. My regret is that Earley's lectures were not taken down, by me or by someone else, verbatim, stenographically (tape recorders not being then available).

The original handwritten notes taken in class number 133 pages written on two sides (total of 265 pages). The original typed notes number 173 pages, single-spaced (but with some partial pages). The notes on my word processor (not including this Introduction) number 168 pages, single-spaced.

A number of historiographic themes or positions are evident, assuming the notes to be accurate: (1) Earley was eclectic; no one theory or explanation of anything was necessarily sufficient to explain all cases or to completely and exclusively explain any one case. (2) He was prepared to distinguish between rhetorical window-dressing and fundamental doctrine or theory. (3) He thought Smith's *Wealth of Nations* replaced the *Theory of Moral Sentiments*, the latter being the work of Smith's youth, with Smith subsequently better informed and his interests redirected by contact with the Physiocrats. This is a view inconsistent with what is now understood of Smith's early lectures and work on *Wealth of Nations* topics and of the relation between the two great books. (4) His analysis of Smith's views on productivity leads to the conclusion that Smith, at least in part, treated society as a whole like a private firm, similar to the Mercantilists. (5) His treatment of Smith's theories of value and of distribution does not fail to indicate conflicts and hiatuses but does attempt to include all of Smith's lines of reasoning and to make as much sense as possible of what he said. (6) Earley discusses Smith's theory of free trade found in pages 421–425 of the Modern Library Edition of the *Wealth of Nations* (Book IV, Chapter II), but the notes record him discussing neither the concept of the invisible hand (of which so much has been made) found on page 423 nor the main context of the concept, the preference for domestic investment based on security considerations. (7) Earley contrasts Smith's analysis, wherein value is, in part, a function of distribution, with Ricardo's, wherein distribution is a function of value – a view different from that following the later work of Piero Sraffa. (8) Ricardo is said not to have an embodied labor theory of value; his is not a theory of the origin of value but of the measurement of value, and Ricardo's labor theory is a cost theory. (9) Earley identifies, rather than simply take for granted, how value/price became the central focus of economic analysis in the nineteenth century. And so on.

Earley's thinking on a number of subjects, some of it original, will be of interest to historians of economic thought and others. Not the least suggestive are his unique view of Ricardian value theory and his view of Classical Political Economy as bourgeois economics. Also, Earley used Keynesian economics to criticize some of Marx's crisis theory. He was especially candid about the motivations generating developments in economic theory and even general philosophy, for example, the sources of the so-called Revolution of 1870 and the attractiveness of positivism.

The reader will find extensive treatment of Joseph Schumpeter and *relatively* limited treatment of Alfred Marshall and John Maynard Keynes. The explanation for this is simple and has two related parts. First and primarily, Earley taught the graduate courses in price theory (microeconomics) and in money, income and price (macroeconomics). The former concentrated on Marshall; indeed, it was largely an exercise in Marshallian economics. The latter did not concentrate as much on Keynes, but his work was heavily covered. Graduate students who took Earley's history of economics course would also be taking his other two courses. Second, Schumpeter, although he died only four years earlier, was not part of current theory, whereas Marshall and, especially, Keynes were. The more contemporary the work covered in the study of the history of economic thought, the less one has to "teach" it; whereas one has to teach Quesnay, Smith, Ricardo and Marx, i.e. go into more detail.

Students who have had my own graduate courses in the history of economic thought may recognize the residual influence, as to content and approach, of Earley's lectures on my own.

I am indebted to Stephen Cullenberg and Robert Pollin for documents providing complete biographical information on Jim Earley, to Margaret Henderson for some initial scanning of the typed notes on to the computer, to Sylvia Samuels for additional scanning, and to Allan Schmid for calling my attention to Samuelson's Commons Award lecture.

SYLLABUS AND BIBLIOGRAPHY
FOR
ECONOMICS 201
<u>THE DEVELOPMENT OF ECONOMICS</u>

James S. Earley
THE UNIVERSITY OF WISCONSIN

(Revised 1952–1953)

Economics 201

September 1952

The Development of Economics

Instructions

The course surveys the history of economic thought as outlined on the following pages. Emphasis is upon the development of "Classical Economics," in the broadest sense of that term. Little attention is given to economic thought before the Mercantilists or to the Historical Schools.

The course has three main objectives: (1) to acquaint the student with the major landmarks in the development of economic thought; (2) to give the student a firmer grasp of the relation of modern economic thought to its intellectual forebears, and thus to increase his understanding of contemporary economics; and (3) to provide training in research in the history of economic thought.

The student should acquaint himself with the attached bibliography and the contents of several of the listed surveys. He is expected to read all of W. C. Mitchell's *Lecture Notes on Types of Economic Theory* (2 Vols) and indicated portions of supplementary reading from the special bibliographies on each topic. References marked with an asterisk (*) are expected to be read as the course proceeds. A number of the works most referred to will be found on reserve in the Quonset Reading Room. Assigned books include Mitchell, Schumpeter's *Ten Great Economists*, Spiegel's *Development of Economic Thought* and Smith's *Wealth of Nations*.

The student is assigned one research paper for the year. (Students taking the course for only one semester must meet this same research requirement.) The objectives here are research training and a firmer grasp of areas of thought of special interest to the student. The subject of the research paper should be chosen in consultation with the instructor. The paper should be at least a modest contribution to knowledge.

Very broad topics militating against intensivity of research will be discouraged. The student should keep in mind the possibility of writing his doctoral dissertation on some phase of the history of economic thought, as well as publication of his research paper. He should try to prepare his paper as if it were to be submitted for publication.

Attention is called to the fact that the history of economic thought provides an especially convenient field for learning and improving foreign languages. A number of surveys in French and German, available in the Library, are listed in the general bibliography. Most of the original works of leading economists who wrote in these languages are also in the library.

Econ 201 September 1952

GENERAL BIBLIOGRAPHY

General Surveys

Cannan, Edwin, A., *Review of Economic Theory* (1930).
Ferguson, John M., *Landmarks of Economic Thought* (1938).
Gide & Rist, *History of Economic Thought* (7th ed., 1948).
Gray, Alexander, *Development of Economic Thought* (1931).
Heimann, Eduard, *History of Economic Doctrines: Introduction to Economic Theory* (1945).
Mitchell, W. C., *Lecture Notes on Types of Economic Theory* (2 Vols) (1949).
Newman, P. S., *Development of Economic Thought* (1952).
Roll, Erich, *History of Economic Thought* (revised 1942).
Scott, W.A., *Development of Economics* (1933).
Whittaker, Edmund, *History of Economic Ideas* (1940).
Spiegel, Henry W., *The Development of Economic Thought* (1952).
Schumpeter, *History of Economic Analysis* (expected in winter 1952).

Additional Bibliography of General Usefulness

Abbott, L. D., (Ed.), *Masterworks of Economics* (1946).
American Economic Association, *Readings in the Theory of Income Distribution* (1946).
Bagehot, Walter, *Economic Studies* (1895).
Beer, M., *Early British Economics* (1938).
Bonar, J., *Philosophy and Political Economy* (1893).
Boucke, C. F., *Development of Economics, 1750–1900* (1921).
Cannan, Edwin, *Theories of Production and Distribution, 1776–1848* (1924).
Commons, John R., *Institutional Economics* (Chaps. I–VIII esp.).
Cossa, Luiga, *Introduction to the Study of Political Economy* (1893).
Dobb, Maurice, *Political Economy and Capitalism* (1937).
Earley et al. *Economic Theory in Review*, Indiana University Press (1950).
Encyclopedia of the Social Sciences
Gemahling, Paul, *Les Grandes Economistes: Textes et Commentaires* (1925).
Gonnard, R., *Histoire des Doctrines Économiques* (3 Vols) (1922).
Gourvitch, Alexander, *Survey of Economic Theory on Technological Changes and Employment* (1940).

Gruchy, Allen G., *Modern Economic Thought: The American Contribution* (1947).
Halevy, Elie, *The Growth of Philosophical Radicalism* (1949 ed.).
Homan, Paul, *Contemporary Economic Thought* (1928).
Ingram, J. K., *History of Political Economy* (1915).
Kinlach, T. F., *Six English Economists* (1926).
Klein, Lawrence, *The Keynesian Revolution* (1947).
Lowe, Adolph, *Economics and Sociology* (1935).
McConnell, John W., *The Basic Teachings of the Great Economists* (1943).
Macleod, N. D., *History of Economics* (1896).
Mints, Lloyd W., *History of Banking Theory in Great Britain and the U.S.* (1945).
Mitchell, W. C., *The Backward Art of Spending Money* (1950 ed.).
Monroe, A. E., *Early Economic Thought* (Readings, prior to Smith).
Monroe, A. E., *Monetary Theory before Adam Smith* (1923).
Myrdal, Gunnar, *Das Politische Element in der National-economischen Doktrinbildung* (1932).
Oncken, A., *Geschichte der Nationalökonomie* (1902).
Patterson, S. H., *Readings in the History of Economic Thought* (1922).
Peck, H. W., *Economic Thought and its Institutional Background* (1935).
Pirou, Gaetan, *Les Doctrines Economiques en France depuis 1870.*
Rist, Charles, *History of Monetary and Credit Theory* (1940).
Sabine, George F., *A History of Political Theory* (Rev. ed.) (1950).
Salin, Edger, *Geschichte der Volkswirtschaftslehre* (3rd ed.) (1944).
Schumpeter, Joseph, Epochen der Dogmen- und Methodengeschichte. In: *Grundriss der Socialökonomik* (Vol. 1) (1914).
Schumpeter, Joseph, *Ten Great Economists: From Marx to Keynes* (1951).
Spann, Othmar, *History of Economics* (1930).
Stark, W., *The Ideal Foundation of Economic Thought* (1943).
Stark, W., *The History of Economics in Relation to Social Development* (1944).
Stephen, Leslie, *The English Utilitarians* (1900).
Stephen, Leslie, *History of English Thought in the 18th Century* (1927).
Stigler, George W., *Production and Distribution Theories* (1941).
Suranyi-Unger, *Economics in the Twentieth Century* (1931).
Tawney, R. H., *Religion and the Rise of Capitalism* (1926).
Teilhac, E., *Pioneers of American Economic Thought in the 19th Century* (1936).
Usher, Abbott, Empiricism. *Journal of Economic History* (1950).
Weber, Max, *Theory of Capitalist Development*, Oxford University Press.
Wermel, *Development of the Classical Wage Theory* (1939).
Zweig, Ferdinand, *Economic Ideas: A Study of Historical Perspectives* (1950).

I. Introduction

Useful Background Chapters in Surveys
Gray, Chaps. I and II.
Haney, Parts A and B.
Heimann, Chap. I.
* Mitchell, Lecture Notes, Vol. I, Chap. I.
Roll, Chaps. I and II.
* Spiegel, *Tawney on Medieval Economic Thought.*
Tawney, *Religion and the Rise of Capitalism.*
Zweig, Chap. I.

*Denotes reading expected of students.

II. Mercantilism

Better Chapters in Surveys
Gray, Chap. III.
Haney, Chaps. VII, VIII.
Heimann, Chap. II.
Johnson, *Predecessors*, Chap. I.
* Mitchell, *Lecture Notes* (Vol. I, Chaps. IV, esp. pp 20–23); Chaps. VII, VII, IX, X (pp. 53–9)
* Roll, Chap III
Scott, Chap, II
* Spiegel, Hecksher on Mercantalism.

Other Sources
Abbott, L. D. (Ed.), *Masterworks of Economics* (condensation of Thomas Mun's England's Treasure by Foreign Trade, pp. 13–37).
Beer, M., *Early British Economics* (1938).
Buck, Philip W., *The Politics of Mercantilism* (1942).
Chalk, Alfred F., Natural Law and the Rise of Economic Individualism in England. *Journal of Political Economy* (August, 1951).
Cole, C. W., *French Mercantilist Doctrines Before Collbert* (1931).
Cole, C. W., *Colbert and a Century of French Mercantilism* (2 Vols) (1939).
Ellsworth, P. T., Part I, The Age of Mercantilism. In: *The International Economy.*
Furniss, E. S., *Position of the Laborer in a System of Nationalism, A Study of the Labor Theories of the Later English Mercantilists* (1920).
Ginsberg, Eli, *The House of Adam Smith*, Chaps. I–IV.

Gregory, T. E., The Economics of Employment in England, 1660–1713. *Economica* (1921), pp. 37–51 (Also in his *Gold, Unemployment and Capitalism*, 1933).
Gourvitch, pp. 20–29.
Heckscher, Eli F., *Mercantilism* (2 Vols) (1931), esp. Vol. I; Introduction, Chaps. I, VIII; Vol. II, Part I, Chap. I; Part V.
Heckscher, Eli F., Mercantilism. In: *Encyclopedia of Social Sciences*.
Horrocks, J. W., *A Short History of Mercantilism* (1924).
Johnson, E. A. J., *Predecessors of Adam Smith* (1937).
Johnson, E. A. J., *American Economic Thought in the 17th Century* (1932).
* Keynes, J. M., *General Theory* (Chap. 23), Notes on Mercantilism, etc., pp. 333–353, 358–362.
Monroe, A. E., *Early Economic Thought* (extract from Serra, pp. 145–167).
Monroe, A. E., *Monetary Theory Before Adam Smith* (1923).
Robertson, H. M. *Aspects of the Rise of Economic Individualism* (1933).
Schmoller, G., *The Mercantile System* (1884).
Sen, Samar Ranjan, Sir James Steuart's General Theory of Employment, Interest and Money. *Economica* (February 1947).
Sewell, H. R., Theory of Value Before Adam Smith. *Publications of the American Economic Association* (3rd series), Vol. II, pp. 633–766 (1901).
Small, Albion W., *The Cameralists* (1909).
*Smith, Adam, *Wealth of Nations*, Book IV: Of Systems of Political Economy, Chaps. I–VIII (condensed in *Masterworks*, pp. 144–168).
Spengler, Joseph J., *French Predecessors of Malthus*, Chaps. I–III.
Stettner, Walter, Sir James Steuart on the Public Debt. *Quarterly Journal of Economics* (May 1945).
Suviranta, Br., *The Theory of the Balance of Trade: A Study in Mercantilism* (1923).
Tawney, R. H., & Power, E., *Tudor Economic Documents* (1935).
Tawney, R. H., *Religion and the Rise of Capitalism* (1948 ed., paper).
Viner, J., *Studies in the Theory of International Trade*, Chaps. 1 and 2.
Viner, J., English Theories of Foreign Trade Before Adam Smith. *Journal of Political Economy* (1930).
Wilson, E. B., John Law and John Keynes. *Quarterly Journal of Economics*, Vol. LXII, No. 3 (1948).

* Indicates reading expected of students.

III. Physiocracy

Chapters in Surveys
* Gide and Rist, Book I, Chapter I.

Gray, Chapter IV.
Heimann, pp. 48–63.
* Roll, pp. 132–142.
Schumpeter, History . . .
Scott, Chapters III, IV.
* Spiegel, Smith and Marx on the Physiocrats.

Other Sources

Abbott, *Masterworks*, pp. 39–61 (Condensation of Turgot's Reflections).
Beer, M., *An Inquiry into Physiocracy*, 1939.
Bloomfield, A. I., The Foreign Trade Doctrines of the Physiocrats. *American Economic Review* (December 1931).
Calvert, George H., *Mirabeau.*
Chinard, G. (Ed.), *The Correspondence of Jefferson and DuPont de Nemours* (1931).
Daire, E., *Les Physiocrates* (2 Vols) (1846).
Gonnard, Vol. II, Book III.
Gurvitch, pp. 29–33.
Higgs, Henry, *The Physiocrats* (1897).
* Monroe (Ed.), *Early Economic Thought*, Quesnay, *Tableau Economique* (pp. 304–348); Turgot, *Reflections*, Sections 49 to 95 (pp. 351–375).
Neill, Thomas P., *The Physiocrats' Concept of Economics.* Quarterly Journal of Economics (November 1949).
Pinkerton, Milo B., *Physiocracy.*
Say, Leon, *Turgot* (English Translation, 1888).
Schumpeter, *Dogmengeschichte.*
* Smith, Adam, *Wealth of Nations*, Book IV, Chap. 9, Of Agricultural Systems.
Spengler, Joseph, The Physiocrats and Say's Law of Markets. *Journal of Political Economy* (September and December 1945).
Spengler, A J., *French Predecessors of Malthus* (esp. Chaps. V–IX).
Stephens, W. W., *Life and Writings of Turgot* (1895).
Ware, A J., The Physiocrats, A Study in Economic Rationalization. *American Economic Review* (December 1931).
Weulersse, *Le Movement Physiocratique en France de 1756 à 1770* (2 Vols) (1910).

Original Works in Library

Du Pont de Nemours, *Physiocratie* (1768).
Le Trosne, *De L'Interet Sociale* (1777).

Mirabeau, *Ami des Hommes* (Rev. ed.), including Explication de la Tableau Economique.
Mirabeau, *Oeuvres* (L'Ami & Des Hommes, La Theorie de l'Impot, La Philosophie Rurale).
Quesnay, *Oeuvres Economique et Philosophiques* (A. Oncken (Ed.), 1888).
Quesney, *Tableau Economique.*
Riviere, *L'Ordre Naturel et Essential des Societes Politiques* (1767).
Turgot, *Oeuvres* (E. Daire (Ed.), 1844).
Turgot, *Reflections on the Formation and Distribution of Riches* (in French also).

IV. The British Background of Classical Economics

Assigned Readings

*Mitchell, Vol. 1, Chaps. IV, VI, VII, VIII, X.
*Heimann, pp. 36–47.
Locke, John, *Second Treatise on Civil Government*, Chap. V: Of Property. (Available in Social Contract; Sir Ernest Barker (Ed.), pp. 16–30, and in several editions of Locke's work in Library.)
Patterson, *Readings*, pp. 2–30 (selections from Mandeville & Hutchison).
*Monroe, *Early Economic Thought*, pp. 310–338, extracts from Hume's Political Discourses, "Of Interest" and "Of the Balance of Trade".

Other Sources

Bryson, Gladys, *Man and Society, The Scottish Inquiry of the Eighteenth Century* (1945).
Cannan, *Introduction to Smith's Wealth of Nations* (Modern Library Edition).
Davidson, Wm. L., *Political Thought in England: The Utilitarians from Bentham to J. S. Mill*, Chaps. I–V.
Higgs, Richard Cantillon. *Economic Journal* (June 1891).
Jevons, W. Stanley, Richard Cantillon and the Nationality of Political Economy. *Contemporary Review* (January 1881), and in Higg's volume reprinting and translating Cantillon's *Essai*.
Johnson, E. A. J., *Predecessors of Adam Smith*, Chap. IX: "Hume, the Synthesist".
Keynes, *General Theory*, pp. 358–362 (Mandeville).
Rotwein, Eugene, *The Economic Thought of David Hume* (1950).
Stark, *Ideal Foundations*, pp. 1–26 (Locke).

Major Original Works in Library

Cantillon, *Essai Sur la Nature due Commerce en General* (text printed in both French and English), Henry Higgs (Ed.) (1931).

Hutcheson, Francis, *System of Moral Philosophy.*

Hume, *Political Discourses.*

Locke, *Two Treatises of Government*, especially Second Treatise.

Mandeville, *Fable of the Bees.*

North, *Discourses upon Trade*, in *Reprints of Economic Tracts.*

Petty, *The Economic Writings of Sir William Petty* (C. H. Hull) (1899).

Smith, *The Theory of Moral Sentiments.*

Smith, *Lectures.*

Turgot, *Reflections on the Formation and Distribution of Riches* (in both French and English).

V. Adam Smith's Wealth of Nations

Better Readings in Surveys

Gide and Rist, Chapter II.

Roll, pp. 143–183.

* Mitchell, Vol. I, Chaps. II, III, IV, V, XI, XII.

* Spiegel, *Douglas on Smith*, pp. 113–143.

** Readings in the Wealth of Nations*

Edwin Cannan edition (Modern Library):

Introduction

Book 1, Chaps. I–IX; Chap. X, (except Part II); Chap, XI, (Introduction, Part I, and Conclusion)

Book II, Introduction, Chaps. I, III, V

Book III, Chap. I

Book IV, Introduction, Chaps. I, II, VIII, IX

Selected Writings on Smith

Bagehot, Walter, Adam Smith and Our Modern Economy. In: *Economic Studies* (1895).

Bonar, J., The Theory of Moral Sentiments by Adam Smith, 1759. In: *Journal of Philosophical Studies* (1925).

Bladen, V. W. In: *Essays in Political Economy*, H. A. Innis (Ed.).

Bryson, G., *Man and Society.*

Cannan, Edwin, Adam Smith as Economist. *Economica* (1925).

Ginsburg, Eli, *The House of Adam Smith.*

Grampp, Wm. D. The Politics of the Classical Economists. *Quarterly Journal of Economics* (November 1948).

Grampp, Wm. D. Adam Smith and the Economic Man. *Journal of Political Economy* (August 1948).

Hasek, Carl W., *Introduction of Adam Smith's Doctrines Into Germany* (1925).

Myint, Hla, The Classical View of the Economic Problem. *Economica* (May 1946).

* Patterson, *Readings* (selections from Smith's Moral Sentiments and Lectures), pp. 32–61.

Rae, John, *Life of Adam Smith* (1895).

Salomon, Albert, Adam Smith as Sociologist. *Social Research*, XII (1945).

Scott, W. R., *Adam Smith as Student and Professor* (1937).

Small, Albion W., *Adam Smith and Modern Sociology* (1907).

Stephen, Sir Leslie, *History of English Thought in the 18th Century* (1927).

* Viner, Jacob, Adam Smith and Laissez Faire. In: *Adam Smith, 1776–1926.*

Other Relevant Original Works

Theory of Moral Sentiments (1759).

Lectures of Adam Smith, Edwin Cannan (Ed.), (1896).

Adam Smith's Moral and Political Philosophy (Major selections from *Moral Sentiments*, *Lectures* and *Wealth of Nations*, (Ed.) with introduction by H. W. Schneider, Hafner Pub. Co., 1948 (paper).

A Treatise on Public Opulence (an early draft, circa 1764, *Wealth of Nations*) published in Scott, W.R., op. cit.

Note: The Modern Library Wealth of Nations is the famous Cannan Edition, complete with Introduction and Notes. Students are expected to possess a copy.

VI. Classical Economic Thought From Smith to Ricardo
(Bentham and Utilitarianism; Rent Theory; Population Theory)

Better Readings in Surveys

* Cannan, *Review of Economic Theory*, Chap. IV (Population), pp. 227–234 (Rent).

Encyclopedia of the Social Sciences (J. Anderson and E. West).

Gide and Rist, pp. 118–138 (Malthus).

Haney, Chapter XI (Bentham).

Scott, Chapter VIII.

* Mitchell, *Lecture Notes* (Vol. I, Chapters XIII–XV) (Background); XVI–XIX incl. (Bentham); XX–XXII incl. (Malthus).

Other Sources

Buer, Mabel C., The Historical Setting of the Malthusian Controversy. *London Essays in Economic.*

Bonar, J., *Philosophy and Political Economy*, Book III, Chap. II; (Bentham and James Mill), and Chap. I, (Malthus).

Davidson, W. L., *Political Thought in England: The Utilitarians*, esp. Chaps. I, II, IV.

Halevy, E., *Growth of Philosophical Radicalism* (esp. Part I, Chaps. I, III; Part II, Chaps. II, III).

Keynes, J. M., Robert Malthus. In: *Essays in Biography.*

* *Masterworks*, condensation of Malthus' *Essay on Population* (8th ed.).

Mitchell, W. C., Bentham's Felicific Calculus. In: *The Backward Art of Spending Money* (1950 ed.); reprinted from *Political Science Quarterly*, Vol. XXXIII, pp. 161–183 (June 1918).

Spengler, *French Predecessors of Malthus.*

Spengler, J. J., Malthus' Total Population Theory: A Restatement and Reappraisal. *Canadian Journal of Political Science* (1945), Vol. II, pp. 83, 234.

Stark, W., Jeremy Bentham as an Economist. *Economic Journal* (April 1941).

Stephen, L., *The English Utilitarians*, Vol. I, esp. Chap. 13.

Stephen, L., *History of English Thought in the 18th Century* (2 Vols).

Stigler, George, The Development of Utility Theory I. *Journal of Political Economy* (August 1950).

Robbins, Lionel, The Optimum Theory of Population. In: *London Essays in Economics.*

Robbins, L., *The Theory of Economic Policy in English Classical Political Economy* (1952).

* Patterson, *Readings*, pp. 101–127 (Godwin), pp. 128–176 (Malthus, Essay, Principles, and Definitions), 178–190 (Bentham).

* Viner, Jacob, Bentham and J. S. Mill. *American Economic Review*, Vol. XXXIX, No. 2 (March 1949), pp. 360–382.

Original Works in Library

Works of Jeremy Bentham, John Bowring (Ed.). (See especially Volume III.)

Stark, W. (Ed.), *Jeremy Bentham's Economic Writings* (2 Vols) (1952).

Anderson, *Recreations in Agriculture.*

Bentham, *Defense of Usury.*

Bentham, *Manual of Political Economy.*

Bentham, *Principles of Morals and Legislation.*

Bentham, *Theory of Legislation.*

Malthus, *Principle of Population* (first and later editions).
Malthus, *Principles of Political Economy*.
Malthus, *An Inquiry into the Nature and Progress of Rent* (1815) (Hollander reprint).
West, *Application of Capital to Land*. In: J. H. Hollander (Ed.), *Reprints of Economic Tracts* (Series 1–2).

VII. David Ricardo

Assigned Readings
* Spiegel, *Development*, McCulloch and Marshall on Ricardo.
Mitchell, *Lecture Notes*, Vol, 1, Chaps. XXIII–XXIX.
* Ricardo, *Principles* (3rd ed.): Chaps. I (On Value), II (On Rent), III (On the Rent of Mines), IV (On Natural and Market Price), V (On Wages), VI (On Profits), XXX (On the Influence of Demand and Supply on Prices), XXXI (On Machinery).

Other Readings in Surveys
Cannan, *Review*, pp. 172–185, 230–249.
Gide and Rist, Book I, Chap. III, Section II.
Roll, pp. 183–207.

Other Readings and Sources
Bagehot, *Economic Studies*, "David Ricardo".
Cannan, *Theories of Production and Distribution* (1776–1848).
Checkland, S. G., The Propagation of Ricardian Economics in England. *Economica* (February 1949).
Horsefield, J. K., The Bankers and the Bullionists in 1819. *Journal of Political Economy* (October 1949).
Knight, F. H., Ricardian Theory of Production and Distribution. *Canadian Journal of Economics and Political Science* (1935).
* Masterworks, condensations: Ricardo, *Principles*, pp. 273–342.
McCulloch, J. R., *Works of David Ricardo* (1846).
Mitchell, W. C., Postulates and Preconceptions of Ricardian Economics. In: *Backward Art of Spending Money*.
Myint, Hla, The Classical View of the Economic Problom. *Economica* (May 1946); *Theories of Welfare Economics* (1948).
Robbins, *The Theory of Economic Policy*.
Shoup, Carl, Ricardo on the Taxation of Profits. *Public Finance*, Vol. V, No. 2 (1950).

Sraffa, P. (Ed.), *The Works and Correspondence of David Ricardo*, 9 Vols, Vol. I, *Principles*; II, *Notes on Malthus*; III, *Pamphlets and Papers, 1809–1811*; IV, *Pamphlets and Papers, 1815–1823*; V, *Speeches and Evidence*; VI–IX, *Letters*.
Stigler, Geo. J., The Ricardian Theory of Value and Distribution. *Journal of Political Economy* (June 1952).
Wermel, *Evolution Of Classical Wage Theory*.

VIII. Post-Ricardian British Economics, 1820–1850

Assigned Readings
* Marshall, *Principles*, Appendix J (the Wages Fund).
* Mitchell, *Lecture Notes*, Vol, 1, Chapters XXX–XXXIX.
* Roll, pp. 212–226, 363–403.
* Spiegel, *Development*, Viner on Bentham and J. S. Mill.

Other Readings in Surveys
Gide and Rist, Book III, Chap. II (J. S. Mill).
Gray, Chap. X.
Scott, Chaps. X and XI.

Other Readings and Sources
Bladen, V. W., John Stuart Mill's Principles: A Centenary Estimate. *American Economic Review* (March 1949).
Bowley, M., *Nassau Senior and Classical Economics*.
Bowley, M., Senior's Contribution to the Methodology of Economics. *Economica* (August 1936), pp. 281–305.
Brebner, J. Bartlet, Laissez Faire and State Intervention in 19th Century Britain. *Journal of Economic History*, Supplement VIII (1948).
Checkland, S. G., The Propagation of Ricardian Economics in England. *Economica* (February 1949).
Checkland, The Birmingham Economists, 1815–1850. *Economic History Review*, Second series, Vol, 1, No. 1 (1948).
Cruikshank, R. J., *Charles Dickens and Early Victorian England* (1949).
Davidson, *Political Thought in England: The Utilitarians*, Chaps VI–X.
Davidson, *Political Thought in England: The Utilitarians from Bentham to Mill*.
DeQuincy, Thomas, *Collected Works* (David Massen (Ed.).), Vol. IX, *Political Economy and Politics*.

Encyclopedia of the Social Sciences (James Mill, McCulloch, Senior, Bailey).

Grampp, Wm., On the Politics of the Political Economists. *Quarterly Journal of Economics* (November 1948).

Halevy, *Philosophical Radicalism*, Part II, Chap. I.

Hayek, F., *John Stuart Mill and Harriet Taylor; Mill's The Temper of our Times.*

Johnson, Harry G., Malthus on the High Price of Provisions. *Canadian Journal of Economics and Political Science* (May 1949).

Johnson, H. G., Demand for Commodities is Not a Demand for Labour. *Economic Journal* (December 1949).

Keynes, *The End of Laissez-Faire*, I, II. III; *Treatise on Money*, Vol. II, pp. 127–129 (The True Wages Fund).

Levy, S. L., *N. W. Senior* (1943).

Longfield, *Lectures on Political Economy* (London School Reprint).

Masterworks, condensation of J. S. Mill's *Principles*, pp. 381–401.

McCulloch, J. R., *Principles of Political Economy.*

Meek, R. R., The Decline of Ricardian Economics in England. *Economica* (February 1950).

Mill, James, *Elements of Political Economy.*

John Stuart Mill, *Principles of Political Economy*; *Autobiography*; *Unsettled Questions in Political Economy*; *Utilitarianism*; *A System of Logic.*

Myint, Hla, The Classical View of the Economic Problem. *Economica* (May 1946); *Theories of Welfare Economics* (1948).

O'Leary, James J., Malthus' General Theory of Employment and the Post-Napoleonic Depressions. *Journal of Economic History*, Vol. 3 (November 1943).

Patterson, *Readings*, pp. 219–296 (James Mill, Senior, J. S. Mill); Appendix, "Popularizations of English Classical Economy" (Jane Marcet and Harriet Martineau).

Pigou, A. C., Mill and the Wages Fund. *Economic Journal* (June 1949).

Robbins, *The Theory of Economic Policy*, esp. Lecture V (J. S. Mill and Socialism).

Seligman, *Essays in Economics*, Chapter III: Some Neglected British Economists.

Senior, *Outline of the Science of Political Economy.*

Sorenson, L. E., Some Classical Economists, Laissez Faire, and the Factory Acts. *Journal of Economic History* (Summer 1952).

Stephen, Sir Leslie, *English Utilitarians*, Vol. II (James Mill, Malthus & Ricardo).

Wermel, *Evolution of Classical Wage Theory.*

IX. Some Highlights of "Classical" Economic Thought On the Continent of Europe, 1776–1850

Assigned Readings

* Gide and Rist, Book 1, Chap. I (pp. 64–68, Condillac); Chap, II (Section IV, J. B. Say, pp. 118–133).

* Gide and Rist, Book II, Chap. IV (Friedrich List); Book III, Chap. I (The Optimists) pp. 329–354.

* Spiegel, List on Say, Cairnes on Bastiat, Schneider on Thünen.

Other Readings and Sources

Böhm-Bawerk, *Capital and Interest.*

Cannan, *Theories of Production and Distributlon*; and *Review of Economic Theory.*

Cossa, Chapters X, XI, XIV, XV (political economy in France, Germany, the United States and Italy, respectively).

Gray, pp. 238–247 (Von Thünen).

Haney, Chapter XVIII (Von Thünen).

Leigh, Arthur H., Von Thünen's Theory of Distribution and the Advent of Marginal Analysis. *Journal of Political Economy*, Vol. LIV, No. 6 (December 1946).

Palyi, Melchior, The Introduction of Adam Smith on the Continent. In: *Adam Smith 1776–1926.*

Patterson, *Readings*, pp. 63–88 (J. B. Say); pp. 379–443 (List, Bastiat).

Roll, pp. 244–248 (List); pp. 347–357 (France); pp. 359–363 (Von Thünen).

X. Marxian Economic Thought

Assigned Readings

* Marx, *Capital*, Vol. 1, Chaps. I (Parts I and 2), II, III (Part 2a), IV to IX inclusive.

* Marx and Engels, *The Communist Manifesto*, excerpt in Patterson, Readings, or complete.

* Schumpeter, The Communist Manifesto in Economics and Sociology. *Journal of Political Economy* (June 1949).

* Schumpeter, Science and Ideology. *American Economic Review* (March 1944).

* Schumpeter, Karl Marx. In: *Ten Great Economists.*

* Spiegel, Veblen on Marx.

* Spiegel, Halevy on Sismondi, Foxwell on the Ricardian Socialists, Cole on Owen.

* Gide and Rist, Book II, Chap. II (Saint-Simon).
* Roll, pp. 249–270 (Sismondi, Proudhon, Thompson, Gray, Bray, Hodgskin).
* Mitchell, Vol. II, Chap. XXVI (Reaction in Germany Against British Classical Economics); Chap XXXI (Veblen Contrasted with Marx).

Classified Readings

A. *Precursors of Marx*

*Gide and Rist, above.
*Roll.
*Spiegel.

B. *Philosophical and Methodological Foundations*

* Marx and Engels, *Communist Manifesto.*
* Mitchell, chapters noted above.
* Schumpeter, Science and Ideology.
* Spiegel, Veblen on Marx.
* Sabine, *History of Political Theory*, Chap. 30 (Hegel); Chap. 33 (Marx and Dialectical Materialism).
* Marcuse, Herbert, *Reason and Revolution* (1941).
* Popper, K. R., *The Open Society and Its Enemies*, Vol. II, esp. Chap. 12 (Sections I, III); Chaps 13–17.
* Russell, Bertrand, *Unpopular Essays*, Philosophy and Politics.
* *Encyclopedia of the Social Sciences*, Hegel, Dialectical Materialism, Evolution.
* Heimann, Chap. VI (Economics as Historical Dialectic of Harmony).

C. *Marxian Economics*

* Marx, *Capital*, chapters above.
* Schumpeter, *Ten Great Economists.*
* Schumpeter, The Communist Manifesto . . ..
* Robinson, Joan, *An Essay on Marxian Economics* (1949).
* Popper, Vol. II, Chap. 20.

D. *Marxian Sociology*

* Schumpeter, all references assigned.
* Spiegel, Veblen on Marx.
* Popper, esp. Chaps 18, 19, 21–25.
* Marcuse.

E. *Other Sources*

Assigned Readings:

Gide and Rist, Book II, Chapter III, Section I (Robert Owen), Section III (Louis Blanc), Chapter V (Proudhon); Book IV, Chap. II (Robertus and LaSalle); Book IV, Chap. II, Sections I and II; Chap. III (Marxism).

Gray, Chap. XI (Marx).

Roll, Chap. VII (Marx).

Marx, *Capital*, Vols. II & III, *A History of Economic Theories* (1952).

Adams, H. P., *Karl Marx in His Earlier Writings* (1940).

Beer, M., *A History of British Socialism* (2 Vols) (1920).

Bladen, V. W., The Centenary of Marx and Mill. *Journal of Economic History*, Supplement VIII (1948).

[Two lines are largely illegible but includes:

Böhm-Bawerk, *Eugen von Karl Marx and the Close of his System* (1898).

Maurice Dobb, *Political Economy and Capitalism* (1945). Classical Political Economy and Classical Political Economy and Marx.]

Dobb, Maurice & Aba Lerner, Controversy. In: *Journal of Political Economy* (1940), under title of "Vulgar Political Economy and Vulgar Marxism".

Gray, Alexander, *The Socialist Tradition* (1946) (esp. Chap. X1 on Early English Socialism).

Laidler, Harry, *A History of Socialist Thought*.

Lange, O., *On the Economic Theory of Socialism*.

Lange, O., Marxian Economics and Modern Economic Theory. *Review of Economic Studies* (June 1935).

Laski, H., *The Communist Manifesto: Socialist Landmark* (1948).

Lenin, *The State and Revolution*.

Lowenthal, E., *The Ricardian Socialists*.

Karx, *Critique of Political Economy* (1859) (English Translation by N. I. Stone, 1904).

Masterworks, condensation of Vol. I of *Capital* (pp. 455–614).

Masterworks, condensation of Robert Owen, *A New View of Society*, pp. 345–378.

Menger, A., *The Right to the Whole Produce of Labor*.

Patterson, *Readings*, Part VII, Section I (Sismondi); Part VIII, Sections 2, 3, 4 (Proudhon, Marx and Engels).

Robinson, Joan, "Marx and Keynes" and "The Labour Theory of Value." In: *Collected Economic Papers* (1951).

Round Table in Commemoration of the Centenary of the Communist Manifesto. *American Economic Review*, Proceedings (May 1949).

Schlesinger, Rudolph, *Marx: His Time and Ours* (1950).

Schumpeter, Jos. A., *Capitalism, Socialism and Democracy*, Part 1, The Marxian Doctrine.

Scott, J. W., *Karl Marx on Value* (1920).

Sweezy, Paul M., Fabian Political Economy. *Journal of Political Economy* (June 1949).

Sweezy, Paul M., *The Theory of Capitalist Development* (1942).

Stark, W. *Ideal Foundations of Economic Thought*, especially on Hodgskin and Thompson, pp. 52–148.

Tuan, Mao-Lan, *Simonde de Sismondi as an Economist.*

Zauberman, A., Economic Thought in the Soviet Union. *Review of Economic Studies* (1948–1949).

XI. "The Revolution of 1870": Precursors, Participants, and Followers

Assigned Readings

* Mitchell, *Lecture Notes*, Vol. II, Chaps II–VIII (Jevons); XXIV (Von Wieser); XXIX–XXX (Walras, Cassel); XVIII (earlier U.S. Economics, and J. B. Clark).

* Spiegel, Fisher on Cournot, Walras on Gossen, Hayek on Menger, Hayek on Weiser, Schumpeter on Böhm-Bawerk, Hicks on Walras, J. M. Clark on J. B. Clark, Demaria on Pareto, Robbins on Wicksteed.

* Schumpeter, *Ten Great Economists* (Walras, Menger, Pareto, Fisher).

Readings in Surveys

Gide and Rist, pp. 63–68 (Condillac).

Gide and Rist, Book V, Introduction and Chap. 1, The Hedonists (esp. for Walras and Pareto and "Psychological Economists").

Gray, Chap. XII, esp. pp. 330–345 (Condillac, Walras, Gossen and Jevons).

Roll, pp. 404–435 (Gossen, Jevons, Menger, Walras); pp. 444–456 (Wieser, Böhm-Bawerk and Parreto).

Scott, Chap. XX (Carl Menger); Chap. XXI (Von Wieser); Chap. XXII Böhm-Bawerk); Chap. XXIII (Sax, Wicksteed); Chap. XXIV (Criticisms and defense).

Other Sources

Clerc, J. O., Walras and Pareto: Their Approach to Applied and Social Economics. *Canadian Journal of Economics and Political Science* (November 1942).

Condillac, *Le Commerce et Le Gouvernement* (1776) in *Mélanges d'Économie Politique* (1847).
Dupuit, *De l'Utilite et de sa Mesure.*
Eckard, W. W., *Economics of W. S. Jevons.*
Knight, F. H., Marginal Utility Economics. In: *Ethics of Competition.*
Patterson, *Readings*, pp. 324–351 (Jevons), pp. 353–378 (Böhm-Bawerk).
Robbins, Lionel, The Place of Jevons in the History of Economic Thought. *The Manchester School*, VII (1935), pp. 1–17.
Robertson, Ross, Mathematical Economics before Cournot. *Journal of Political Economy* (December 1949).
Schumpeter, J. A., Vilfredo Pareto (1848–1923). *Quarterly Journal of Economics* (May 1949).
Seligman, Some Neglected British Economists. In: *Essays in Economics*, esp. pp. 81–94, 111–121 (Samuel Bailey, W. F. Lloyd, Mountifort Longfield, Isaac Butt).
Stark, W., *Ideal Foundations*, pp. 149–195 (Gossen).
Stigler, Chap. II (W. S. Jevins) ; also Chaps III, VI, VII, VIII, X (Wicksteed, Menger, Von Wieser, Böhm-Bawerk, and Wicksell, respectively).
Stigler, The Economics of Carl Menger. *Journal of Political Economy* (April 1937).
Stigler, The Development of Utility Theory, I and II. *Journal of Political Economy*, Vol. LVIII (1950).
Veblen, T., The Limitations of Marginal Utility. *Journal of Political Economy* (1909). In: *The Place of Science in Modern Civilization* (1919) and in: *What Veblen Taught* (1936).
Spiegel, *Development*, Keynes on Jevons, Frisch on Wicksell.
Schumpeter, *Ten Great Economists*, on Böhm-Bawerk, on Wieser.

XII. The Neoclassical School

Assigned Readings

* Mitchell, *Lecture Notes*, Vol. II, Chaps. X-XVII (Marshall).
* Schumpeter, *Ten Great Economists* (Alfred Marshall, 1842–1924).
* Spiegel, *Development*, Viner on Marshall, Colin Clark on Pigou.

Readings in Surveys

Heimann, pp. 184–214.
Homan, Paul, *Contemporary Economic Thought*, Alfred Marshall'.
Scott, pp. 291–296 (Cairnes).

Other Sources

Bladen, V. W., Mill to Marshall: The Conversion of the Economists. *Journal of Economic History*, Vol. I, Suppl.

Cairnes, J. E., *The Logical Method of Political Economy.*

Davenport, H. J., *The Economics of Alfred Marshall.*

Encyclopedia of the Social Sciences, Economics – The Cambridge School.

Frisch, R., Alfred Marshall's Theory of Value. *Quarterly Journal of Economics* (November 1950).

Keynes, J. M., Alfred Marshall, 1842–1924. In: *Memorials*, Keynes, *Essays in Biography*, and *Economic Journal* (September 1924).

Marshall, *Principles of Economics.*

Alfred Marshall, 1842–1924. In: *Economic Journal* (December 1942) (esp. G. F. Shove, The Place of Marshall's Principles in the Development of Economic Theory, pp. 294–329).

Oppenheimer, Franz, A Post-Mortem on Cambridge Economics. *American Journal of Economics and Sociology*, Vols. I & II.

Parsons, Talcott, *The Structure of Social Action*, Part II, Chap. IV.

* Patterson, *Readings*, pp. 297–322.

Pigou, *Economics of Welfare*, Chaps I and II.

Pigou, A. C., *Memorials of Alfred Marshall*, esp The Present Position of Economics (1885) and The Older Generation of Economists and the New (1899).

XIII. "The Schumpeterian System"

Readings in Surveys

Newman, P. C., *Development of Economic Thought* (1952), Chap. 31.

* Heimann, pp. 219–226.

* Gide and Rist, pp. 713–724.

Works about Schumpeter and his Economics

* Clemence, R. V., & Doody, F. S., *The Schumpeterian System* (1950), Parts I and II (pp. 1–21).

Harris, Seymour (Ed.), *Schumpeter: Social Scientist* (1951) (Most of this material appears also in Review of Economics and Statistics, May, 1951); includes:

Erich Schneider, *Schumpeter's Early German Work* (1906–1917).

Fritz Machlup, Schumpeter's Economic Methodology.

A. P. Usher, Historical Applications of the Theory of Economic Development.

Arthur Smithies, Schumpeter and Keynes.
P. R. Sweezy, Schumpeter's Theory of Innovations.
D. McCord Wright, Schumpeter's Political Philosophy.
E. S. Mason, Schumpeter on Monopoly and the Large Firm.

Haberler, G., Joseph Alois Schumpeter, 1883–1950. *Quarterly Journal of Economics* (August 1950).

Keirstead, B. S., *The Theory of Economic Change* (1948).

Kuznets, Simon, Schumpeter's Business Cycles. *American Economic Review* (June 1940).

Smithies, Arthur, Joseph Alois Schumpeter. *American Economic Review* (September 1950).

Solo, Carolyn S., Innovation in the Capitalist Process: A Critique of the Schumpeterian Theory. *Quarterly Journal of Economics* (August 1951).

Taymans, A. C., Tarde and Schumpeter: A Similar Vision. *Quarterly Journal of Economics* (Nov. 1950).

Taylor, O. H., Schumpeter and Marx: Imperialism and Social Classes in the Schumpeterian System. *Quarterly Journal of Economics* (November 1951).

Sweezy, Paul R., *The Theory of Capitalist Development* (1942).

Usher, A. P., The Significance of Modern Empiricism for History and. Economics. *Journal of Economic History* (November 1949).

Essays in Honor of Joseph A. Schumpeter. *Review of Economics and Statistics* (February 1943).

Sweezy, Paul, Professor Schumpeter's Theory of Innovation. *Review of Economics and Statistics* (February 1943).

Selected Works by Schumpeter

Capitalism, Socialism and Democracy, 2nd ed. (1947); 3rd ed. (1950), Harper & Bros., esp. Part II: Can Capitalism Survive? (Chaps VI, VII, VIII, XI, XII, XIII, XIV).

Business Cycles (2 Vols) (1939), esp. Vol. I, Chaps I, II, III, IV, and VI sections A & B, esp. pp. 220–231).

The Theory of Economic Development (English ed.), Harvard University Press (1934, reprinted 1949), especially Chaps I and II.

Ten Great Economists: From Marx to Keynes (1951) (Includes essays on Marx, Walras, Menger, Marshall, Pareto, Böhm-Bawerk, Taussig, Fisher, Mitchell, and Keynes).

* Science and Ideology. *American Economic Review* (March 1949).

* The Communist Manifesto in Economics and Sociology. *Journal of Political Economy* (June 1949).

* The Explanation of the Business Cycle. *Economica* (December 1927).

* The Analysis of Economic Change. *Review of Economics and Statistics* (May 1935, reprinted in H. Ellis (Ed.), *Readings in Business Cycle Theory*, 1944).

* Review of the Troops: A Chapter from the History of Economic Analysis. *Quarterly Journal of Economics* (May 1951).

* Epochen der Dogmen- und Methodengeschichte. In: Grundriss der Socialökonomie, Vol. 1 (1914).

Das Wesen un der Hauptinhalt der Theoretischen Nationalökonomie (1906).

A History of Economic Analysis (announced but not yet published).

John Maynard Keynes: 1863–1946. *American Economic Review* (September 1946).

Theoretical Problems of Economic Growth. *Journal of Economic History*, Supplement VII (1947).

The Instability of Capitalism. *Economic Journal* (September 1928).

XIV. "The Keynesian Revolution"

General

* Roll, pp. 524–542.

* Heimann, Chapter II.

Gide and Rist, pp. 738–749.

* Dillard, Dudley, *The Economics of John Maynard Keynes* (1948), esp. Chaps 1–3 and 12.

Klein, Lawrence R., *The Keynesian Revolution* (1947), esp. Chaps I–III and XII.

Harris, Seymour (Ed.), *The New Economics: Keynes' Influence on Theory and Public Policy* (1947).

Biographical and Interpretative

Harrod, R.F., *The Life of John Maynard Keynes* (1951).

Schumpeter J. A., John Maynard Keynes, 1883–1946. *American Economic Review* (September 1946) and in: *The New Economics*.

Sweezy, Paul M., Keynes, The Economist. In: *The New Economics*.

Robinson, E. A. G., John Maynard Keynes, 1883–1946. *Economic Journal* (March 1947).

Williams, John H., An Appraisal of Keynesian Economics. *American Economic Review*, Proceedings (May 1948).

Williams, John H., An Economist's Confessions. *American Economic Review* (March 1952).

Smithies, Arthur, Schumpeter and Keynes. In: *Schumpeter: Social Scientist.*
Smithies, A., Reflections on the Works and Influence of John Maynard Keynes. *Quarterly Journal of Economics* (Nov. 1951).

Works of Keynes
* *The Economic Consequences of the Peace* (1919), esp. Chap. II.
* *Monetary Reform* (1923), esp. Preface and Chap. I ("Consequences to Society of Changes in the Value of Money").
* *The End of Laissez-Faire* (1926) (abbreviated in *Essays in Persuasion*).
A Treatise on Money (2 Vols) (1930), esp. Vol. I , Book III (The Fundamental Equations).
* *Essays in Persuasion* (1932), esp. II (4–7); IV, "Politics," V, "No Future".
* *The Means to Prosperity* (1933), (37 pages).
* *Essays in Biography* (1933), esp. Malthus, Marshall.
The General Theory of Employment, Interest and Money (1936), esp. Chaps 1, 2, 3, 13 (and appendix), 18, 22, and 24 (Social Philosophy).
The Theory of the Rate of Interest. In: Gayer, A. D. (Ed.), *The Lessons of Monetary Experience* (1937).
How to Pay for the War (1940).
* *Two Memoirs*, David Garnet (Ed.) (1951), esp. II, My Early Beliefs.

[Editor's note: Only minor corrections have been made to the original]

James S. Earley
LECTURE NOTES
Economics 201
DEVELOPMENT OF ECONOMICS
Notes Taken by Warren J. Samuels

Lecture

Introductory

Two short papers, one per semester, on earlier and later development of economics. Not longer than 12 pages (not arbitrary). On some phase of economic thought not later than 1850 (J. S. Mill, List, Bastiat for first semester, etc.).

See also instructions etc. in Syllabus. The texts are:
Gide and Rist; Newman, Readings; Smith, Wealth of Nations; Spiegel and Mitchell are supplementary texts. Other general works (orientation and newer books), and their primary use, are:

Heilbroner: Good for earlier period, the role of economists in period 1500–1900 in development of general social ideas.
Hutchison: history of economic analysis, 1870–1929.
L. Robbins: theory of economic policy of English classical political economists, 1952.
Schumpeter: History of Economic Analysis; Economic Doctrine and Method, translated.
Schumpeter: AER 3–49, "Science and Ideology": How economic theories arise and change and the reasons for which economic theories are imbued with ideological elements: economics must be developed anew for changing situations, new generations, despite attempts of some to straight-jacket economics by declaring the universality of one system; instead reflect ideological and social constitutions; processes of genesis and change are most interesting.

Lecture
Schumpeter, History of Economic Analysis, pp. 3–50 (Part One): read to get general ideas, etc.

J. A. Schumpeter, "Science and Ideology," AER March 1949

In his *History of Economic Analysis*, Schumpeter draws a distinction between three types of studies of the development of economic ideas:

(1) histories of systems of political economy;
(2) histories of economic thought;
(3) histories of economic analysis.

By systems of political economy he meant coordinated policies concerning economic affairs on the part of government (similar to Smith, whose fourth book is entitled "Of Systems of Political Economy"); these differ as to what they are "maximizing," such as agriculture, foreign trade balance, free trade (laissez-faire), socialism, communism, fascism.

By economic thought Schumpeter meant the whole conglomeration of all thoughts people have about economic affairs, public and private, objective and subjective, etc. This area he recognized to be of little value due to the incoherence and lack of scientific foundation, thus lacking respectability, inherent in such study.

By economic analysis, and Schumpeter would confine his treatment as the true scientist to this field, he would study the way in which scientific apparatus and conclusions have developed through time; thus he held scientific economics to be distinct from views on policy, predilections, prejudices, and private interests.

Schumpeter doesn't mean to confine his attention to what we call today "economic theory;" rather he has three or four classifications of analytical work in economic analysis: (1) economic history; (2) economic statistics; (3) economic theory (covering concepts and their interrelations; broad behavioral principles; simplified models of economic structure); and (4) economic sociology, i.e. how did people come to behave in economic affairs as they do; the study of the history and forms of economic behavior.

Schumpeter felt all these areas of economic analysis were scientific, with common characteristics of development and analysis. The pattern thereof is what he describes and defends in his article, "Science and Ideology" – on the "sociology of knowledge," i.e. how knowledge comes about.

Professor Earley presents the thesis of the article as a three-stage development.

In the first stage, an economist – any social scientist – has a "vision" which is "prescientific," not derived from any long study and analysis, but a mixture of perceptions and prescientific "knowledge" – more accurately, partly perceptive and partly intuitive – a common-sense knowledge of sorts. This may be a modification of something presented before by others). In any event, the scientist has a set of related phenomena that he wishes to analyze.

The second stage is that of model-building in which he takes the material from the "vision" and tries to construct it into an interconnected system of relations and interrelations, having a certain form and causal sequence, and concerning which he can make an explanation – the scientific step using all available scientific techniques and methods – science. Economic analysis is, therefore, devising and using these techniques to build models that are explanations or rationalizations of the vision. [In a note at this point I typed: "But does the economic scientist get any more out of the hat than what he puts into it?" I do not know if the query is due to Earley or myself.]

The third stage is the subjection of the model to testing: econometrics, statistics, history, etc.

In the *History of Economic Analysis*, Schumpeter deals with the visions (where from), the methods (how built), and the models of the economists. He admits that the process of the development of economic analysis is not wholly scientific, that it differs markedly from the history of physics; this is because the "visions" are ideologically conditioned to a greater or lesser extent and that such is in the very nature of the thing. The vision is explainable by the particular position in which, e.g. the Physiocrats were in: a weakening crown, their suspicion of something "wrong," the popular study of the circulation of blood and digestion in the body; hence Quesnay got the idea of circularity in a system getting "fuel" and using it up required its replacement. Marx's particular bent is due to personal and contemporary social and economic reasons causing him to see the capitalistic process as one of labor exploitation. He articulated it during the rest of his life, in *Capital*.

Keynes, says Schumpeter, got his vision of a chronically ill world by living in a country actually suffering in such a manner. A thorough Marshallian, he saw, however, that Marshall's theory was unable to cope with such a situation. He threw aside the received doctrine, coming out with a radically different model. Earley doubts Schumpeter's claim that Keynes had his vision as late as post-World War I. [Original notes read: "Earley doubts JMK's early vision post WWI claimed by JAS."]

Therefore, says Schumpeter, we must trace the extent to which the ideological has affected economic thought. He feels, however, that the second and third stages of economic analysis will eradicate the ideological bias. The analysis is neutral and is comparable to the apparatus used in other sciences.

Therefore we do get something respectable from the standpoint of science after all.

Professor Earley commented that this view fits pretty well in some cases and not too well in others. Intellectual bias isn't found solely in the initial vision and it may be more durable and therefore more difficult to eradicate. It is not necessarily precognitive; it may be distillations from earlier analysis, not a burst of genius but an accretion process, especially in recent years.

Schumpeter's *History*, Professor Earley went on to say, reflects his life; a student of Böhm-Bawerk, in seminars with Marxists, he saw Europe's economy developing in a way different from both the received doctrine and that of the Marxists. His vision, therefore, is a reaction to his environment. As with Keynes, the new vision comes not from dissatisfaction with the given scientific apparatus but from seeing something "wrong" with the environment.

Furthermore, Professor Earley pointed out, Schumpeter is not clear as to the effect of how people are trained, which leads them to something new.

Schumpeter's, therefore, is not an accretion phenomenon but, similar to other concepts of his, one of innovation, from the pioneering patentee.

Lecture

Consult Syllabus. Recommended reading on Mercantilism: Smith, Part IV, Introduction; Chapters 1, 2, 3 (Part I, omitting digression on banks, and Part 2), 5 (omit digression), 8.

Smith: Mercantilism as emanation of thinking and interests of mercantile class, not as expression of philosophy of statehood. [My note in margin: "Why not the two 'theories' aiding each other?"]

Concluding ideas on Schumpeter's analysis: Alternative ways of looking at and analyzing the problem regarding the history of economic thought:

(1) Objective conditions in the society in which the thought arises: trade, prosperity, etc. of particular industries, underemployment – general economic history as framework of economic thought; the salient features and salient problems.
  (a) Mitchell: especially in early period, growth of individual in England and chapters on institutional change.
  (b) Ricardian economics as aftermath of Napoleonic War.

(2) Stress on developments in associated disciplines as showing how they came to look at the world the way they did, the scientific environment of their time.
  (a) Physiocrats reflected Newton and Lavoisier in physics and biology.
  (b) Marx reflected Hegelian philosophy.
  (c) Marshall reflected the new biology of the later 19th century.

(3) Class origins of the individual who is writing or the group who form a school.
  (a) Schumpeter's idea is that class may influence, but not have a fundamental influence on the product, which is primarily analytical and from which the ideological is shorn.

(b) Marx: main ideas reflect class interest.

(4) Economic theories evolved by building block or incremental process in which they are built upon predecessors' intellectual structures which to them have weaknesses. Apply to special cases and expand the analytical framework, in manner similar to physical and biological sciences. Not a steady or even growth, but a progressive development building upon past theories.

Professor Earley's sole comment was that it was hard to interpret along any one line and have it fit all cases.

MERCANTILISM

Summaries of various analyses of mercantilism: [Part of typed notes, not of original class notes]

(a) T. E. Gregory ("The Economics of Employment in England, 1660–1713," *Economica*, 1921) concluded that underemploy-ment was one cause.
(b) G. Schmoller (*The Mercantile System*, 1884) argued that mercantilism was a political thing, that state-making or -building was the important impetus; that economic interests were handmaidens to the rise of power of the crown.
(c) E. Heckscher: the result of free-wheeling economy, especially of various economic groups of the time.
(d) H. M. Robertson: (*Aspects of the Rise of Economic Individualism*, 1933) questions Weber's thesis of the Protestant Ethic.
(e) A. W. Small (*The Cameralists*, 1909): was more directly concerned with the increase of the power of the crown: political and administrative motives predominate.
(f) J. Viner ("English Theories of Trade Before Smith", *JPE*, 1930): reflected thinking of mercantile classes, not the court; similar to Heckscher.
(g) Adam Smith: mercantilism as the emanation of thinking and interests of mercantile class, not as an expression of the philosophy of statehood.

Interpretations: Schmoller and Small (political) versus Heckscher, Viner and Smith (economic).

Why start a history of the development of economic thought with the Mercantilists, and not Adam Smith, the Physiocrats, or Xenophon, Plato or Aristotle?

(1) Trace mainly classical tradition, differentiating between the classical, and the historical and institutional schools; earlier ideas have had more influence on those two schools; mercantilism thus stands out as founder of the discipline:
   (a) The first group to look upon an increase in wealth as a good in itself – an independent object worth following, whether for the glory of the crown, national strength, or the interests of the mercantile groups; increase of wealth worthwhile – their focus if not their paramount analysis: similar to Machiavelli's isolation of politics.
   (b) Studied with method not fundamentally different from those used since; analyze economic processes and infer what will happen if such and such is done; analytical and not merely descriptive, e.g. balance of trade and effects of certain policies – started discussion; a form that could be tested; not in juridical or moral or social principles.
   (c) Recognized money was a central element in economic machine and there was a unit of account in their thinking (independent of subjective elements) and can do things by managing the unit of account; a view having longevity despite reaction to it.
   (d) Theories based on notion of economic behavior, viz., merchants and manufacturers would behave in own pecuniary interest so you could depend on it. Use it in ways administered to wider good than individual would by himself.
   (e) Held provocative ideas on issues giving forth to Physiocratic and classical thinking:
      (1) nature of wealth;
      (2) relation of business principles and economic welfare of the community;
      (3) issue of free trade versus protection;
      (4) government intervention.

Provided material on which later economics was built; must view Physiocracy against background of mercantilism, the same with Smith.

(2) Interest in the theory of employment developed in recent years shows that mercantilists held ideas similar to Keynes on employment, money and the interest rate, and economic development.
(3) Have widest influence of any school on government policies, less on economic analysis proper but still substantial, especially as getting ball rolling.

Mercantilist thought seemed to grow out of two factors:

(1) The environmental elements of:
   (a) the problems and interests of a growing group of capitalists and the problems of the oligarchies in which they lived (England, Spain, Holland, France);
   (b) and the problems of the public administrator.
(2) Concepts derived from the theory of private enterprise, seeking to apply them to the analysis of the economy as a whole, regarding money, money and savings, profit or surplus – more important than gross turnover, importance of liquid position (Viner, Schumpeter). Merchants looked at problems at large in same way they looked at the problems of their own business – favorable balance of trade, etc. They analyzed, theorized and then people whittled at them as they thought they weren't satisfactory; see example of naive vision as beginning of economic science.

Distinction between channel mercantilism, cameralism and bullionism:

(1) Channel mercantilism: mainly low countries and Britain, but also France; countries engaged in the overseas trade; classical tradition in broad sense goes from this to ideas of British and Italian writers emphasizing concepts of wealth – clear mercantile notion.
(2) Cameralism and Colbertism: emphasized state-making problems and those of the public administrator and tend to more integrated analysis, as in historical and institutional economics.

In this course by "mercantilism" shall mean channel mercantilism.

Lecture

PHYSIOCRACY

General Introduction

I. Various Concepts of Their "Rights" as the Founders of Economics

Gide and Rist

The Physiocrats discovered or saw the economy as a natural order; more complete than the Mercantilists, an interrelated system.

The Physiocratic system is "natural" in a sense not easy to specify. Ideas of natural laws governing economic affairs are not peculiar to the Physiocrats, but they held a complete system, governed by immutable and universal laws, similar to physical and biological laws; not natural laws in the limited sense of Locke or Smith; best described as closely analogous but not similar to the physical universe. They had two notions, or visions in the Schumpeterian sense, first, that economic and social order is just as regular and impersonal as the Newtonian system and therefore just as subject to scientific study and generalization; and second, that this order had characteristics of a living organism and the study of economics can properly deal with the physiology of this organism.

One idea that they held is that the actual same physical laws governed economic order as governed the physical and biological orders; their concept of wealth is material, production is a technological process, and human institutions are not too significant in the economic process.

Hard to agree, but close approach; Gide and Rist disagree.

Government should not interfere with the natural actions of individuals; if it does so, waste, poverty and loss of welfare would ensue.

Fundamentally a divine order; hard to show to what extent this was dressing on their doctrines to make it attractive to all.

Had idea of a unified science of society; Mercier seems to so imply, but this influence wasn't powerful as sociology developed much later and from different origins.

Karl Marx

In declaring the Physiocrats the founders of economics Marx gives three reasons (quotes, etc. may be found in his *Theories of Surplus Value*):

First, the analysis of capital and its role within bourgeois horizons is the product of the Physiocrats. They saw capitalist production as existing independent of volition; derived from necessities of production and social life and these were eternal and natural.

Second, though they turned the capitalist form of production into an eternal and natural form, they had the merit to conceive them as physiological forms of social life independent of individual or group volitions and politics, etc. This is in line with Marx's idea of inevitable technological movement and the need for social forms to be in line therewith – a natural order independent of man's will.

Third, notable for finding a surplus – to them use values – in the process of production itself but not in exchange. Whereas Mercantilism taught that surpluses came from exchange with other countries – the favorable balance was their net product – and advantage derived from trade, Marx considered the surplus to come from the production process itself. Thus Marx commended the Physiocrats for their emphasis on surplus as an end product and finding it in production and not in exchange.

The notion of "surplus" a significant variable in the history of economic thought.

Marx, therefore, credited the Physiocrats for their analysis of capital, their notion of a proper order of economic society independent of the volition of man, and their theory of surplus or net product. Their ideas coincided in brief with those of his own – the concept of a "surplus" derived from production and the "vision" of the capitalist form of production as existing independent of human volition, derived from the necessities of production and social life, and which were eternal and natural; all lent something to the Marxian economic analysis.

Joseph A. Schumpeter

First, they made economics a "natural" science, i.e. a study by the methods of the natural sciences, abstracted for study from questions as to what ought to be; set up apparatus to use basic methods of measure and interrelationships used in the natural sciences.

Second, discovered the circular flow of economic life – the basis of Schumpeter's own theory.

Whereas Mercantilists dealt with parts of the economy, theirs was not a "closed system," for, although it analyzed the processes of production internally (domestically), the product went abroad. They did not conceive of the economy as a self-sustaining circular process as did the Physiocrats, who saw a "closed economy," a complete system in and of itself, like a circuit, in which the processes continually repeated themselves.

This to Schumpeter is the basis for proper monetary theory, cycle theory and the theory of economic development.

[(Eliminates problems incumbent upon the inclusion of consideration of an international economic system.) In typed version, not in original notes.]

Professor Earley thinks that they might be called the first macroeconomists: total national income and its reproduction, and what made it greater or less. Also that Leontieff's input-output is based on their fundamental conception, in effect a modern Tableau.

The arguments of Gide and Rist, Marx, and Schumpeter, are strong; but even if they are qualified, the Physiocrats did much that was new and gave economics a push in new directions that were followed for a long time.

In addition the following are the basic characteristics of the Physiocrats:

(1) Primarily influential in starting the vogue – which took a long time to catch on – of economic analysis by model-building. Theirs was complete, had a particular form, and showed, they thought, the entire economic system at work.

This was part of the background for Schumpeter and Leontieff; and gave Adam Smith a point of view, having him work out the theory of the workings of the price system in a way different than he would have done otherwise on a different foundation, namely that of Great Britain.

(2) The notion of general equilibrium, in which all processes are interdependent and reach a general equilibrium position. Theirs was the prototype of the system of Walras, and possibly of national accounting.
(3) They were the founders of the deductive method (in economics); with a few simple concepts and postulates, they tried to derive a great body of theorems.
(4) Pierced the "veil of money" and went beyond so-called monetary transactions to analyze real processes.

Thus, they were the founders of highly theoretical method and still also of notions permitting measurement. Schumpeter, like Marx, was very sympathetic to the Physiocrats. Schumpeter saw them as the predecessors of the first econometricians.

II. Several Important Concepts

Income and Wealth: (and hence value).

To the Phyiocrats wealth was strictly material, excluding money and only in the backs of some of their minds were there any ideas of maximizing utility.

Income ran parallel to that of wealth, but modelled in part on Mercantilist doctrine, i.e. a net income concept, based not on money but on material goods of a certain sort. Income was a net product, an increment of physical or material wealth; income, therefore, an increase in wealth.

These concepts are significantly different from modern views. Income as used in contemporary thought comprises in some sense all of what is produced and not just that which is left over as a surplus. Value and its significance are either monetary or psychological in measure, notably the latter. The Physiocrats did not explicitly deny psychological valuation, but rather took it for granted, placing their emphasis on real wealth.

Modern thought derives wealth from income; Physiocracy, on the other hand, derived income from wealth. For us, wealth comes from income; for them, income was a net addition to wealth; for us, therefore, income is a flow of value from which wealth is derived by capitalizing income. They viewed simply from the facet of physical form; the other processes of economic life – exchange and fabrication – can't be considered productive.

Thus, it was natural for them to visualize only agricultural activities (also the extractive industries, fishing and mining) as productive; the others considered sterile.

Nevertheless this "productivity" or wealth or net income was not seen as coming solely from nature. Three elements seen as entering into the production of wealth: labor, capital and nature.

Labor: only the labor of agricultural labor was productive, or rather only agricultural labor was conducive to the creation of a net product. The keep or maintenance or substance of labor equated with the input of labor. The net product or surplus left over was not accredited to labor but to the natural factor with which labor cooperated; still, labor was essential in the process.

Capital: likewise capital was considered productive if employed where a surplus was produced, that is, devoted to agriculture. Marx has given us the idea that they really concentrated on capital – that they put it into productive activities to get an increase in income and thus wealth, otherwise capital would be reduced if employed in non-productive industries. Capital set labor in motion, especially advances in agricultural production, the factor starting the process and keeping it going. Capital was working capital in their system; labor and capital applied to land was productive, with capital the key, setting labor in motion.

Their peculiar notion of nature producing a surplus necessitated the distinction between agricultural and fabricating activity.

Furthermore, what was saved was also productive, a surplus over that which was necessary to keep the process going. Their dilemma was that profits and interest might also be saved; their answer, however, was that in agriculture saving was automatic and required no abstinence.

We see a mixture, therefore, of essentially Physiocratic ideas with capitalist notions: the surplus was viewed as a desideratum, capital was seen as setting in labor in motion, and savings as a key economic process.

Lecture

Physiocratic Theory of Income

The Physiocrats had: (1) a theory of income and what constituted income intimately attached to their theory of reproduction; (2) a theory of how this income circulated (income flow); and (3) a theory of the role of capital and of consumption insofar as capital and consumption expenditures affected the level of income. The first two were explicit in the *Tableau Economique*; the third was not explicit.

At this point, Professor Earley went into the versions of the *Tableau* as presented first in Roll (pp. 136–137) and second in Gide & Rist (pp. 19–20). The outcome of the comparison was that Roll says that the *Tableau* deals only with those parts of production that circulate, hence only 2L are deducted as expenses; whereas Gide & Rist see the investment manufactured by the sterile class and sold to the cultivators as expense to the latter, totalling 3L in expenses.

The Physiocrats recognized that agricultural labor was productive, but that sterile industry was not productive. The *avances annuelles* are made by capitalists rather than by the ultimate owners of the land; the proprietors are simply consumers. The Physiocrats were worried about the latter spending their income on sterile production. The Physiocrats had a notion of a *bon prix*, the good price, but they had no price theory concerning products and factors, i.e. had no theory of distribution. (Gide & Rist mistaken when they said the Physiocrats did have a theory of distribution.) They had only one element of a theory of distribution – all factors other than land get their expenses – a crude cost-of-production concept.

Earley's own interpretation of the *Tableau Economique* had the following sequence:

(1) The cultivators pay $2M in rent to the proprietors.
(2) The proprietors spend $1M on food from the cultivators and $1M on manufactured goods from the sterile class.
(3) The sterile class spends the $1M on food from the cultivators.
(4) The cultivators spend $1M on manufactured goods from the sterile class.
(5) The sterile class spends $1M on raw materials from the cultivators.

Also, $2M of food is produced by the cultivators that does not circulate.

Income analysis:

$5M produced (4 food plus 1 raw materials)
$3M deducted as expenses
―――――――――
$2M net product

Modern income concepts:

two food (non-circulating)
two food (one and one)
two manufactured goods (one and one)

six gross national product
less one replacement

five national income net

Lecture

Physiocratic Income Concepts, Their Rationale and How They Differ from Modern Income Concepts

The Physiocrats were moving away from the concept held by the Mercantilists. The only significant income concept of the Mercantilists was a favorable balance of trade; all domestic transactions and processes are significant only as means to the end of a favorable balance of trade. Comparable to the *produit net*. The maximization and increase of the favorable balance of foreign trade was the end of Mercantilist policies. Consumption was a means to an end and had no value in itself. Investment activities were likewise instrumental in increasing the favorable balance of trade. The favorable balance of trade was the myopia of Mercantilism.

The Mercantilist failure to see the significance of economic aspects in the large was greater than the failure involved in their fixation on money. Money to them was a measure of the profit rather than being the profit itself; money was beneficial to profit, not worthwhile in itself (only for what it could be used for). Still they identified money with the favorable balance of trade and wealth.

The Physiocrats felt that the focus on money needed rectifying and that not the favorable balance of trade but some measure of domestic production is significant. Theirs is a special view concerning the measurement of income stemming from their reaction to Mercantilism, but more from their naturalist agrarian astigmatism that confined it to physical production. They concluded there was neither advantage nor disadvantage from international trade, and that internally they should get away from a monetary for a real or physical measurement.

France was then predominantly agricultural and in the midst of an agricultural revolution, which involved a more capitalistic organization of agriculture. This, coupled with contemporary advances in physiology, resulted in the Physiocratic system. Mercantilism, on the other hand, was influenced by the rise in commerce and by the development of business principles of operation.

The Physiocrats moved nevertheless towards a contemporary view, advancing more from the Mercantilist view; their ideas are not wholly unlike the views of today regarding production and the significance of different economic activities.

What was left out in their production measures, and why they are included now:

I. Physiocratic

A. Gross product

1. Food:

1M to proprietors
1M to sterile classes
2M to cultivators in agriculture (not necessarily all food)

2. Raw materials: for manufacturing: 1M

The Physiocratic analysis omitted the production of the sterile classes and that of the proprietors, if the latter were not strictly idle. Their reasoning was that five million livres is the total of physical production, that manufacturing and services were merely derivatives of the raw material and food consumed in their production.

B. Net product: two different concepts

1. 2M food plus 1M raw material = 3M net product:

Production above requirement for agricultural consumption, that which circulates, excluding the 2M used by cultivators that is non-circulating

2. 2M: originally in rent, food and raw materials going to proprietary class

II. Modern

Gross National Product

Consumption:

1M food, proprietors
1M food, sterile class
1M manufactured goods, proprietors
2M food, etc., cultivators

5M total consumption

Investment:

1M gross investment (manufactured goods used in cultivator sector)

GNP: 6M Gross National Product

This analysis, however, neglects the consumption of manufactured goods, and services, by the sterile classes.

Net national income:

GNP = 6M
– 1M (less gross investment, manufactured goods used by cultivators as replacement – depreciation, etc.)

5M Net National Income

The modern net income figure equals their gross income figure, but such is not necessarily the case. The modern net is quite different from either the A or B net income figures given above. Modern national income, 5M, consists of the sum of distributive shares: proprietary rent, 2M, plus the wages, profits and interest going to the agricultural and sterile classes, 3M.

Thus, the modern analysis attributes productivity to the sterile classes, something absent from the Physiocratic scheme. This may be analyzed in the following way: The sterile classes receive as inputs one million in food and one million in raw materials. The modern analysis assumes the one million in foodstuffs to be used on consumption, a sector quite apart from the production of goods. The one million of raw materials, on the other hand, are transformed by the sterile classy, to continue to use the Physiocratic terminology, into two millions of manufactured goods, which are exchanged for an equal amount of cash first from the proprietors and second from the cultivators. This, therefore, imputes an increment in value to the raw materials equal to one million cash that could come only from the process of manufacturing itself, i.e. from labor (omitting the question of industrial capital). The Physiocrats would deny the possibility of the two foregoing transactions, for, according to their scheme, the one million of raw materials could only sell for one billion in cash. [Likely my work, not notes from lectures.]

Lecture

Professor Earley brought up my comment, expressed at the end of the last lecture, concerning productivity in the sterile sector through using the modern GNP concept. "The Physiocrats will not attribute to the consumption of the sterile sector any productivity similar to that of the cultivators; sterile consumption is unproductive consumption," to quote Professor Earley.

Quesnay, he said, in answer to another question, did not quite definitely hold to a labor theory of value. The only productivity he envisioned was that of labor engaged in agriculture, and even there because nature was the essentially productive element. Later classicists, he pointed out, like Adam Smith, differentiated between productive and non-productive consumption and production, such as Smith's servant in a household; to Smith, the wealth of a nation was the gross product less the contribution of the non-productive group.

The *Tableau Economique* (using the translation of Quesnay in Newman) yields a theory of capital.

Immediately we see the significant role implicit to capital in the Physiocratic scheme. Quesnay has three types of capital. First, the cultivators produce because of the *avances annuel*, which is circulating capital, distinguished from the more permanent or fixed capital, the *avances primitive*, that the proprietors expended many years before and which must be replaced periodically (hence the economic justification of the earning of rent); and the expenditures by government on public works, roads, etc. enhancing the land, the *avances fonciere*.

The Physiocrats were very outspoken on the necessity of sufficient fixed capital and annual advances for production to be undertaken.

The net product is a surplus concept, but of actual consumed goods, not goods amassed and accumulated. There were advances in manufacturing and trade as well, but these are just repaid, as they produce no *produit net*. Capital is involved in agricultural and sterile sectors, and gets a return in both, though greater return in agriculture, i.e. rent. Sufficient fixed capital and annual advances are necessary. Advances are made in manufacturing and trade as well; but are just repaid, producing no net product.

The annual advances are merely the net product returning to the soil in the form of expenditure in the agricultural sector by the other two groups, so the circulatory system can maintain the advances necessary for the repetition of the net product

Capital must be attracted and expenditures must be made in the agricultural sector in order to keep it prosperous, i.e. purchasing power must be maintained.

The peculiar property of agriculture is that it uses the advances and reproduces them double, one half for their own sustenance and payment of rent and one half for the purchase of manufactured goods. [In brackets I wrote: Physiocrats confused as to time period: annual advance, yet many growing seasons.]

The Physiocratss may be said, without a great deal of accuracy admittedly, to have anticipated the Classicists on: (1) demand and supply; (2) the division of capital and its importance; and (3) the share of income going to the capitalists.

Marx held that the two important contributions of the Physiocrats were: (a) their concept of capital and its importance (they saw it as a physiological thing whereas he saw it as the product of institutions); and (b) their concept of surplus value, i.e. of a surplus.

Decadence will reduce net product. Undesirable and upsetting expenditures on products of the sterile sector – ostentation – means failure of the net product to return to agriculture.

Lecture

Theory of Capital

Two key features of the Physiocratic theory represented in the *Tableau* and in ancillary writings are: (1) the great importance given to investment; and (2) the great importance given also to consumption, and the necessary adequacy of both investment and consumption expenditures.

Turgot aptly develops the Physiocratic theory of investment and explains the need for the return of capital and the encouragement of investment in agriculture. There is a tri-partite division of capital: (1) what is called today circulating capital; (2) fixed capital; and (3) primitive proprietary investment (draining, clearing etc.). The third capital classification includes also government expenditures on canals, roads, and other public works.

They had the notion that the flow of capital to agriculture keeps the economy running, annual advances in particular setting agriculture in motion. Here we have the first current of a wages fund theory, though it is not tied up with the level of wages.

Turgot sees a necessary return to capital whether invested in agriculture or industry, which he explains is not "disposable," i.e. it is not strictly speaking part of the net product and hence subject to the single tax. Entrepreneurial wages, risk payment plus some capital return (interest rate), are not the only thing required, says Turgot. Capitalists have alternative opportunities for investing – in agriculture or manufacturing or commerce – and hence a certain premium or interest rate has to be paid in any line of industry to attract capital – an opportunity cost theory. This additional sum comes from the agricultural sector and is a share of the agricultural net product, but is not a part thereof for it is necessary to be paid. [Evident confusion.]

Turgot did not connect the need for interest with the requirement of evoking savings; some words seem to imply it, but the idea is not emphasized at all, in contrast to Smith and the classicists; there is no argument that parsimony is the secret of economic progress for a community. Real progress, for the Physiocrats, came from the productivity of agriculture and the direction of as much resources as possible into agriculture, not from saving per se.

They were quite equivocal, saying that interest must be paid in agriculture as an expense because capital could earn something elsewhere.

Consumption and Saving and Monetary Theory

The Physiocrats stressed the importance of keeping sufficient consumption expenditures coming into agriculture. Theirs was not, however, a theory of over-saving regarding depression. Their concern was for the consumption of agricultural production. It was not savings as such but monetary hoardings that they were worried about.

The usual interpretation of their system is that they put everything in real terms, with money a mere *numeraire* to facilitate transactions; therefore monetary affairs weren't important. This fits in with their anti-Mercantilist and naturalistic point of view.

But they were worried over monetary derangements disturbing the natural order. (1) Quesnay proposed a curb on the export of money capital, quite contrary to his general notion of free trade and laissez-faire. (2) Quesnay wanted to have a maximum interest rate set; his concern was that the money-lenders' rates were likely to be high. This shows his worry over conditions in the money market. (3) He also warned that savings might be withdrawn from circulation and be rendered sterile.

Three rules which Quesnay lays down on this subject are: (1) There should be no sterile savings curtailing the circulation, exchange and distribution of savings and profits. (2) He warned against the accumulation of monetary fortunes. (3) He wanted to keep the "lower orders" income up so as to keep their consumption up – somewhat of a mal-distribution theory of income.

Thus, Quesnay (1) worries that underconsumption might result from a mal-distribution of income; (2) worries over disturbing conditions in the markets; (3) worries over hoarding resulting from the large accumulation of capital. He was furthermore worried that savings wouldn't enter into circulation, though not the adequacy of savings.

Quesnay had some of the notions, says Schumpeter, of Keynes. Although Professor Earley says we can question the exactitude of the parallelism, the final answer is not on the side of those believing that savings equals investment automatically, or the more savings the better, or that the interest rate is perfectly adjusted by the saving and investment mechanism. Here their theory is quite modern; although the British classicists moved in a different direction from them, some modern income theory is in a sense a return to their approach.

The *Tableau Economique* is no theory of distribution, though the Physiocrats did have quite definite ideas underlying their theory.

They had, first, a subsistence theory of wages, with only agricultural labor being productive. They had a "risk and trouble" theory of the supply of capital, and perhaps an alternative-cost idea also. Their view was that the net product of agriculture was the only disposable income, though this was not consistently carried out. They recognized that saving did take place outside of agriculture, for income was not equal to consumption in the sterile classes – but this, they held, was not part of the true net product.

Their ideas on saving in relation to net product and supply of capital are quite confused. Accumulation by the merchants is not a net product but a redistribution of income, a profit made over someone else.

[The following notes are in the margin, but I am uncertain whether they record Earley's lecture or my own thoughts, except for the last part.] "As is" or "ought" plus recommendations for transition. *Tableau Economique*: Processes and significance as things are; hurt by unfortunate public and private policies and practices. Natural, but hard to get people to abide by it. Partial contradiction; Physiocrats had no faith in it – Earley.

Lecture

Recapitulation of the Physiocrats

I.

Schumpeter's thesis of the development of scientific knowledge may be applied to the Physiocrats. His thesis is that inventive individuals have a perceptual image, a vision, about how the phenomena they are interested in actually operate; that this is a naive observation, i.e. not built on a completely analytical observation – pre-analytical; a picture of these phenomena, a pattern, the crucial thread. Then the observer devises a model or schema representing the working out of the details and interrelationships or ramifications of the phenomena. The model is then subjected to analytical examination.

Other people, later and with different visions, test and analyze, etc., the model, and in such a developing process derive a schema closer to reality, eliminating the ideological element introduced at the first stage, gradually eliminated in the process of analysis.

Schumpeter's thesis may be applied to the Physiocrats as they are the first group to have a dominating point of view, conceptual as distinct from normative. They were not really the first, the Mercantilists were; but they had a better worked out model. [In margin: "Question of purpose of model building."]

First, Schumpeter's thesis is very plausible when applied to the Physiocrats. They had little analytical material to work with, there was more room for the ideological element, and there was no academic tradition in the schools and training.

Second, in relation to the Mercantilists, they had a polar character – they changed the approach of economics from one pole to another: from the analogy of the mercantile establishment making money, profit, etc., to the closed-up system in which nature was primary, with emphasis on real goods.

Third, the influence of biological discoveries and the fact that Quesnay was himself a physician.

Fourth, the gross objective environment of the time with its great disorder, especially in agriculture, could easily lead to this kind of vision in which the soil was the basis of the economy.

Fifth, their literal way of carrying through their analysis in the *Tableau*, i.e. their minute explanations and definitions that are used to bolster their argument.

Sixth, the high degree of consistency between their analysis and their recommendations is suggestive of a person getting an idea and following it out without caution.

Seventh, they did have an elaborate model in the *Tableau*.

I.

The ideological element fits in well with their analysis, their notion of the natural order and with their laissez-faire: free enterprise and government non-intervention – a competitive order. The natural order as a concept of social organization jives well with mechanistic theorizing. From the Physiocratic objectives regarding social policy and over class bias, their natural order arises easily, too. Jives well with their view of basic economic organization. [In margin: "?-Teleological-deterministic, not mechanistic."]

It was important to get the sterile work done as cheaply as possible; therefore the idea of enforcing competition in the manufacturing and commercial sectors, forcing or promoting efficiency in those sectors. The Colbertist system had avowedly tried to initiate and maintain inefficient manufacturing through tariffs, bounties and monopolies. This raised the real cost of the services of the sterile sector; this was easily seen by the Physiocrats. Similarly, international trade, the opening up of borders to get the agricultural sector supplied from abroad if cheaper and to secure wide markets for agricultural products (elimination of domestic and foreign barriers to sale of agricultural production), was an important policy recommendation. Also propounded was the reduction of government expenditures, as their cost fell on agriculture: let the economy run itself, with government limiting itself to order-keeping and defence. Free trade versus protection was the main element of their laissez-faire.

They defended the property rights of the proprietary class; they were not revolutionists, rather they were very orthodox, much pro the status quo, and didn't want to upset the status quo too badly. The justification of landowners otherwise appearing to be useless and parasitic, was made by adhering to the notion of laissez-faire, which required private property (with its major form being land).

They had a utilitarian ethic (like most intellectuals then in France) and psychology – felt people tried to maximize pleasure and minimize pain – a calculating rationality; and that therefore men could be depended upon to work out their own solutions to the economic problems confronting them better than servants of the crown.

Their analysis shows visionary defects in that it isn't consistent; yet, on the other hand, where it was convenient or desirable to go contrary to the laissez-faire doctrines, they did, such as setting a maximum interest rate, banning the export of money capital. They recognized the natural order and rationality, yet also recognized hoarding, mal-distribution of income, and insufficient flow of capital to agriculture, as possible occurrences. Thus, when they were afraid of a particular event, especially regarding agriculture, they were ready to depart from laissez-faire.

Therefore, Schumpeter in this matter is applicable to the Physiocrats.

Recapitulation (Evaluation)

(1) The Physiocrats were innovators of first-rate importance in economic analysis. They were the first economic model builders and their analysis is significant as a completely interdependent economic system, something not achieved by the Mercantilists.

(2) They analyzed expenditure and income flows as a means to understand the operation of the economy; while this type of analysis fell into disuse, it is now popular again.

(3) They made notable though only partially satisfactory advances in the concepts of income and wealth. They were far superior to the Mercantilists in visualizing income as a flow, not a balance at the end of the period – a flow of income, of consumers' goods, used to carry the economy over, if properly distributed, into the next period.

(4) They originated the view of capital as setting labor into motion, seeing that the economic structure depended upon the direction of those outlays of capital.
(5) They started a ferment of economic theorizing at the time and thereafter. Their influence on Smith was powerful.

Regarding Smith's *Moral Sentiments* as a complement or change of mind regarding the *Wealth of Nations*, Professor Earley thinks Smith got a jolt from his sojourn into France and his contact with the Physiocrats. His friend Hume had turned from general philosophical work to particular issues of the day. The *Moral Sentiments* was merely the work of his youth, fitting into the vogue of the time; and different from his lectures.

Lecture

LOCKE, MANDEVILLE, HUTCHESON AND HUME; INTRODUCTION TO ADAM SMITH

In addition to the influence of the Mercantilists and the Physiocrats on Adam Smith, a great influence was exerted from "British Moral Philosophy."

John Locke

Philosopher and psychologist, for whom moral philosophy was in part a psychological discipline. He attempted to interpret and lay down maxims of social conduct on psychological principles, beliefs regarding the nature of man, and philosophical ideas based on this notion of man's psychological nature.

In general it may be said that the British natural order was similar to the social order flowing from the nature of man.

Locke began the analysis in his approach to a utilitarian social philosophy, his views on the origin of government, the basis and justification of property, and his theory of value.

Locke was not much of an economist. He was predominantly a Mercantilist: as a Whig braintruster, he defended their strongly mercantilistic policies: trade regulation, great emphasis on the import of money.

His political point of view was in furtherance of the views of the rising capitalists versus the monarchical principle and against the secular power of the church. He was the Philosopher of the Glorious Revolution of 1688–1690, when Britain became a parliamentary government.

Locke's significance lies in his social philosophy and psychology, his views of property and of value growing out of them.

(1) Value, to Locke, reflected psychological conditions; a subjective cast was given to economics (pain and trouble, etc. regarding working) that was absent in Mercantilism and not prominent in Physiocracy. From this time on pain-cost notions – requirements that have to be met to get work done – were basic in classical thinking – until the mid-19th century. Value and scarcity were a function of psychological disinclination, etc.; Smith, and others, picked up this notion.
(2) He had the notion that government gets its power from the consent of the governed, i.e. deliberately constituted with a contract actually present, in furtherance of individual interests – not distinct from interests of men but an instrument of the general population for furtherance of the total population.

He saw a state of nature and natural law that it was necessary to obey in the natural state. Society developed to further the needs of individuals different from other needs – sustenance, etc. – and therefore formed government reflecting man's needs as human psychological being.

(3) His justification of property in the natural state was that it derives its value due to the trouble expended to get it.

The same conditions are reflected in civil society, though it was not a mirror image of natural state: the ultimate purpose of civil society came from the nature of man and man's needs.

In the state of nature, the origin and justification of property came from labor, which conferred the right to appropriate that which was previously held in common. The original measure of value is also labor; his labor theory of value was therefore traced back to the state of nature.

In civil government, property rights are set by compact, values are still primarily explained by labor, and distributive shares are by the compact, not strictly on labor.

Bernard Mandeville, "Fable of the Bees"

His proposition is that men's psychological propensities govern their social activities. They are selfish propensities. These propensities are mixed, with many bad passions. Still, the resultant of all the propensities, and particularly the desire of each to get ahead, will lead to prosperity: *The Fable of the Bees*. Self-love and vanity are seen as the basis of both human behavior and the human economy. The best balance of interests comes from the least interference by government and moralists: vile ingredients compose a wholesome mixture.

Has utilitarian emphasis: judge "good" by its effects on people and not by preconceived doctrines of good and bad; build moral philosophy not on a priori preachments but on what was and is.

Evaluation and contribution: Mandeville saw a clear connection between human passions and economic behavior and thereby founded social analysis on psychology.

Francis Hutcheson

Was Smith's teacher; his law of nature and concept of moral philosophy are representative of Smith's thinking.

Law of Nature: that we should find the rules of good conduct for both individuals and society by observation and not by revelation or scripture; i.e. use the same scientific method in social and moral problems as in the physical sciences. Discovered by looking at nature and will come through men; therefore not natural laws but laws of nature, i.e. not *strictu sensu*. These laws would be in accordance with the nature of mankind and would work and minister to their welfare.

Moral Philosophy: general happiness or partial good consistent with general good; stated for first time what became Bentham's utilitarian principle: the greatest good for the greatest number. He taught prudence, temperance, thrift and equality.

He recognized value in use and value in exchange; believed that the origin of capital is in saving and that the division of labor is a fundamental economic principle; and held a labor theory of value.

Summary of Hutcheson

(1) His labor theory of value was endemic to the whole group, a subjective theory with the view of the crucial factor in economic activity being getting people to work; connected with utilitarian calculus – usefulness but also cost (with more emphasis on cost), seen subjectively.
(2) Recognized or believed that it is best to order things in accordance with man's nature and not remake him.
(3) Set up a new science with normative values through things as they are, not as they should be through prescription.
(4) Individualism a strong current.

Introduction to Adam Smith

Smith worked on the sources and writers of the time; history, statistics, etc., the Mercantile system and its principles and fate, the Physiocratic system, etc. Brought together many strands of ideas and much factual material information, historical and contemporary, in the *Wealth of Nations*.

Lecture

Guest Lecturer: Professor Rotwein [based on outlines copied from board plus lecture notes]

David Hume (1711–1776)

Major writings:

Treatise on Human Nature, 1739.
Essays Moral and Political, 1742.
Inquiry Concerning Human Understanding, 1748.
Inquiry Concerning Human Morals, 1751.
Political Discourses (Economic Essays), 1752.
Essays Moral, Political and Literary, 1753.
History of England, 1760's (at ends of chapters, attempts to distill "laws" and sequences).

Hume's Science of Human Experience:

A. Principles of Human Nature:
   (1) Human understanding (Book I, Treatise);
   (2) Human passion (Book II, Treatise).

Laws of Human Behavior:

A. Morals (Book III, Treatise);
B. Politics (Essays, mainly);
C. Aesthetics (Essays).

Hume's Economics:

(1) Economic Psychology: natural history of rise and progress of commerce; causes of labor.
(2) Political Economy: applications of supra to major economic problems:
   (a) monetary theory;

    (b) interest theory;
    (c) shifting and incidence of taxes;
    (d) free versus controlled markets;
    (e) fiscal policy.
(3) Economic Philosophy: application of supra to evaluation of commercial society:
    (a) utilitarian ethics;
    (b) individual happiness;
    (c) effects on society as a whole.

Hume's Philosophical System as a Whole:

A. Critical of highly rationalistic and speculative philosophical systems; adheres to empirically based system.
    (1) Empirical analysis of human nature of primary concern: all experience is human experience and human and at center of own experience: therefore science of human nature is center of all sciences.
B. Treatise: foundations of science of man, developed in Essays:
    (1) saw as basis for further sciences:
        (a) morals (ethics);
        (b) politics;
        (c) aesthetics (criticism).
C. System: essence of man consists of principles of human nature and laws of human behavior:
    (1) principles of human nature:
        (a) elements and relations common to all mankind:
            i. human understanding;
            ii. human passions, emotions.
    (2) laws of human behavior:
        (a) constructs based on use of principles of human nature to explain particular situations;
        (b) develops certain uniformities of response of human beings:
            i. "profit maximization";
        (c) these laws are the subject of the three groups of sciences.
    (3) these principles and laws constitute the science of human experiences, of which the outstanding element is psychology.

Concerning the nature of the science of human experience, of great importance is history. The laws, e.g. profit maximization, per se, presuppose certain static conditions and institutions and a given stage of development of history. The historical laws of human behavior deal with the importance of changing circumstances and situations on human responses; they explain change and in particular changing human behavior patterns.

The use of the term "natural law" in the outline above (natural history of rise and progress of commerce) refers to the recurrent, repeated, and correlated-with-certain-circumstances phenomena of history. Hume uses the technique of natural histories in presenting his laws of human behavior. In his system, there is marked psychological emphasis, especially regarding changes in habits, customs and manners.

Hume's Economic Thought:

A. Economic Psychology:
- (1) Concerned with motives underlying economic activity and behavior:
  - (a) "causes of labor:" links economic analysis to science of man (Book II).
- (2) Presents causes of labor thusly:
  - (a) nucleus in natural history of rise and progress of commerce: how the rise in trade affected human nature and how this in turn affected economic behavior.

B. Political Economy
- (1) Uses perspective of natural history to analyze economic problem areas.
- (2) Repeated emphasis on development and change in criticism of contemporary policy recommendations.
- (3) Problem: Money
  - (a) Short run: little or no significance of increase in quantity of money: quantity theory of money.
  - (b) Long run: continued increase in quantity of money would stimulate spirit of industry, increase employment; significant regarding behavior patterns in affect on employment and labor.
- (4) Problem: Interest Rate
  - (a) Function of changes in supply and demand of savings:
    - i. Agrarian society: landlord is key figure but is idle, therefore is spendthrift and demand is high and supply low, hence interest rate high;
    - ii. Mercantile and industrial society: merchant and producer are key, with economy an enjoyable game with acquisition as trophy: demand is low, supply high, with interest rate low and with its tendency being to fall.

(5) Problem: Free Trade
   (a) Most conducive to economic development and growth – basis of his advocacy (Smith: specialization and consequent increase in wealth the basis);
   (b) Answers Mercantilist argument as stagnation.

C. Economic Philosophy
   (1) Justification of commercial and industrial society in terms of moral and ethical considerations.
      (a) Smith doesn't answer the problem of the desire to increase wealth: the "das Adam Smith problem" of the hiatus between the disdain in the *Theory of Moral Sentiments* and the lack of justification for increasing wealth, and the theory contained in the *Wealth of Nations*.
   (2) Justification based on utilitarianism (Book III, Principles of Morals):
      (a) By historical comparison, saw middle ages as worse than contemporary times;
      (b) Attributed the advance to the advent of commerce and industry and materialism on human happiness and in relation to the causes of labor:
         i. "industry, knowledge and humanity" linked together – the desire for luxury.

General Significance of Hume:
(1) A mercantilist but also concerned with economic growth and with the motives for economic activity.
(2) Major contribution is using different approach: economic psychology:
   (a) had superior "vision" of economic psychology in his time;
   (b) had superior understanding of the relationships of historical movements;
   (c) showed how to amalgamate history and psychology as basis of science of economics.
(3) Didn't treat economics as anything but interdisciplinary – no separate sciences except for analytical and presentational purposes.
(4) His vision, outlined in toto above.

Lecture

ADAM SMITH

Similar to the Physiocratic natural order is Smith's "simple and obvious system of natural liberty;" his was to replace the Mercantilist commercial and Physiocratic agricultural systems:

(1) There is little evidence of divine thinking on his part; he did not derive his thinking from any notion of an underlying divine order.
(2) We must conclude that Smith had no notion that society was a replica of any biological or physiological order of things. This is clear in his criticism of the Physiocrats and in his own formulation of revenue, value and the purpose of economic activity.
(3) His idea wasn't one of a social order that man would naturally discover, set up and adhere to. He had no notion of the harmony of interests that might lead to the belief that all would agree on a particular system. On the contrary, his work is shot through with notions of class conflicts.

To John Locke the natural law, based on the natural order, is the state of things in nature when man lived alone without government and positive law to govern him. He derived government in part from things in the natural state, men getting together to increase their security, protect themselves, but with rights stemming from the state of nature.

His view of the social contract was that the regulation by government be in accord with the contract protecting these natural rights.

Smith, on the other hand, had antithetical views on these lines. As is evident in his *Lectures*, he was a practical man to whom no state of nature existed; the origin of government is in something else.

To Smith, natural rights was a limited concept implying no absolute liberties and freedom in the nature of things; he distinguished between natural rights and acquired rights. Natural rights had to do with protection of one's person and reputation from injury; acquired rights, with the protection of one's real and personal property.

To Smith the origin of natural rights is not doubted; the origin of acquired rights: property and civil government depend on each other; reservation and inequality of property first formed government – no deep philosophical justification.

As to the social contract concept, Smith argued "no" on three grounds: (1) the original contractual government was peculiar only to Great Britain; (2) posterity has nothing to do with it even if it did happen; (3) states continue jurisdiction over people who have left it.

To Smith the principles of *authority* and *utility* rather than contract and natural rights (Hume) are the source of the social contract, of government.

Hume felt that historically governments were founded on conquest, but from the normative point of view, i.e. the best governmental form, utility would be important. To both Hume and Smith, therefore, the question of utility is what will serve well for mankind; monarchy is based on the one – authority (force, tradition) – and democracy, the other – utility.

Smith's defense of the system of natural liberty is based on two things: (1) general social utility; and (2) individual liberty of action and expression, i.e. yields an opportunity for self-development and initiative as far as possible. Utility mixed with liberty reflected the general social philosophy of the time in which the individual, self-importance and satisfaction were major elements.

The concepts of natural law and natural rights were not used in the *Wealth of Nations*, only the "simple and obvious system of natural liberty."

Smith's Psychological Foundations:

The system of natural liberty was based, for the purpose of social utility, on man's nature as a human being – his "passions" or his psychological propensities.

Man, to Smith, had a mixed bag of propensities: for maximizing wealth there are both harmful and conducive qualities present. The system of natural liberty was a shrewd method of harnessing and releasing the favorable propensities, i.e. favorable to greater national wealth, and for suppressing the others, less favorable or unfavorable.

The good characteristics were:

(a) *Man's drive to better his condition*, which was constant and therefore dependable; his notion of a partially motivated economic man.
(b) *Propensity to "truck, barter and exchange:"* crucial because of emphasis on the division of labor; originally gives occasion to division of labor; wasn't sure whether this was innate or derivative from culture in which man lived (cf. p. 14, *Wealth of Nations*).
(c) *Propensity to save*: the frugal man or the Scotsman; to augment fortunes the only way is to save and accumulate.
(d) *Prudence*: contrasts prudence and misconduct, the latter consisting of bad judgment, behaving in unintelligent way; would be judicious, although at times dubious of man's good judgment (p. 107, *Wealth of Nations*).

The unfortunate bad qualities were: (judgment solely based on increasing the wealth of nations, not some other notion of the good life or moral qualities):

(a) *Propensity to get something for nothing*, to live at our ease; to maximize gains, minimize cost; to reap what we have never sowed (p. 716, *Wealth of Nations*).
(b) *Spirit to monopolize:* opposite to notion of propensity to compete; natural order, if left alone, would be cartelized. Not an absolute, but bred by

conditions; especially in manufacturing and trade, less in agrarian employments, and least in labor, partly due to lack of sophistication.

(c) *Tendency to be hypocritical, deceitful, rationalizing conduct:* Evils of Mercantilist system where government dispenses favors upon special interests, gives sway to corrupt legislatures; therefore have to keep things in open.

Smith's system, therefore, is the "simple and obvious system of natural liberty" and his "invisible hand" is the rough hand of competition; the individual does things necessarily for the benefit of mankind; without the hand there would be a different system injurious to wealth though still in accord with man's nature (calling to the fore other human propensities); to increase wealth we need to use the proper system, the prototype of positive laissez-faire.

Lecture

Adam Smith's Notion of Competition:

To Adam Smith, the hard fist of competition was the invisible hand that coordinated self-interest, propelling individual action into social good. This invisible hand was not of divine origin, however.

The first element in his concept of competition was the freedom of labor, the freedom to apply one's labor to whatever activity one thinks will yield the highest income. Labor therefore is the foundation of the economy. Value is predominantly, though sometimes exclusively, a function of labor – the toil and trouble taken to produce. To Smith the division of labor is the secret of higher productivity. The laboring classes, the most numerous, were therefore the most important. Laborers were equated with consumers – a general consumer interest over the special producer interest that dominated Mercantilism.

Of great importance to him, therefore, was the occupational and geographical division of *mobile* labor.

Property, following John Locke, was important, but derived itself from labor (pp. 121–122, *Wealth of Nations*) and in this sense is therefore "sacred."

The second element, due to the realistically observed immobility of labor geographically and occupationally, was the free movement of capital across national boundaries, so as to seek the use yielding the maximum return. The competition of foreign capital is incentive to domestic capital. This element is of great importance, for the allocation of capital determined the allocation of labor, for capital sets labor in motion. Thus, Smith would do away with the privileges of local monopolies to allow the entrance of capital, domestic and foreign.

Smith's argument for free trade was, therefore, analytical in nature. In order to make use of the maximum return within and between nations, free flow of resources, mobility, free entry and egress would have to be allowed.

There is little in this concept of "perfect knowledge," "foresight," "divisibility," and "atomistic" which were forthcoming as later refinements; rather, Smith's was the long run structural standpoint.

To Smith, competition required the managers of firms to have the most direct possible interest in the profits of the enterprises they were managing. The corporate form of organization was suspect to Smith because of the separation of ownership and management – the latter were not keenly affected in their pocketbook by their decisions.

Concerning the business unit that is small relative to the size of the market as a whole, Smith saw the division of labor limited by the extent of the market, and if the market is small (due to poor communication and transportation, or restrictions on trade), the advantages of the division of labor are reduced. Therefore it was beneficial to widen the geographical domain of trade, for only by a large market area can we reap the benefits of large-scale enterprise through the division of labor within the plant without undermining the competitive principle.

Thus, Smith was not worried over the monopoloid structure of the economy under Mercantilism because it prevented the exploitation of internal economies of scale; rather, he was suspicious of large-scale organizations per se; he didn't envision large-scale mass production techniques. Rather he was interested in external economies through better allocation of resources. Smith was not the prophet of large units, despite his pin study; Marx, coming later, had a different vantage point.

Smith's Concept of Income:

Differences in fundamental economic viewpoints come out most clearly when one considers alternative ideas on "income," i.e. "production," "consumption," etc.

Smith's prototype of the income concept is the one that has continued to the present day, with several notable exceptions, Irving Fisher among them.

Smith represents almost the full antithesis to the Mercantilists, but not the complete antithesis. Smith took over their notion that "productive" and "income" are found in the market – a notion quite different from the notions of the Physiocrats and the Marxians, who do not equate value (and income) with price. Income to Smith is the result of pecuniary transactions. Smith is concerned only: (a) that we can't identify income with mere money income, as money has no importance regarding real value – it is only a counter; and (b) that income results from work, productive rather than trading operations.

Smith thus introduces: (a) the psychological point of view regarding income – in terms of value in the sense of importance to human beings as they see it, rather than in physical terms; and (b) the shift from the class interest of producers and hence profit as a surplus coming from trade and exchange to the notion of a consumer, with income determined through the consumer, not viewed as a business enterpriser but as the final beneficiary of the economic system.

Income therefore was in the form of the "conveniences, necessities and amusements" of life.

The measuring rod of any commodity in the market value of the final product depends on its yielding utility, to use a later term, and having therefore a price – which constitutes income.

We can differentiate Smith's notion from the Physiocratic concept in that the idea of physical production is still there but the amount of income is determined by value and hence on the psychic point of view.

A second motif we can find in Smith is that much prior literature, especially in the preceding century, identified specifically the problem of value in the economic sense. Hence value is the central concept, yielding the key to what is productive, and at the same time is a measure thereof, a cogent point of view in that value is derived from the ultimate users, a unifying principle for the theory of value and the theory of distribution, and the value mechanism through the notion of the market as a natural price through the flow of resources, etc., and a focus for the best policy – the competitive price system.

Production therefore, is anything that adds to value; the sum of productive activities that have or yield utilities yields the total revenue and is identical thereto. Locke and Petty were therefore anticipators of Smith on value. Smith did, it will be seen, place special emphasis on the productivity in durables production.

Lecture

Adam Smith's Concept of Income (continued):

The concept of income held by Adam Smith is close to the modern concept – unlike the Mercantilist and Physiocratic notions.

(1) The Distinction Between Gross and Net Revenue.

Smith saw the revenue of society as the sum of the shares or the total of the product valued at market price – adding up the shares – wages, profit and rent

– or adding up the value-added through the different stages of production to the final disposition of the finished goods.

With regard to the inclusion of "services' ("the conveniences, necessities and amusements of life"), he apparently includes the value of services that vanish in the instant of their production, i.e. he includes both services and physical commodities as long as they are vendable and have a market value. As later discussion will evidence, he does not include "non-productive" services – those of the clergy, lawyers, rulers, entertainers, etc.

Smith includes as income all services and products exchanged in pecuniary transactions, i.e. for money, not given in barter or as gifts.

Net Revenue is the residual after deducting from *Gross Revenue* the expenses of maintaining fixed and circulating capital, i.e. depreciation plus the cost of maintaining circulating capital (p. 271).

Real wealth, therefore, is in proportion to net revenue; wealth is productivity, not a stock, rather a flow of goods to be consumed either now or eventually.

Net revenue is the sum of the income shares in a real sense; the summing up of each individual's net income (his gross income less his expenses).

Circulating capital does not represent a drain against gross revenue, i.e. deducted to get net revenue, except the money element. To Smith the four elements composing "circulating capital" are money, provisions, materials, and finished products; the latter three do not represent a drain upon gross revenue. These three may go into fixed capital or into stocks reserved for immediate consumption.

These elements of circulating capital are then a "perpetual fund" unless they are converted into fixed capital or into consumption – all that has to be done is to maintain them at a fixed level. The *Classicists* later had the notion that saving was tied up with this.

On the other hand, the maintenance of a commodity money has a cost, though negligible over the long run, of obtaining, maintaining and replacing (where perishable) the commodity so used.

Although the concept, etc. is not used, or stated, we can infer opportunity cost herein.

This concept of income held by Smith is the same or close to the currently held point of view in national income accounting, regarding deduction of depreciation: GNP minus depreciation yields NNP.

(2) Qualifications Put on Different Economic Activities through Degree of Productivity.

It may be assumed that Smith felt it incumbent to answer a question raised by both the Mercantilists and the Physiocrats, viz., what is productive labor?

First, Smith discounted the criterion of labor producing psychic value. He preferred to limit the analysis to where one can apply the pecuniary test; he thereby excluded the services of housewives. His reasoning is that value is a central concept and since he doesn't think much of calculating use values he prefers exchange values, i.e. price, and since the services of housewives have no exchange value they must be excluded.

Second, he therefore used the market test of value.

Third, he would apply the same test as in a private concern, i.e. exclude from productive that which is clearly an expense; he would confine revenue to what has actual pecuniary value. Thus, he distinguishes between types of production.

Productive to Smith is that which results in a vendible, tangible, durable commodity; this is because: (a) to Smith the accumulation of the power to produce income is the strategic economic activity – the heaping-up complex but not of a virulent sort; and (b) capital was conceived as setting labor in motion, and therefore providing capital for the next period was productive as it led to labor being employed productively in the next period instead of not productively (pp. 314–317).

This notion of productive and non-productive labor is closely related to the accumulation of capital (II.3). This is where his analogy with the firm enters in: unproductiveness relates to the inability to bring in profit. He brings in the vision, similar to that of the Mercantilists, that society as a whole is like a private firm.

He views capital as playing a strategic social role in providing employment for labor; similar to the Physiocratic advances which carry the system as a whole through the productive process. This he shows through productive labor used as capital: whereas when it is used as consumption satisfying capital it depletes the productivity of the nation, for this use doesn't increase future productivity.

Thus, he aims at maximizing gross revenue through time, not in money or goods terms but a maximum level of income – with the strategic role of capital accumulation: (a) increasing the productivity of labor; and (b) setting labor in motion, assuring its being used in a productive way.

Smith is not a half-way materialist, but a thoroughgoing Scotch capitalist; he wants to accumulate the power to produce in the future and thereby increase the wealth of nations, increasing net national income; he is not worried about under-consumption.

His system may seem artificial but as a vision of an economy working and progressing it is perfectly consistent – through the accumulation of capital.

Lecture

Smith's Theory of Capital, Capital Accumulation, and its Relation to the Allocation of Resources and Employment:

In connection with Smith's theory of capital there are two prominent motifs: (a) the division of labor; and (b) the strategic importance of capital in connection with accumulation.

As to the source of capital, Smith see it in "parsimony" and not prodigality (p. 321); his emphasis on frugality, i.e. saving, is, to reverse history, the anti-Keynesian point of view. Smith's emphasis on parsimony rather than industry (in the sense of activity or enterprise) was the antithesis of the Mercantilists' viewpoint: industry merely provides the subject which saving accumulates. The larger the saving, therefore, the larger the allocation of resources devoted to "productive" activity, productive meaning yielding a tangible vendible commodity, either consumer or producer goods. Saving, then, to Smith was also consumed, but by a different set of people – people who would make a productive use of it. Capital may produce, at a profit, either capital (producer) or consumer goods – hence it is productive. His concept, though, seems to be more than mere physical productivity – there is also a revenue-value strand running through his statements. To Smith, those activities that lead to capital accumulation are superior to others.

Smith gives importance (pp. 362–367) to circulating capital as supporting fixed capital, both existing for the goal of maintaining and increasing the stock of consumer goods. Circulating capital is the key – a fixation in later classical theory: Ricardo, McCulloch, Marx.

Smith calls for accumulation – saving – to improve the allocation of labor and its dexterity and productivity; it also increases the capital stock which sets labor in motion; he also has the idea that savings, then accumulation, is beneficial for employment. In this respect Smith is as usual thinking of his adversaries, writing from the persuasive standpoint, for many earlier writers thought frugality – saving – was injurious to employment. Demand for labor, for Smith came from the demand for capital and not from the demand for goods.

The argument for the superiority of the use of capital in agriculture was made in terms that agriculture was such that a given amount of capital employed therein sets in motion a larger quantity of labor than in foreign trade, e.g. The demand for capital, not the demand for goods, constitutes the demand for labor and therefore that demand for capital which sets in motion the most labor is best.

The modern concept holds that the function of capital is to save productive power, free labor, increase labor productivity, allowing a larger product with given resources. That capital which is most economical in the use of labor is therefore best. Thus, the modern concept concentrates on the function of *fixed* capital and its abridgement of labor – its roundaboutness. The classical theory on the other hand was such that capital was primarily *circulating* capital. The shift in point of view from circulating capital to fixed capital is an important change in economic thinking, and was post-Marxian.

Smith did not stress the employment level, i.e. using wasteful capital, using capital that used the most possible labor. Smith saw brisk competition for labor between productive and unproductive uses and therefore argued strongly that savings increases the efficient use of labor and would pull labor away from the production of luxuries, etc. into the greater production of circulating capital and thus more fixed capital, hence to a higher level of income (measured in consumer goods). Smith was arguing for the frugal disposition of resources and not for a high demand for luxuries (and, necessarily, employment).

We have to conclude therefore that Smith was tied up in inconsistencies; e.g. (a) given employment, that capital is best which uses maximum labor – a poor sole criterion even from his standpoint; and (b) regarding relative quantities of capital vis-à-vis labor in various employments, failed to note that foreign trade was the last stage of production and not just having a higher labor/capital ratio.

There is in Smith also the anomaly in holding agriculture superior to manufacturing and trade by the criterion of setting more labor in motion and in pointing out that manufacturing and trading (classes) have the highest propensity to save (landlords are spendthrifts) and have the propensity to invest in their enterprises as well as the best managerial efficiency (Book III, Chapter IV). Smith concludes (Book III) that urban life is conducive to saving and the careful use of resources as well as accumulation, but that systems favoring the towns over the country have retarded the growth of opulence and accumulation. His argument here is weak in view of his emphasis on saving, good and prudent content, etc. Under his system, he could answer, though, the nation would have advanced even further.

Regarding the effects of changing circulating capital into fixed capital on employment since the former sets labor in motion: less of a "wages fund" – Ricardo. Marx – increased exploitation, and falling rate of profitability: would go on as productivity is increased, which requires increased saving.

Lecture

Smith's Distribution Theory:

Smith placed great importance on saving and had great concern lest it be impaired and reduced, but did not develop a cost theory of the supply of capital, of savings (Senior), nor did he fear a stationary state created by capital accumulation (Ricardo, James Mill, J. S. Mill).

This was due to his view of human nature, that man's nature in large part was naturally parsimonious, of an instinct to save so as to get ahead. Thus, he had *no impatience cost of abstinence, and the reward for saving is not for him related to the real cost thereof.* Any lack of saving is due rather to bad institutions: Mercantilist restrictions reducing the income from which saving comes and from the waste resulting from institutional derangements putting resources in the hands of prodigals such as bad banking, spendthrift government.

Thus, there is *no true marginal cost of capital; yet he explains profit as a natural component of price. Smith makes note of profits for enterprise in the form of wages of management and payment for risk.*

He further saw the falling rate of profit but still continued increasing saving, no hoarding.

Thus, Smith put great emphasis on saving but didn't see any price for it. His analysis is better than the Physiocratic analysis in terms of the framework in which it stood, especially in relation to the use of savings (not only in agriculture).

Smith's Value Analysis:

In Smith value becomes for the first time the central element in economic theory; Condillac, Turgot and others, though, developed "value" earlier.

Smith has several roles for his value analysis:

(1) *Value is fundamentally tied up with his concept of income*:
   (a) income is value produced; the criterion of income depended, therefore, on market price;
   (b) total revenue was the sum, therefore, of value added (produced), of income shares;
   (c) of great methodological importance in bourgeois economics.

(2) *An analytical tool* used in his theories of distribution, incidence of taxation, advisability of free trade and protection, etc.

(3) *As an explanatory principle* concerning the control mechanism in the economic system, an economy organized around exchange and pricing.
(4) *As a norm* for the valuation of institutions and policies: "justice" of distribution, of taxes; productive versus unproductive activities.

Smith's uses of value have set the pattern for contemporary economic analysis.

Value is approached by Smith from the principle of the division of labor, which principle makes the exchange process fundamental in all economic relationships throughout the entire economy.

The need to examine value arises, first, from the phenomenon of the division of labor taking place through exchange involving value (i.e. a new means of analysis), and second, following the tradition that economists should explain value (Locke, Petty, Cantillon all discussed the riddle of the determinants of value) (i.e. following tradition).

To explain numerous ambiguities and consequent inconsistencies, it is useful to see two levels of value analysis:

(1) the traditional problem of value – his labor theory of value;
(2) value in his theoretical system – a supply-and-demand pecuniary cost theory.

Labor Theory of Value:

In making labor the fundamental creative force of goods in the real sense Smith was reacting against Mercantilism and Physiocracy (neither trade nor land). On page one of his general Introduction, Smith calls attention to the fund of labor that is the original source from which the wealth of nations is created. Labor produces use-value.

Smith had two forms of labor theory: (a) embodied labor theory; and (b) labor command theory. When Smith refers to the "source" – "original fund" – creating things and values, he uses the embodied labor theory; when he seeks to measure value, one the other hand, he uses his labor command theory. Historically the former concerns primitive society; the latter, a developed capitalist system.

Smith, thus, gives great impetus to an exploitation theory of the operation of capitalism. Marx can therefore be traced back to the ideas on property in Locke and Smith, rather than to Ricardo. With a commodity embodying two hours of labor, cet. par., commanding four hours of labor, a share is going to a party other than productive labor, i.e. exploitation.

Smith discusses the labor theory of value when referring to a determination of value independent of monetary considerations; labor was to Smith a better criterion than corn. He uses this theory (labor) regarding primitive conditions, when slapping slothful *rentiers* and monopolistic capitalists, but not in his economic analysis. Part, therefore, of "das Adam Smith problem" consists of where his emphasis really lay.

Under the labor theory of value, profits and rents are deductions from the production of labor. On the other hand, his theory of income is built on the sum of revenues going to the different classes, not on a labor theory of value.

Smith builds his value theory on cost (adding up costs), not on a marginal imputation process moving from product to factors of production; i.e. on values, shares, prices of the various productive factors – quite different from the later Austrian study of the "natural prices" of factors required to make a product.

Smith had the notion of an equilibrium value of productive factors and of products without any clear working out of the determination of equilibrium conditions.

Lecture

Smith's Value Theories, continued:

It is difficult to determine Smith's degree of seriousness regarding his ideas on labor in different settings.

We can conclude though that his greater emphasis on value theory is an "entrepreneurial cost theory." His is a theory of value based on a "cost" approach and not on demand-supply monetary or factor imputation approaches.

Smith uses both real and opportunity cost propositions in elaborating his entrepreneurial cost theory; these are by no means necessarily incompatible. The latter is often forgotten (Book I, Chapter VII, especially pp. 55ff).

Smith differentiates between natural and market prices regarding allocation of resources. Thus, regarding his distribution analysis, different principles apply to each factor and one can't therefore arrive at real cost by adding up money costs – but only by adding up *natural prices*. The market cost of each factor is the price they can obtain elsewhere, their opportunity cost – best seen in his analysis of the shifting of capital through profit, page 55.

Smith's Hiatus on Value:

An hiatus is evident in both Locke and Smith regarding labor as the source of value – their differentiating between the state of nature (primitive society) and civil society (modern economic society).

First, Smith does not present or endeavor to present a critique of existing society through justice and equity, although he couldn't forbear making remarks thereon.

Second, Smith had three relevant aims:

(a) Discrediting Mercantilism through both analytical and empirical-historical arguments – by which he needed a theory of value in the technical sense to show the wastes of the Mercantilist system compared with his simple and obvious system of natural liberty.
(b) He built a theory of value and distribution fairly accurate at a high level of abstraction as to the way capitalist society was put together and ran. He thus used a labor theory of value but didn't realize the shortcomings thereof.
(c) He tried to develop a theory of value as a guideline for policy in a capitalist society to maximize the wealth of nations.

Concerning tools as representing the labor used in their production in the productive process, profits according to Smith bear no particular relation to the labor therein but to the size of the stock and its value, i.e. its relative supply.

Lecture

Smith's Value Theory (continued):

Smith, thus, has both a notion of natural value and a labor theory of value and, regarding the latter, apparatus by which value gravitates to natural levels allocating resources to maximize the level of revenue.

Smith's is a notion of the summation of individual factor costs, each cost individually determined; this concept of cost is not a unitary concept derived from a "natural level" but more like modern equilibrium analysis in which factor cost of different products differs between products (per quantities used, relative advantages and disadvantages in different uses, and reflecting opportunity costs of factors in different uses). Thus "cost" includes notions of: (a) productivity in this use; and (b) value in other uses. They tend toward a natural level in each use and flow – allocate – between all uses gravitating to some natural or central level. (Analysis conducted in Chapter VII, most explicit on pp. 60–61 regarding rent.)

General Theories of Wages, Profits and Rent:

While Smith has a "real cost" doctrine only regarding wages, later classicists included capital and entrepreneurship. In Smith there is a general level of wages – a central point about which wages in different lines lie – determined by factors important in regard to later thinking:

(1) An upward sloping supply curve of labor in general, that as wage rates are raised, the supply of labor is higher, that high wages are not self-defeating but rather create future development and opulence – the foundation for an optimistic view of the effects of increasing opulence on general welfare. This soundness given to a high wage policy was fundamentally opposite to the Mercantilist point of view and policy.
(2) The natural rate of wages is therefore not a fixed rate, but depends on the supply and demand for labor, and not on any mechanical or biological basis of labor; Smith has the idea of a minimum of subsistence but it is not a necessary rate, for the wage rate can diverge from it.
(3) For Smith the crucial relationship is an embryonic wages fund, the relationship between the quantity of savings and the amount of stock (Chapter VIII); his is not a strict wages fund analysis for his emphasis is on the growth of capital and not on size per se – for a stationary supply of capital (and hence a stationary demand for labor) however high it may be means low wages, through an effective tacit conspiracy to keep wages down on the part of employers.
(4) While, again, notions of subsistence do enter the picture, Smith also speaks of the "toil and trouble" of labor – later its "disutility."

Other than wages Smith has no underlying real cost theory except regarding a notion of the wages of entrepreneurship differing from the profits of stock.

Hence his is neither a labor cost theory nor a full fledged real cost theory.

Rent:

Different from the other distributive shares, it is price determined, i.e. high price creates high rent and not vice versa – a concept later held and developed by Ricardo.

In addition, also different from the other factors of production, rent seems also to be a monopoly price – Senior, J. S. Mill.

The modern view is that there is no monopoly unless it is all in one hand (effectively).

In any case, it is an unearned distributive share attributed to the bounty of nature, the lucky owners receiving the rent, and in proportion to its differential fertility, etc. Smith is thus in agreement with Malthus that rent derives from the bounty of land and not from scarcity or differential qualities, i.e. from the niggardliness of nature as Ricardo held, and which formed the basis of Henry George's single tax.

Nevertheless, there is no explicit idea in Smith of the diminishing returns of land.

Profits:

In Smith there is a hint of the notion of risk, irksomeness and wages of management. But in essence profit is the return to property as such, and not an interest rate in the monetary sense: the interest rate is derivative, as in the Keynesian schemata, from the rate of profits on property and moves in general with the profit rate.

The payment of interest is the payment for an advance by the workers who need to have materials, tools, and living provided during the production period. Though part of the produce is paid to the owners of stock for their advances, the payment as such is not, according to Smith, a necessary required supply price of capital; there is no underlying real cost notion, rather it is along the lines of opportunity cost to meet the alternative uses of capital. Smith's historical analysis leaves the door open for notions of exploitation.

In addition Smith held that wages and profits move inversely, not in accordance with the reasoning of Ricardo (inevitable conflict in dividing up a fixed pie), but because both are subject to an underlying cause: the growth of capital relative to growth in population.

Concerning the differing interests of the different social groups (pp. 248 et seq.) Smith shows a definite anti-capitalist bias: whereas both the workers and landowners want a progressive society, i.e. increasing opulence, the capitalists' rate of profit falls in rich countries, i.e. increases with scarcity, for opulence reduces the rate of profit.

Lecture

Smith on Free Trade (pp. 421–425):

Free trade is perhaps the area of Smith's greatest influence on policy.

Smith uses the theory of natural price and the way in which resources are allocated in a competitive system through the relationship between prices and costs in different lines of activity. Smith has no explicit doctrine of comparative cost, but such notion is very implicitly contained and has two branches, the static and the temporal.

Static: Smith uses the analogy of the individual writ large for the nation as a whole: since it is clearly advantageous for an individual to buy some of his needs rather than make them all, paying with receipts from the sale of the product he produces as a specialist, "what is prudent for the individual can't be folly for a large kingdom."

(a) Every individual tries to allocate his capital so as to maximize his net return, and each is in the best possible position to determine the best way to devote his capital.
(b) Capital sets labor in motion.
(c) Thus, under free trade and competition labor is so set to produce that which produces the greatest value, the widest profit margins, and as such will produce the greatest mass of value. Decisions are thus made by on-the-whole prudent investors; agriculture and labor being more passive and not knowing their own best interest.

Smith (pp. 421–425) seems to imply that what can be cheaply produced absolutely in each area will be so produced and exchange will be undertaken, i.e. produce through specialization what will produce more revenue.

Regarding the doctrine of natural (equilibrium) prices, and the natural levels of wages, rents and profits in different areas, Smith's argument is that where all value relationships are in accordance with the natural rates, then the maximum total value is assured, that money price levels of different countries are kept in some systematic relationship through the specie flow mechanism (similar to Hume), and there will be a flow of resources to where they will produce a maximum return and hence maximize revenue.

Thus, although there is lacking the neat demonstration such as found in Ricardo, Smith uses the same argument for international and domestic free trade – based on comparative costs.

Temporal: Smith recognizes the importance of capital development and is also very doctrinaire on the subject (pp. 346–347, 421–425).

Smith has a hierarchy of the uses of capital: first, agriculture; second, manufacturing (city growth); and third, the carrying (foreign) trade: the hierarchy is in terms both of the quantity of labor set in motion and of adding value to the annual produce.

Capital would flow first to agriculture, and in sequence to manufacturing and then foreign trade. Capital, coming out of saving, will increase fastest when the original capital is most remuneratively used; hence no artificial – Mercantilist – means should be used to create a diversified economy. Arguing for free trade, Smith thus negates the infant industry argument for protection.

Smith's crucial assumptions:

(1) *Underemployment*: Smith is not worried about the problem that has become a frequent argument for protection. Smith got around the problem (p. 424) by saying industry is in proportion to the capital that employs it, i.e. capital

rather than consumption provides the market for labor – hence more savings means more employment.

(2) *Saving to Smith is uniquely related to the level of real income*: thus a higher income leads to a higher saving which increases the rate of capitalization and leads to a faster growing employment. Smith sees no slip possible between saving and investment; furthermore the distribution of income among the different classes has no influence on capital development (important in modern theory) so that redistribution will not increase capitalization and employment.

(3) Smith further denies that the pace of capital development, investment, is a function of profit rates of potential investors, innovators, entrepreneurs – that it is a mere function of aggregate real income.

(4) There is further an implicit denial of dynamic virtues to any type of activity. Current protectionist argument is in part that manufacturing is more amenable to innovation and progress, faster improving than agriculture, and if resources are shifted to manufacturing the economy and income will grow faster; Smith, however, declared that growth is always faster if progress is in accordance with his system of natural liberty.

This, however, involves Smith in a dilemma, for he also postulates that greatest saving is derived from manufacturing and trade and not in agriculture – which would support the protectionist argument.

Methodology of Smith:

Smith is essentially prescriptive, which he makes attractive by using deductive economic analysis and history.

His prescriptions are in the main of a negative nature.

Lecture

Smith on Free Trade (continued):

An examination of Smith's writing on free trade and its benefits, especially his analysis on page 425 ("By means of . . .") where he deals with the "temporal" side, indicates that Smith thought in terms of comparative advantage and not in terms of absolute advantage (cost) concerning international trade; that differences in trade come from comparative advantages so that income is maximized by producing on a comparative basis.

It is paradoxical that Smith failed to take into account the Marshallian distinction between industries of increasing and decreasing returns, i.e. a country, following the guideposts of comparative advantages, might confine itself to raw-material production activities and would thereby lose the advantages obtainable at home in producing in lines characterized by increasing returns. This latter is a sound foundation for the infant industry argument, i.e. the raw-material producing country will over time retain such production and not have the advantages resulting from devoting its resources in that activity which is characterized by increasing returns. Here, therefore, Smith was not correct.

[Here I placed a note, of uncertain source:] The idea of comparative advantage implies that free trade is best at any moment of time. Smith, however, extends this to advantages through time doing what is best at the particular moment of time. This extension, however, is invalid where there are differing laws of returns with internal benefits accruing through increasing returns.

In another sense of increasing returns, there may be certain types of industry particularly amenable to innovation and the building up of know-how. Thus, by not stimulating these industries a country's progress will be slowed up, for with such stimulation there would be a higher pace of innovation, etc.

To the above objection Smith, however, has some rebuttal, centering on the wider degree of international trading. He would argue that the productivity of labor depends on the degree of the division of labor which in turn is a function of the extent of the market and that consequently an autarchic system prevents world-wide advantages of the division of labor whereas the system of free trade would open up markets to permit it. And, in fact, some of the external economies of production are associated with the growth of the extent of the market: thus, if some regions cannot manufacture efficiently, to stimulate such production might result in increasing returns in time but, on the other hand, they would be foregoing the advantages of the division of labor and the extent of the market gotten through free trade.

Smith's case therefore doesn't rest solely on the comparative-advantage argument but also on the extent of the market and the territorial division of labor.

Smith's Monetary and Banking Theory:

Banking Theory:

Smith's ideas on banking were highly influential on later thought. He originated, at least by virtue of his high authority, the notion that credit used for capital purchases merely acts as a medium of exchange similar to coin, which it merely replaced, and has no effect on the structure of production and is therefore not dangerous by way of inflation or deflation. His reasoning is: (a) that the notes issued by the bank circulate only to return to the bank for payment; and (b) that the banks can displace only an equal quantity of coin; loss however will result if there is an undue expansion of notes. Thus, long term loans will upset the structure of production, lead to speculation and perhaps to mal-investment and crises. This analysis is the theoretical foundation of classical banking theory, although he is not generally noted as the basis of the real basis or needs-of-trade theory which holds that because there is no associated danger there is no need to place limits on short term loans.

General Monetary Theory:

Smith is generally considered as being a non-quantity-theory thinker. Two reasons for this are: (1) that he traced the value of gold and silver to causes similar to those determining the value of other commodities; and (2) Smith makes no explicit statement concerning the rise in prices subsequent to an increase in the quantity of money similar to what had already been formulated explicitly by his friend David Hume, nor does Smith make any explicit statement of the price-specie flow mechanism regulating the distribution of precious metals between countries through changes in the price levels involving the quantity theory of money.

Professor Earley, however, feels that a close analysis of Smith would justify the conclusion he has made (in an unpublished article) that Smith was a quantity theorist, his analysis resting on quantity theory ideas.

In his *Lectures*, Smith stated the importance of the quantity theory and of the price-specie flow mechanism of Hume.

In the *Wealth of Nations* Smith repeatedly speaks of the distribution of precious metals in accordance with "effectual demand" and that a nation must maintain and augment its quantity of money. Distribution by nations' "effectual demands" is in quantities proportional to the values created in those different communities – i.e. through some real term, "real national income." This implies that the units of internationally traded goods (at least those) would have equal prices in terms of the precious metals.

Thus, if a nation increases in supply of notes it would simply lose a portion of its specie to other countries: it would have more money than is proportional to its effectual demand the excess of which would be turned into bullion and shipped abroad by the people thus causing prices to rise, an adverse balance of trade, and a redistribution of money.

The same is true with regard to a particular region within a country.

Several alternative explanations for the explicit neglect of the quantity theory in the Wealth of Nations are:

(a) That Smith was bent on playing down the importance of money and didn't want to talk in anything but real terms (effectual demand)
(b) That Smith merely took Hume's analysis for granted in writing his work [In note: Including the thought that Smith thought that his anti-Mercantilist argument was more important than that of Hume.]
(c) That Smith didn't want to give Hume too much credit, and thus displayed the analysis in a new cast.

The first two are thought to be more likely explanations, but it is known that Smith was not overly generous in acknowledging debts to predecessors or colleagues.

Lecture

Book V of the *Wealth of Nations*:

The last Book of the *Wealth of Nations*, little read, contains considerable material, some of which is important, in part because it expounds somewhat on Smith's analysis in the earlier sections.

(1) Concerning the needs for defense, just administration, public works and public institutions, the three functions of government recognized by Smith, he reiterates Locke's view that expenses for the administration of justice grow out of the need for the protection of property, that civil government is essentially for the protection of those who have property against those who would infringe or take that property away.

Although Smith has a strong inclination to the benefit theory of taxation, he is not doctrinaire, for he sees the benefit theory as leading to grave injustices.

(2) Concerning government expenditure towards facilitating general commerce, Smith has the principle of increasing returns as trade increases. Such indiscriminate benefits are an exception to the rule of individual enterprise – justified on the theory that they would not be remunerative for private enterprise to undertake.

However, particular favoritism is strongly opposed, for it would lead to Mercantilist practices and a consequent misallocation of resources.

(3) On education, Smith advocates payment out of common funds for the education of the "common people" but a fee system for those who can afford, paid to the tutors directly.
(4) On religion, Smith envisions "atomistic competition" as a desirable situation, crying out against a situation with a few strong sects (p. 745).
(5) Taxes and Public Credit: this is the area where Smith's earlier analysis enters.

One of Smith's primary maxims, there are four, is his advocacy of the ability-to-pay principle; he comes out for both progressive and proportional taxes but is against regressive taxes on equity grounds.

Smith's analysis of incidence is along the same lines as his analysis of distribution:

The incidence of taxes on the produce of land or rents and ground rents is on the surplus – because of the inelastic supply of land.

The incidence of taxes on the profits of stock and the wages of management is such that the wages of management are not fit for taxation because competition tended to reduce them to a minimum, but interest is a fit subject for taxation since it has no cost associated with the provision of capital other than regarding risk and the toil and trouble of management. He concludes that a tax on interest wouldn't reduce the supply of capital, although, since the incidence is on the owners of stock, two limits are: (a) determining the building of stock; and (b) stock might migrate abroad.

Considering a general tax on profits against a particular tax on the profits of certain industries, Smith applies opportunity-cost doctrine such that the latter particular tax would fall on consumers since the returns on capital tend to equalize and therefore capital would move and prices would include the tax component; the particular tax would not, however, affect the general rate of interest.

A tax on wages, which Smith is strongly against, is opposed on social grounds, as on the whole Smith is an egalitarian in his social philosophy, as well as on its implication of being destructive of employment (pp. 815–817). Although Smith argues that the tax will finally be paid by the landlords or by the consumers and not by the workers or the owners of stock, he nowhere attempts to justify his statement that a tax on wages would destroy employment opportunities, i.e. occasion a decrease in the demand for labor. His analysis seems to contain some Keynesian elements, at least implicitly.

General taxes on necessary commodities are considered similar to taxes on wages: wage rates rise and the incidence is on consumers and landlords.

A luxury tax raises the price of luxuries only and has no effect on wages.

A tax on imports diverts the economy from the best allocation of resources.

A tax on monopoly goods is a tax on the monopolist.

Smith thus follows his value theory consistently except with regard to wages where there is a hiatus.

On public credit, Smith is attacking the uses of public credit of the Mercantilists against whom he cannot refrain from commenting. He criticizes two major theses: first, that public debts are a blessing in that they create capital; and second, that debt service is no net detriment to the economy, that it is merely a transfer. The Mercantilist view is that of the functional finance theorists today: that we can stimulate the economy by high liquid resources, e.g. public debts, and the payment of taxes to pay interest thereon is only a transfer. Smith criticizes public debts as oppressive and that they will ruin a nation in the long run. He sees in them the transfer of revenue from productive capital to unproductive government expenditure, or that they are merely unnecessary and would be used anyway and are really being misdirected by government use thereof (p. 877).

Two notions on capital are contained in his analysis: (a) that capital consists of a real fund and the government can do nothing to increase it for it can only be increased by savings out of revenue; and (b) that once saved it is inevitable that the fund be used to employ productive labor – governmental use destroys it.

Hence saving, not effective demand, determines the use of capital. Smith seems to be assuming that the demand for labor comes from land and capital (which he calls the two sources of revenue) and not from the purchasing power of the interest receivers. On this, Ricardo agreed with Smith and Malthus disagreed.

Smith further criticizes debt service (pp. 879–881) as Mercantilist sophistry that constitutes a Peter-Paul transaction, i.e. a mere transfer. He further criticizes public creditors as having no interest in the productive process and its direction and benefits, for the public creditor gets his revenue regardless of general prosperity.

Lecture

Concluding Remarks on Smithian Economics:

First, Smith was substantially inductive in character; his analysis was based on observations of human character, the working of institutions, economic history – this was the foundation on which Smith built his theoretical structure, which was not highly abstract and deductive, like the systems of Bentham and Ricardo.

Second, there are numerous hiatuses in his thinking, considered only as an analytical structure.

(a) There are, first, considerable ambiguities, duplications and inconsistencies in Smith's theoretical propositions on value and distribution. There are a multiplicity of value theories and multiple propositions on rent and wages. Furthermore, his effort to derive a real-cost theory of value is without any homogeneous entity necessary to represent real cost.
(b) Smith also lacks any cost theory of interest, or of profits including interest.
(c) Although Smith has the notion of marginal transference and the notion of opportunity cost guiding allocation of resources and influencing value, he has no clear (explicit) notion of the "margin."
(d) Concerning wealth and income, Smith's distinction between productive and unproductive labor is unsatisfactory; furthermore, there is no close analysis of the psychological components of income (as through marginal utility or a similar analysis), and he holds the odd view that nature cooperates only in agriculture.
(e) Smith has the idea that capital sets labor in motion, but has no clear development of the relation between demand and the employment of labor or other productive factors.
(f) There is a certain degree of naivete in Smith's reliance on laissez faire to procure the conditions of competition, especially concerning the conditions of large-scale-production, and human nature and monopoly. Indeed, Smith doesn't work out the theory of monopoly at all carefully.

Third, Smith's monumental characteristic lies in his enormous innovative virtues: in a real sense Smith founded the kind of economics that has continued down to recent times and still persists in economic theorizing.

In answer to a question, Professor Earley stated that in Smith there is no basis for a labor theory of value except in the ideological sense present in several chapters in the *Wealth of Nations*, and then only in the sense of a precedent.

In answer to the query why Smith is so outstanding an author, Professor Earley laid out the following reasons: (a) That coming when it did, the *Wealth of Nations* was a most persuasive piece of work, which is not to detract from the fine writing style of Smith, however. Although Cantillon, Turgot and the Physiocrats expressed many of the same ideas earlier, their ideas were not in the right garb or at the right time. (b) That Smith synthesized many partial ideas and brought them together – ideas of those writers just above plus Petty and Mandeville; Smith thus built a larger system. (c) That Smith built a very usable kind of apparatus for economic analysis.

In answer to the question, why didn't Smith follow the utilitarian approach, Professor Earley spoke as follows: The major reason for Smith not following the approach of the utilitarians was because of the nature of the problems in which he was interested, that is, the primary problem of increasing total output, increasing the wealth of nations – problems of production – and the secondary problem (only secondary) of the distribution of income – and both problems can be dealt with only very obliquely and, in Professor Earley's view, not satisfactorily by the marginal-demand approach.

Only when the imputation process was worked out could we get from production to distribution by the marginal-demand approach, and then only deductively and still unable to deal with problems of the total level of output, technology, growth of capital, and certain important and interesting aspects of the division of labor, and still quite far from an institutional study bearing on the level of production and on distribution.

Smith saw that the primary task of the economist was to work out ways to increase output through time.

Smith's key factors were: (1) the growth of capital (saving); (2) the increase in the division of labor; and (3) competition.

Only the last can be well analyzed by marginal demand and imputation which can indicate the virtues of competition through some welfare analysis.

Only through a gradual process of dealing with, say, the distributive process or the value problem, and a long process of economics becoming academic and divorced from its innovative aspects, from problems of government policy and problems of the day, do you get the marginal approach.

Bentham has his felicific calculus, utility, and the notion of measuring utility by money, but he had no marginal concept and was not a marginalist.

Theory will evolve from strategic social problem in formative period, later to become formalized by being embedded in an academic curriculum. Later, new problems and new visions, worked over and joined. When lack of problems – highly abstruse and refined theorizing, complex models; in depression, social movement, prosperity – new visions come out. Theories have most common sense in their inception – reflect new situations. Then comes gradual degradation as conditions change and theory becomes more and more worked over. No straight line trend toward a more satisfactory theory except in working out certain models. Schumpeter right only if conditions didn't change.

Lecture

RICARDO AND HIS PREDECESSORS AND CONTEMPORARIES: CLASSICAL POLITICAL ECONOMY

Developments Between the Wealth of Nations and Ricardo's Principles:

Four names are significant in the period between Smith and Ricardo: Jeremy Bentham, James Anderson, Sir Edward West, and T. R. Malthus (on population).

Before examining these economists it is necessary to look at the period of history that was 1776 to 1815 – a period of considerable disturbance in the economic affairs of Europe, in England as well as on the Continent.

First, there was the further development of industrial capitalism, especially in Great Britain but also, though to a lesser extent, on the Continent.

Second, the Napoleonic wars particularly upset economic affairs and served to call attention to new problems: *Agriculture*: high prices, need for high production, introduction of intensified capitalistic agriculture, rise of rents, growth of conflict between industrial and landlord classes. *International Trade*: embargoes, trade restrictions, etc. Monetary: depreciation of currency, instability. In addition there was a tremendous boom that eventually cracked and thus led to a period of great instability and much controversy.

Third, as W. C. Mitchell points out (*Lecture Notes*), the French Revolution occurred and engendered a reaction in England – an England fearsome of the breakdown of basic institutions by the application of "fraternity, equality." This engendered repressive legislation on labor and counter agitation in response. These measures were quite definitely contrary to the philosophy of Adam Smith, who looked for the general welfare of the masses.

Fourth, the growth of individualism.

This fourth point, the growth of individualism – developed in Mitchell's *Lecture Notes* – brings the discussion to economic thinking during this period. On the Continent the absorption of the basic ideas of Adam Smith was not long in coming; J. B. Say, as well as writers in Germany, tried to improve on Smith for Continental readers.

Jeremy Bentham: Utilitarianism

Although Bentham exerted but slight influence on technical economics, for there was no taking up of the marginal methodology based upon his thinking, he nevertheless exerted great personal influence – the group known as the "Philosophical Radicals" grew up about Bentham: Ricardo, McCulloch, James

Mill, John Stuart Mill, and also, to a degree, Malthus – the leading economists of the first sixty-seventy years of nineteenth century English Political Economy.

Bentham may be said to have made three contributions to economics:

First, part one, Bentham is noted for his methodological individualism: that he viewed social analysis, both normative and analytical, from the standpoint of the individual. Methodological individualism is in Bentham in its extreme form: the individual is seen as the atom of which society is composed. Part two, his view of human nature is that of the economic man – the rational calculator of pleasures and pains. While simpler than the thinking of, say, Smith and Hume, it is nicely conceived for economic analysis.

Second, Bentham had a great effect on social philosophy, i.e. the sociology underlying economic analysis: social welfare for Bentham was based on individual satisfaction summed up: the greatest happiness principle. Although such thinking had predecessors in the Physiocrats, Smith and Hume, economic thinking tended from the time of Bentham on to exalt the value of economic freedom for the individual.

Third, Bentham gave political economy the confidence that economic science could be built on scientific foundations similar to, say, Physics. Thus Bentham rejected thinking along the lines of natural rights and having argument proceed from first principles, preferring to using money such that economics can be objective and quantitative. Nevertheless, Bentham in fact – as well as utilitarianism in general – as a social philosophy – rests on an adopted first principle – despite Bentham's protestations against such analysis.

Proceeding to Bentham's economics proper, his Manual was based on Smith's *Wealth of Nations*, but extended and made more doctrinaire Smith's views on the basis of his felicific calculus.

Economics did, however, contribute to his social philosophy: he concluded, through Smith, that freedom is best in economic affairs, although this is quite different from his conclusions elsewhere. Freedom was an element of happiness but also a stimulus to the growth of capital. Inequality was recognized to be a detriment to the greatest happiness but was said to be a necessary sacrifice to achieve freedom and security of property, and, in the long run, increasing opulence and, though he offers no proof, equality as property accumulates: economic advance brings about general advance including better income distribution.

Bentham may be contrasted with Smith on two points: First, Bentham concluded, quite contrary to Smith's conclusions on the subject, that a smaller population with a higher per capita income is better than a larger population.

Smith, on the other hand, held that a large and increasing population was symptomatic of prosperity and opulence. Second, Bentham was internationalist in outlook – again in contradistinction from Smith. Bentham spoke of the "world's wealth," that all men are of the same importance, that free trade would mean harmony, peace and the general good of the world which was of much more importance than the reactions, etc., in particular countries. Smith, as is obvious, spoke of the wealth of *nations*, and only briefly (see above) delved into the realm of international relations of the economic variety.

Lecture

Ideas on the Theories of Rent and Population between Adam Smith and David Ricardo:

The present topic may be analyzed in three phases:

(1) The Physiocrats, except Turgot, didn't recognize explicitly the principle of diminishing returns, but felt that rent was a bounty, a true net product; rent was paid because the land produces more than subsistence, a productive surplus, and that it was natural for this productive surplus to go to the landowners.
(2) James Anderson and Malthus: recognized the differential nature of rent but on the extensive margin only; combined with the view that it was a bounty, with no diminishing returns – similar to the Physiocrats.
(3) Ricardians, though anticipated by West and to some degree by Malthus: diminishing returns and scarcity of good land (due to population growth) led to emergence and growth of rent over time.

James Anderson

A late eighteenth-century scientific farmer and pamphleteer. Adam Smith had criticized the corn bounty and was answered by Anderson on theoretical principles: Anderson maintained that land varied in fertility (differences in grades); to encourage sufficient agricultural production – to ward off famine – it was necessary to cultivate inferior land to the degree (amount) necessary to provide adequate food in the worse years of crop result. Cost tends to equalize price at the margin; the differential return was a surplus, bounty, and didn't deprive anyone of anything. He didn't recognize diminishing returns on all lands; saw increasing returns throughout. West and Ricardo hit upon this analytical fallacy that neglected diminishing returns on the intensive margin.

Sir Edward West

Writing in 1813, a few years before Ricardo, West pointed out that diminishing returns at the intensive margin was the strategic margin and that it led to the recourse to the poorer lands – the extensive margin. This was later taken over by Ricardo as the differential principle. This was not due to the absence of all land being of equal fertility but to diminishing returns.

It is important to note at this point that the analytical model of the period saw doses of labor and capital as applied to land, labor and capital usually referred to as "capital" application on basis of capital setting labor in motion.

There were also at this time certain parliamentary investigations into agriculture that laid the ostensible empirical basis for the theories of West and Ricardo (1813, 1814 investigations). These hearings revealed:

(a) wide differences in land fertility in the basic crops;
(b) that crop yield was a function of the quantity of capital applied;
(c) that the application of capital to land was a function of the expectation of profit;
(d) that the determination of price determined cultivation;
(e) it was argued, at least, that some lands yielded only a return to capital and no rent.

This was the first general recognition that English farming was capitalist and not feudal.

Malthus and his Population Theory

Several notes on things not always mentioned:

(1) Concerning the apparent inconsistency on his view of human nature: Malthus pretty much agreed with Bentham on self-interest, calculation and profit maximization, yet, as W. C. Mitchell points out, his early population theory implies than man is irrational.

This may be explained as follows: Malthus envisioned human nature – man – as a mixed creature – this was said by both Malthus and Bentham – although emphasis on the felicific calculus crystallized this human nature to a calculating maximizer or "economic man."

(2) The preventive check in the first edition of the Theory of Population is therein said to be operative in the educated and domestic servant classes – indicating

> an element of rationality. Trouble, however, lay in the fact that it became transformed into a vice – illegitimacy, abortion and contraception. "The people weren't moral enough to be rational in a moral way." In the second edition, the general growth of restraint was accompanied by an increase in morality in the community as a whole: thus he had a hope that population might not outrun the food supply. ("Workingmen of the world, awake; you have only your vices to lose!")

It is important to note the change in the wage theory from a physiological minimum of subsistence to a standard of life level – which was taken over by the Ricardians; this new proposition was still a rigid level of habits, changeable only over a long period of time.

In both editions, though primarily the first, Malthus says that there is something beneficent behind the struggle between population and food – such that man can develop his higher faculties – this was a very popular line of reasoning at the time. The idea in general was suggestive to Darwin.

(3) Malthus did not invoke the principle of diminishing returns in support of his population theory; the theory rests on pure ratios – arithmetical versus geometrical – and not on diminishing returns, says Cannan

Professor Earley stated that Malthus' theory was more a temporal theory, one through time, a general law of supply. Malthus, Professor Earley said, did everything but actually bring in the principle per se. He (Earley) also suggested that Malthus' principle was prognostic in character and therefore it was not necessary to bring it in. Furthermore the principle of diminishing returns implies that there is no technological change, which was not a good assumption for his time; indeed for the nineteenth century it was a poor principle.

The significance of Malthus' population doctrine for economic thinking:

(1) The cast it lent to economic thinking: from Smith's optimism to a more sober look.
(2) It was the key element in the Ricardian theory of distribution and on the basis of either the subsistence theory of wages or a given-standard-of-life theory one has the key element in Ricardian theory: bound to have diminishing returns and distribution of income shifting as Ricardo said it would.

Summary of lecture to this point:

(1) principle of population;
(2) principle of diminishing returns;

(3) clear application of marginal principle, in Turgot but especially in West, and only in agriculture – diminishing returns peculiar to agriculture only: Ricardo worked out his whole system of distribution and value on the principle of diminishing returns in agriculture alone and on the population theory.

Introduction to Ricardo:

First of all, Ricardo was basically a utilitarian but took it less seriously than did Bentham or James Mill.

Second, unlike Smith and the Physiocrats, Ricardo did not raise any question concerning the institutional structure; he took capitalism for granted. He was not interested in the institutional structure, but, however, he did recognize class conflict.

Third, Ricardo was a long-run theorist; concerning production theory and even concerning the general principles of economic organization, Ricardo felt Smith was satisfactory. For Ricardo the problem necessary to work out was the theory of distribution.

Finally, Ricardo's standpoint was not that of the theorist, but from the corn-law controversy he turned to economic writings as he was unable by himself to handle it. Although it may be that he had reached his conclusions beforehand, he needed an analytical structure.

<u>Lecture</u>

Ricardo

General Characteristics of Ricardo's Thought:

Ricardo evidenced a lack of concern for social institutions in relation to economic theory, i.e. he may be said to have taken capitalism for granted as the best economic organization of society: indeed, Ricardo saw no reconstruction of society from his work. All his reforms are compatible with a laissez faire system: the abolition of the corn laws (free trade in agriculture); banking system reform to yield sounder and reliable currency; poor law reform to combat the Malthusian specter and increase individualism.

Ricardo developed his economics on the basis of a capitalistic class structure: landlords, wage earners and capitalists: and he saw their interests with a bias towards the interests of the capitalists and the laborers against that of the landlords – he was a capitalist and utilitarian social theorist, following Bentham and Smith (regarding labor).

Ricardo also took for granted the competitive economic structure, and considered the competition therein to be increasing, giving his structure and proposals validity: he could therefore theorize using a competitive model (as the closest approximation to the real world). Competition to Ricardo was natural in the Benthamite sense: the self-interested calculating individual not likely to unite with others. (This characterization of the Benthamite economic man, as the rationally calculating individual always looking to his self-interest, is in somewhat sharp differentiation from the "economic man" of Adam Smith: Smith's is a complexly motivated man some of whose propensities are indolence, getting ahead, against the rigors of competition and prone to join with his fellows against the public interest, usually prudent and careful but not a pleasure-pain machine except perhaps in devotion of his capital to different uses.)

Ricardo was also an "innovator" in the tasks he set before himself as an economist. Previously economists examined value, distribution, allocation, money, monopoly versus competition, etc.; Ricardo, on the other hand, while not neglecting all of these elements of economic analysis, worked out the dynamics of competition in a rigorous form derived from his theories of value and distribution, i.e. what is inherent in capitalism as a system moving through time with the absence of exogenous change. The Mercantilists were interested in such a problem but didn't develop it; the Physiocrats also did not examine the long-run tendencies of capitalist institutions. Smith is diffuse and indefinite on the subject, not integrating his views thereon. Ricardo gave a new chapter to economics – the theory of long run capitalist equilibrium.

Ricardo's Theory of Value:

Although it may be considered the hub of his theoretical system, Ricardo's theory of value, as Professor Sraffa has pointed out (Introduction to Volume I of the nine-volume set on Ricardo), is one of the last things he worked out. The *Principles* grew out of his earlier essay on the relation between the price of corn and the profits of stock, in which he declared that if agriculture is protected and if the population grew, the price of corn would rise (since more would be needed), and producing under decreasing returns, a larger share of the social product would go to the workers (though not better off since the prices they paid would be higher), and the surplus would go to the landlords and consequently the profits of stock would be adversely affected. Under the pressuring of James Mill, Ricardo had to meet with the problem of explaining price and the laws of value. Thus, he undertook to read Adam Smith (whom he probably had only read partially before), Colonel Torrens and Buchanan, and worked out his theory of value. Concerning the Schumpeterian thesis, if he had a vision at all (re: diminishing returns, population principle, final result) his value theory was worked out with the purpose of proving the theories of his earlier essay – a special purpose value theory – his value affects capital, distribution, etc., as population grows bringing in decreasing returns. Thus, he uses his value theory in a systematic way to develop the principles of the distribution of income. Compare the foregoing with the case of Smith where values were built up from the natural component parts of distribution – where the value system is not used to explain the distributive process.

Ricardo's is a cost theory of value, in which scarcity and notably costs govern value, and in which he differentiates between the short and the long run and between competition and monopoly.

Ricardo's labor theory, to begin, is definitely not meant to be an embodied labor theory of value – there is no relation between labor input and value created (pp. 46–47, Sraffa). Rather it is a theory of relative labor values – values in proportion to labor requirements. He also rejects Smith's labor command theory. Value is a price relationship between goods; the distribution of revenue is not associated with any labor theory of value.

Why then is Ricardo so often taken to be an embodied labor theorist?

(1) Because of careless and awkward exposition by Ricardo and equally careless reading thereof, especially to identify Ricardo with Smith and Locke.

(2) The ideological astigmatism wherein Ricardo must have meant it because it makes sense, or because Marx said he did.

(3) (a) Analytically, he seemed to seek a cost theory of value and distribution but only explained labor cost.

(b) He did conceive of a concept of absolute value, a scale to measure price changes.

(c) He does treat capital as accumulated labor:

(i) from Smith, working capital (circulating capital) is considered proportional to labor;

(ii) concern with the integration of the whole economic process saw capital as the product of the previous stages of production – value added from the original source of previous labor (this applied to working capital, not fixed capital: he finally admitted that changes in capital (variable/constant capital) (or time) would change the relative values).

The above analysis follows the argumentation of Ricardo's disciples, James Mill and McCulloch.

(iii) he saw an unequal organic composition of capital as altering the relation between labor and value.

(d) Because readers tend to look at the Principles in which he does use the labor theory of value to develop the principles of distribution.

Many argue that a labor theory of value implies that all value is from labor; but we can have an imputation theory or a relative value system (no adding up) as did Ricardo.

Lecture

Ricardian Value Theory (continued):

Ricardo worked out his value theory in developing his argument that as population increases and/or agricultural imports are restricted, rent would increase and therefore the rate of profits would decrease: operating through diminishing returns to land and Ricardian rent theory. This was the thesis in his pamphlet on the corn law and the profits of stock; but as he endeavored to expand the thesis into what was essentially his *Principles*, he saw he had to solve the problem of value. This he sought, modified and incorporated into his thesis a compatible value theory – pretty much the one he found in Smith.

Ricardo saw the need to develop a general theory of value – the relative values of different products at any one point in time: value in the relative sense – exchange value, not absolute value.

Thus, Ricardo has a cost theory – utility he says is per se, insufficient; cost to Ricardo was labor plus profit – not the amount of labor incorporated. This cost of labor plus profit had to be modified for differences in the ratios of fixed capital to labor, or to labor plus circulating capital. (No modification was necessary for circulating capital, for it was proportional to the quantity and the duration – time – of labor.) Other modifications had to be introduced, he saw, concerning differences in durability (depreciation) of fixed capital and the rate of turnover of circulating capital. Thus, he doesn't say that the relative quantities of labor incorporated therein is the sole determinant of relative values of commodities; but he does say that labor is the most important and that differences arise from these three other sources, the modifications just mentioned.

Ricardo equated differences in grades of labor through the higgling and bargaining of the market into different wage rates – therefore it can be said that the quantity of labor is the same after making allowances for such differences. Concerning the question as to what happens to relative values through time as conditions of production change, Ricardo would negate the claim that the non-homogeneity of labor presented an obstacle by stating that the various grades of labor are apt to be the same throughout and therefore would be reflected in the wage-rate structure. Thus, any change in relative value would be due therefore to changes in the amount of labor needed in production: the wage structure, i.e. does not change over time. Therefore his abstraction from the non-homogeneity of labor is not too violent.

If the wage rate rose there would not be any necessary change in all values, but it would imply a shift in values in accordance with the relative compositions of labor and the other factors: a high wage rate implies a lower rate of profit and therefore if the wage rate rose (because prices of agricultural products rose) relative to the rate of profits, goods with a low capital/labor ratio (much labor relative to capital) would increase in relative price.

Ricardo is always talking of relative returns – rates – proportion of the total. Profit is the return on non-land property; the rate of profit is the relation between the profit share of total product and the share going to labor – not a rate of return on cost.

Ricardo's theory of value is a theory of value worked out as a matter of comparative statics, if you will, rather than a general theory. It is essentially a two-good case: agricultural and manufactured products. There is nothing concerning, say, relative values of different agricultural products. Rent is a surplus because there is no opportunity cost of land regarding alternative uses in manufacturing: there is no transfer earnings on land as between agricultural and manufacturing uses.

Thus, his value theory doesn't seem to be connected to general doctrinal matters of value, and what constitutes value, nor with the forces in the value mechanism determining the distribution of income. Ricardo has only a relative labor theory; only later was he concerned with an absolute determinant of value – and he concluded that it couldn't be done.

With his theory being in essence that as capital increases and population increases rent rises and profits fall, the key factor being diminishing returns on land, and the morals being: (a) prevent population growth; and (b) free important of agricultural products, the distribution of income doesn't depend on the value mechanism but upon his concepts, the rate of profit as a share, the subsistence theory of wages, and diminishing returns in agriculture, with more to the workers and landowners, the reason for the increase to the workers (increase in wage rate) being the rise in the prices of agricultural goods. I.e. Ricardo's theory of value is not intimately related to the forces in the value mechanism determining the distribution of income.

Lecture

Ricardian Value and Distribution Theory and Its Application to His Dynamic Theory of the Long Run:

Recapitulating Ricardo's theory of value, in the first place, his is a form of labor value theory, but it is very complex and highly qualified. As earlier notes will evidence, relative values are not strictly in accordance with labor input; however, labor is still the most important element, says Ricardo, and suffices for a simple analysis.

In this connection it is to be noted that Ricardo eliminates rent entirely by the doctrine that rent doesn't enter into cost of production – that at the margin rent is not a part of marginal cost – which is derived from his differential theory of rent. The only rent recognized, furthermore, is his "payment to 'land' " rather than, following Marshall, Pareto, Joan Robinson, a "leading species of a large genus."

A second important characteristic of Ricardian value theory is that his is a "two-good" case – relative valuation of generalized agricultural produce and manufactured goods. Only the former uses an appreciable quantity of land; the former is also representative of the wages of labor – corn. The latter presumably uses no land. Whereas the former is produced under conditions of increasing costs (decreasing returns), the latter is produced under very different conditions – we can reasonably assume he implied constant costs. Also involved in this two-good system is the assumption that labor and capital are in the long run perfectly mobile between the two and that therefore their returns are equal or tend to equality.

A third characteristic is how relative values shift in the long run due to changes in population, the supply of capital and the availability of land for producing agricultural products. Ricardo was not interested in the relative costs of various commodities, but rather in the relative costs of these two goods – agricultural and manufactured goods as social commodity categories.

From this analysis of value and from his theorizing on distribution, Ricardo derived several long-run theorems. With the accumulation of capital, the increase of population and the limitation of available land, there would be a shift in the shares of the total product such that rent would increase, profits would decrease and real per capita wages would not be greatly affected.

Profit, it should be pointed out, meant to Ricardo the total return to non-land property – a highly global and long run concept: Smith's rate of profits on stock made more abstract. His rate of profit was the proportion profit bore to the total outlay on the wages fund – not a profit uniquely on wages fund but on all capital investment, both circulating and fixed, but a rate calculated only on variable capital. Thus, a fall in the rate of profit meant a fall in the proportion of capital income borne to the wages fund.

Thus, as capital accumulates, population will increase, and therefore agricultural products must be produced, but under diminishing returns. This raises the marginal cost of producing a unit of agricultural products and consequently their price. To maintain the real wage rate of the workers there is a need for the wage rate in money terms to increase at the margin. Thus, there will be a lower share going to the capitalists compared to their outlay on the wages fund: the price of agricultural products rises relative to the price of manufactured goods and real wage cost thus rises relative to the value of manufacturing output even though labor gets no more – a constant living standard. Thus, the rate of profits falls: the fundamental cause is the diminishing returns in agriculture that can't be avoided if population grows relative to the available land.

Furthermore, any improvement in techniques – increasing productivity – will not help the capitalist in the long run, especially as long as they are in non-agricultural sectors, because such improvements will further reduce the value of manufactured products relative to agricultural goods, for competition drives prices down to the new cost level. Improvements in agriculture, on the other hand, can delay or alleviate conditions but Ricardo felt that they would not be sufficient in the fact of substantial increases in population.

<u>**Lecture**</u>

Ricardo on the Effect of the Introduction of Machinery on Labor, Chapter XXVI:

Here Ricardo seems to be quite heterodox, and such was the opinion of his theorizing at the time, e.g. by McCulloch.

There are two income concepts of Ricardo's to be identified in connection with his chapter on machinery, the first "gross product," and the second "net product." Gross product has to do with the total production of the period and consists of both consumption and investment goods, net of maintenance of capital, depreciation. Ricardo's gross concept is seen to be similar to Adam Smith's net product concept.

Ricardo's net product is more closely allied to the Physiocratic notion, not Smith's; it is that part of gross product that is a profit or excess over labor cost – the value of rent plus profit – the landlord-capitalist's net income – all per period. Thus Ricardo has extended the Physiocratic concept to include the return to capital as part of the net product but he continues the bifurcation between the wages of labor as a cost and what is left over, failing in this instance to follow Smith. (For Smith's analysis see page 271 of *Wealth of Nations*, Modern Library Edition.)

This net product includes the consumption of the landlords and capitalists, and is not in the form of a surplus at the end of the period, for it may be entirely consumed in the period; in this respect it is neither similar to the Mercantilist's favorable balance of trade – it is not built up and it includes consumption goods – nor is it similar to the Physiocratic notions on the subject.

It is quite apparent that, for Ricardo, capital sets labor in motion, but the net product here is not that capital available to labor but is a profit to the landlord-capitalist.

Ricardo lacks the view that the net product is the real end of economic activity or an increase thereof is especially desirable itself; it is gross product in which he is interested as a measure of the welfare of the working class (here he is similar again to neither the Mercantilists nor the Physiocrats) but he does distinguish gross product from labor cost of production – see above definition.

To Marx the real net product was this net product in the Ricardian sense – with no clear differentiation between rent and profit; and the end of capitalist activity is to increase the net product – surplus value – in the process of production. Marx thus owes more to this chapter than to anything else in Ricardo. Ricardo, although he thoroughly recognized that for the capitalist it is net product that is important, felt that for economic policy gross product was more important. In Ricardo, circulating capital, not net product, fixes the demand for labor; for Marx, the demand for labor is a function of the expectation of the rate of profit on capital, i.e. the rate of surplus value on labor use.

From this net product, savings are made; and savings in this Ricardian model come entirely from the landlord and the capitalist. New investment is from this saving out of net product, saving being net production less consumption. Furthermore, saving is equal to investment because all saving is invested; the problem is not due to over-saving but to the conversion of circulating capital to fixed capital with a consequent reduction in employment, as will be seen. For Malthus, as we have seen, it was the lack of effective demand, and the maldistribution of income and the over-saving engendered thereby. To Ricardo, however, the business "cycle" might be caused by: (1) the conversion of circulating capital to fixed capital; (2) the cessation of war spending; and (3) a change in the pattern of expenditure, say from menial workers to others. In Ricardo there was no inevitable tendency to underemployment and certainly no cyclical element.

The Ricardian Model on the Introduction of Machinery and its Effect on Labor:

Ricardo assumes to begin with circulating capital – the wages fund – of 13000; fixed capital of 7000; the sum of both of which being 20000; in addition he assumes a rate of profit of 10%.

Period One: The 13000 wages fund – acquired through the sale of commodities to the laborers the proceeds of which buy the services of the laborers – produces value in the amount of 15000, 2000 being the profit, which, when applied to the total capital of 20000 yields the rate of profit of ten percent. The landlord-capitalist realizes his profit by consuming it; there are no savings as yet.

Gross product is 15000; net product is 2000 (15000 net of labor cost of 13000); the wages fund is still 13000 (2000 of the 15000 is consumed). If this same process is repeated there is no trouble as the same results will be repeated; if there is saving it will result in a larger wages fund which will increase the demand for labor – following Smith completely.

Period Two: Now one-half of the labor is employed to build machinery, the other half on food; again 13000 is paid out, with 15000 coming in (7500 circulating capital, 7500 fixed capital – the machine). However, there is nothing yet to affect the demand for labor; net product is still 2000; gross product is also unchanged. He again assumes that the net income of the capitalist is realized by consuming 2000 of the 7500 circulating capital, net of maintenance of fixed capital.

Period Three: But now the capitalist has only 5500 circulating capital left to lay out as the wages fund. Mechanically, Ricardo assumes that due to the increased productivity because of the use of the machine, the 5500 circulating capital produces 7500, permitting at least the mere maintenance of the former net product, but on an employment of less labor – per Marx, the rate of surplus value or of exploitation (sv/vc) has risen. The rate of profit has also continued the same, 2000 on 20000 (5500 plus 7500 plus 7000).

On the basis of this, Ricardo admits his earlier error that the introduction of fixed capital – machinery – still left the same circulating capital intact and wouldn't injure the workers except through temporary dislocation, but would lower prices and perhaps increase the wage rate through increased saving. He overlooked that labor demand is a function of circulating capital and not the total capital (circulating capital plus fixed capital) and that the capitalists were interested in the maintenance of the net product whereas the maintenance of welfare is a function of gross product.

Although it is chronic and therefore requires continual adjustment, Ricardo feels that it is a short run problem, for in the long run population will fall to full employment. The problem can also be eliminated, paradoxically, by increased saving out of net product to increase the wages fund. Practically, he sees that there is only a gradual process of using part of the net product to increase machinery and thus the employment situation is relatively stable.

Lecture

Ricardo reached similar conclusions concerning the introduction of machinery and its effects on labor concerning: (1) the effects of the introduction of horses in agriculture in place of manpower, which represented a decrease in the wages fund; and (2) the cessation of the expenditures associated with war and the effects thereof. On this last point, Ricardo argued that if you finance the war out of revenue, by taxes, and not out of capital, such will increase the demand for labor, i.e. the same production of goods but more or increased demand for workers – the needs of the armed forces – which might increase the wage rate or might raise the level of employment depending upon employment conditions at the outbreak of hostilities. In any case, there would be a net increase in the demand for labor. Difficulties he saw arising when the war spending ceased: deflation and distress among the workers. Although he neglected the problem of inflation, he did see that if there was an increased demand for menial servants, such would better the situation of labor.

Qualifications of his thesis by Ricardo:

Ricardo substantially qualified his thesis that by itself would indicate a good deal of heterodoxy and consequently he is not as highly heterodox as one might imagine from the above. [The notes read that the qualifications are "substantial therefore not highly heterodox." It is quite possible that the second and third uses of "heterodox" in this paragraph should be "orthodox."]

Looking at the behavior of the net product and of saving, he felt that if net product increased greatly, such would lessen the diminution of the wages fund, given the consumption of the landlords and capitalists. Furthermore, if savings were made out of the net product, and are added to the wages fund and thus to the demand for labor, such would serve to counterbalance the disemployment caused by the introduction of machinery converting circulating capital to fixed capital. Thus, to Ricardo, savings can help when added to the wages fund, to circulating capital.

Furthermore, it is likely that the introduction of machinery will increase the rate of saving, for a number of reasons. First, it will lower the price of goods and increase their quantity purchasable with any given income, i.e. real income will rise, and hence savings – beneficially – will also rise. Second, in addition to this, if the net product rises in value terms, and if the income of the landlord capitalists rise, then savings will increase even more aside from the real rise in income.

On another track, Ricardo felt that the introduction of machinery isn't a conversion process, i.e. abrupt, but a steady slower process in which savings takes the form of investment in machinery gradually rather than being used to fully increase the wages fund: thus there is no (sharp) decrease in the demand for labor – it is simply that the demand for labor wouldn't grow as fast as capital grew; this he felt is not nearly as serious and might well be affected by improvements in productivity and increased saving, as above. Still there would be the long run tendency as capital increased for the demand for labor not to be as buoyant as the increase in savings would indicate. As capital accumulated, population would increase, thus leading to diminishing returns in agriculture which would imply that the prices of agricultural products would rise, and make it more profitable to use machinery rather than labor since the cost of labor would be going up in relation to machinery – thus, the constant tendency to go to machinery – similar to Marx.

Professor Earley pointed out that from Smith to J. S. Mill, with increasing clarity, the trend in economic thought was toward the concept that the demand for labor was derived from the demand for capital and away from the concept that the demand for goods is derived from the demand for labor. [Sic].

Ricardo, it was pointed out, among other things, neglected the idea that the use of labor in the production of machinery (the demand for labor being in part at least derived from the demand for machinery) would keep up the demand for labor in the aggregate, i.e. there would be no unemployment because of the introduction of machinery. Professor Earley raised two questions in this respect, however: (1) what about the marginal efficiency of capital as the ratio of fixed capital to labor rose; and (2) will the supply of wage goods be maintained, i.e. scarce consumer goods in relation to demand even with continued effective demand. (My thought is that there would be an unstable but highly expansionary situation, with an increasing marginal efficiency of capital.)

Defects in Ricardo's Analysis:

(1) It is based on the wages fund notion of the demand for labor, that the wages fund represents the demand for labor.
(2) He overlooked the substitution of labor for capital as a function of relative prices in the short run (he does have it in the long run) for, as the wage rate fell, such would affect and offset the substitution of machinery for labor.
(3) He omits all monetary effects of changes, e.g. on price and profit levels.
(4) Because of his notions of the wages fund, etc., he neglects the problem of aggregate effective demand: he sees an increase in saving as helping the situation – contrary to modern theory. However on almost all other points, Ricardo is quite orthodox: (1) he uses the wages fund theory of labor demand; (2) that capital sets labor in motion – the source of effective demand; (3) the labor theory of value; but savings for him is still the solution.
(5) Cannot analyze short-run adjustment problems using his structure, though better over long run when he is more suggestive of the peculiar tendencies of a capitalist economy.

Lecture

Ricardo on Foreign Trade:

In his discussion of foreign trade, Ricardo treats: (1) the effects on domestic values; (2) the effects on the domestic price level; and (3) the effects on national income and effective demand. His conclusion is that it is merely a monetary phenomenon, with its results similar to those which would have occurred if barter was the method of exchange.

He levied a devastating attack on the Mercantilist criticism of free trade: free trade, he taught, would not impair production and employment, it won't upset the domestic economy, and it doesn't affect the principles of value, distribution and effective demand which he developed earlier on the basis of barter exchange: monetary movements do not cause unfavorable reactions. Although the benefits of free trade are by no means fully treated by Ricardo, he does visualize an increasing real income and therefore saving, and that it will raise profits only if it serves to lower the production cost in agriculture. All trading is therefore alike. However, he does realize that because resources are not fully mobile, the value principles in the trading countries will not be identical or similar: there can be different wage rates, profit rates, etc., and still have a balance – but these differences will not be an upsetting factor.

Money, therefore, is a mere *numeraire*; he subscribes to the quantity theory of money: there is no incompatibility of cost of production theory and quantity theory, but he uses the quantity theory.

If there is an imbalance in international trade, money will flow so as to balance it: but product value ratios will be unaffected by the money flow even though dollar prices will vary until total trade is balanced. The basis for trade in all cases is the comparative advantage. Ricardo's in this instance is a long-run theory, although he doesn't bring it out. The analysis here is based on Hume's earlier work, plus Ricardo's own value theory and comparative cost theory (contributed by Thornton).

He concludes that free trade is optimal for long-run welfare, particularly in agriculture – and to keep up the profit rate in manufacturing. The only real problem to Ricardo was population control. He thoroughly assumed competitive conditions.

His then were the classical policy recommendations: (1) free trade; and (2) population control.

Conclusions on Ricardo:

That Ricardo has maintained a commanding figure is easily seen:

(1) He was the first to apply the marginal technique of analysis to value theory even though it was done only partially; value became with Ricardo a function of the marginal cost of production – food in particular; and in the principles of distribution upon an agricultural basis.
(2) He attempted an integration of value and distribution theory.
(3) His was the first real effort to concentrate economic analysis on the theory of distribution; Smith's earlier attempt was nowhere near as complete.
(4) His was the first striking theory of the long run trends of capitalism.
(5) His was the pioneer in international trade theory; Hume and Smith were fairly good but Ricardo was more rigorous.

With regard to number 4, that his was the first striking theory of the long-run trends of capitalism, it is important to note that his was long-run moving trends, not any long-run equilibrium positions. Even though he was crude, simple and excluded many of the most important elements, he set the problem and influenced Marx and others. Briefly, Ricardo omitted: (1) the principle of diminishing marginal productivity of capital as capital accumulates – he had the profit rate decreasing because of diminishing returns in agriculture; (2) problems of aggregate level of effective demand. Ricardo, though, was not as pessimistic as was the first edition of Malthus – he was more similar to the second edition.

The Physiocrats and Smith first formulated the basic notions of income and income flows. Ricardo's distribution and value theory marked a significant advance, vigorous but erroneous. For the Physiocrats, the distribution of income was a function of consumption by classes. An increase in luxury consumption meant an increase in income for the sterile class but an overall decrease in income. For Ricardo, the distribution of income is more a theory of income and of capital formation.

Lecture

The Fruits of the Evolution of Economics as a System of Analysis Through David Ricardo:

(1) conceptions of the economy;
(2) models and analytical devices developed;
(3) theorems derived.

(1) The growth of the conception of a basically capitalist economy as a mechanism subject to systematic study as a whole; that economic processes are interrelated and can be generalized.
   (a) Especially by the Physiocrats: concept of circular-flow economy; continuous production and flow of goods, and use of capital, the way the product is distributed, the role of capital, and of land, and how consumption is related to production. An income and production system. Developed a model of the economy in the *Tableau* that was a fruit of their initial ideas as to how the economic system functioned, which led also to a complete doctrinal system. The Physiocrats well illustrate Schumpeter's thesis in "Science and Ideology," *American Economic Review*, March 1949.
   (b) Smith conceived the full form of the economy as a price and distribution system: the role of price, the parts of price as determining the distributive shares, and of the price system as regulating the economy, including value and allocation.
(2) The discovery of the role of value or price as the key concept in economic analysis. The Physiocrats made little use of it due to their concept of wealth, not market or psychological but physical. Smith developed the outlines of

the price system and investigated prices as the key focus of economic study. It is, however, to be found earlier in Petty, Locke and Cantillon. In Smith, though, there is a demonstration of its systematic use throughout the entire economy. Thus, economics became a study of the theory of value and its ramifications. In addition, the key role of value and price was also seen as a key control device as well as a focus of study and analysis. Value study was the starting point of Ricardo and Marx, especially in their study of the dynamic elements of the economic system.

(3) The establishment of concepts of wealth and income, i.e. what constituted wealth and income.
   (a) To the Mercantilists, income, i.e. that income relevant for economic policy, was a net surplus or favorable balance from the viewpoint of the national economy as a result of international trade.
   (b) To the Physiocrats, income was a net creation per period for the entire system of a physical production in a net product, instrumental in creating more income. Thus, they moved from money to physical magnitudes.
   (c) Smith has the basic notion of income that has been predominant since his time, that of a flow of product or revenue, over the period, plus any net investment therein, in which the unit of valuation is a unit of account reflecting not changes in dollar or money values but of real values; this then combined both market and psychological elements: income as a psychic stream of goods with emphasis on, for Smith, the material, relegating services to a lower position as they vanished in the instant of their creation and were not suitable for capital accumulation.

(4) The discovery of the principle of diminishing returns as a basic principle of operation of the economy – the leading principle of classical economics. Possessed earlier by Turgot; used later by West, Malthus and Ricardo. Though he applied the principle only to land, it was the backbone of Ricardo's theoretical system, together with Malthusian population theory (second-edition version), a modified labor theory of value, and a simplified two-good case, from which he derived his model for analysis. The real basis, of course, for Malthusian population doctrine is diminishing returns in agriculture.

(5) A beginning of the marginal analysis. Although there is some suggestion thereof in Turgot, and it is somewhat in Bentham, it was West and Ricardo, especially Ricardo, who is noteworthy here: the combination of the labor theory of value and the law of diminishing returns is the basis for his theory of distribution and his dynamic analysis, all resting on the marginal cost of agricultural production.

Lecture

Attributes of the Evolved Classical Theoretical Model, Especially that of Ricardo:

(1) The Ricardian model, as well as that of Adam Smith, followed the Physiocratic vantage point in one important respect, namely, the utilization of an agricultural model of the economy. This is characterized by: (a) the period of production over which labor is maintained pending the fruits of production and capital as a fund which carries the factors of production through this period, the wages fund concept in which capital is the wherewithal of employment; (b) capital as machinery, much less technique and stored-up knowledge, is not important; (c) the notion of the capitalist enterprise is also simple, built on an agricultural institutional structure: a coordinator applying labor and capital to land, with no risk element involved; and (d) the idea of flows – wages fund, e.g. It might be added that it was Say, Saint-Simon, and Marx who really introduced the factory and the capitalist enterprise in the modern form into economic analysis.
(2) While their analysis is not macroeconomics in the sense of a study of the levels of income and of employment, their's is not microeconomics: for there is little analysis of the individual consumer or businessman. They work with broad aggregates or classes – most striking in Ricardo, whose two-good case of agricultural and nonagricultural goods forms the basis of his analysis of value and distribution. The Austrians and Marshall turned to microeconomic analysis. To the classicists, labor, capitalist and landlord represented three great classes that for them were economically homogeneous; Marx further simplified the class structure of society.
(3) Their model was of a productive process rather than of an exchange process. To them the basic economic problem was one of producing more goods and services, notably foodstuffs. Their only real interest in value theory lies in their use of value theory in analyzing the production problem. This is seen also in the great extent new capital accumulation, rather than a proper allocation of resources, was held up as the generator of economic progress, i.e. capital accumulation, not the avoidance of waste.
(4) Their model was designed for and applied to long run problems, including the evolutionary problems of capitalism; there is little analysis of the short run and of short-run fluctuations, this being the origin of the famous conflict between Ricardo and Malthus.

The Doctrinal Position of Classical Political Economy Through Ricardo:

(1) Capital is seen as the prime mover, as playing the strategic role in the economy: indeed, capital accumulation was seen as the road to the wealth of nations by Smith and by Ricardo. Capital sets labor in motion and also increases the productivity of labor. Capital comes from saving and therefore saving is a strategic economic function, as distinct, say, from enterprise. The rate of capital accumulation was a function of the rate of profit on non-land property. To this, however, there were two great obstacles: (a) diminishing returns, confined to land, which limited living standards; and (b) diminishing returns reducing the rate of profit. Thus, the necessary policy seemed to be obvious: limit population growth and enhance capital accumulation.
(2) On value theory, the cost approach was thought sufficient, although the components thereof are not clear. For Ricardo, it was composed of labor and profit both relative and determined by relative labor requirements. Nothing clear is attributed to capital. There is much ambiguity and obscurity. The labor theory stands out, but in an impure form. Smith was much less monistic and therefore is more satisfactory: value determined by the sum of supply prices.
(3) On distribution theory, there is a hodgepodge of principles. The marginal productivity principle is applied to the theory of rent, but otherwise they were off in various directions. Wages evoked two theories, though they can be formally reconciled: (a) the standard of life, a modification of the subsistence minimum concept; and (b) the wages fund. Profit was a residuum determined by the marginal cost of food and the landlords' share, with no cost clearly identified with it.
(4) On monetary theory, they accepted the quantity theory of money.
(5) On cycle theory, there was none, except in the thinking of "heretics," which signifies the presence of the problem: the qualifications of Ricardo on machinery and of Malthus, the louder dissenter.

The theorems of classical political economy became their policy prescriptions:

(a) free trade;
(b) control or suppression of monopoly (diminishing returns on land, not competition, drove the rate of profit down);
(c) control of population;
(d) keep up the rate of profit (and enhance capital accumulation and the demand for labor);
(e) sound money.

Further, men like Smith saw monopoly as: (a) representing a wasteful allocation of resources; (b) defeating free trade efforts; and (c) as inequitable, as they were prescribing for the general welfare.

Components of their Ideology:

(a) strongly individualistic;
(b) utilitarian;
(c) thrift is the economic virtue par excellence;
(d) internationalist;
(e) ostensibly not class oriented, though it is hard to argue that its accord with the interests of a class didn't beget the support of that class for their doctrines and policy;
(f) a temperate positive laissez faire.

Shortcomings:

(a) neglected the problems of demand;
(b) confused value and distribution theory;
(c) exclusive attention to the long run;
(d) exclusive attention to the competitive case;
(e) serious inadequacies even within their cost theory of value:
   (i) non-homogeneity of factors;
   (ii) no cost element in profit;
   (iii) two wage theories, though they can formally be reconciled.

James Mill and McCulloch

It may be said that they bear the same position to Ricardo as the Keynesians do to Keynes: the popularizers, textbook writers and expounders of the doctrine. The Ricardians came out with nothing new but a popularized David Ricardo. They tidied up Ricardo and drove home his policy recommendations.

Among their doctrinal characteristics, the Ricardians insisted on: (1) a pure labor theory of value; and (2) the primacy of the wages-fund doctrine. Their pure labor theory of value was important in doctrinal history, serving to give credibility to the ideas that value was created solely out of labor and that value accorded relatively and absolutely with labor embodied in every product. McCulloch's value theory was taken over by Marx.

The primacy of the wages-fund doctrine was emphasized in relation to social policy, on which they argued that anything infringing on savings was undesirable, thus extolling thrift. They likewise argued that interventionism by government, such as the factory acts, and labor organizations would be abortive of the permanently rising welfare of the laboring classes. There are responsible for the doctrinaire laissez-faire position associated with classical economics, and for Marx's criticism of "vulgar political economy." They consistently argued capitalist class interests, arguing down the working class; they were thorough capitalist-class oriented.

Lecture

James Mill

In addition to his textbook organization, Mill's *Elements* presented "messages" concerning: (1) the function of capital; (2) the theory of value; and (3) the wages fund theory.

(1) *The Function of Capital*: Although Ricardo, following Smith, laid emphasis on the primacy of circulating capital, James Mill felt that all capital has the role of bridging time. He identified fixed capital with circulating capital, permitting labor to produce. All capital therefore has value and a claim to a distributive share.
(2) *Theory of Value*: Mill tries to remove Ricardo's qualifications. It is a theory of relative value, not a proposition that total value is attributable to labor. Mill sought to eliminate Ricardo's technical qualifications by which value differs from the quantity of labor: fixed capital, time, and durability.

Both James Mill and McCulloch held that all value is a function of relative labor inputs, not absolute labor inputs. This is closer to the Marxian view than was Ricardo, but it was not an embodied-labor theory, it was one of relative value. Capital did impute value. They had no intention of attacking the existing distribution; they dealt only with the technical question of relative labor input and value. Their argument ran along the following lines:

(a) Cost of production determines exchange value.
(b) Exchange value is determined by the quantity of labor: either total cost is labor cost or any other cost is strictly in accordance with labor input; they chose the latter alternative.
(c) Capital (land rent, following Ricardo, is residual and is eliminated) is produced by labor; labor is the original source of capital.

(d) This capital is used with more labor to produce goods.
(e) Payments to capital are simply a payment in proportion to the stored-up labor; capital ratios may vary, but they reflect accumulated labor.

At this point, it is difficult to see any difference with the ideas of Karl Marx. But it is implicit that the return to capital is a payment for the act of saving, for the function of capital is to bridge time. Capital makes an independent contribution, but one proportioned by the quantity of labor. Total value is determined by labor, the return to capital added on in proportion to labor input.

The foregoing argument has the following defects:

(a) The "accumulated" labor is already paid for.
(b) Profit is earned in capitalism without any current labor, whereas, according to James Mill, capital is used along with labor.
(c) The capital return doesn't die out with the death of the capitalist but is a perpetual one proportioned to the value of the stock, as Smith saw, not merely a terminable annuity.
(d) Profit is not correlated by Mill with the input of capital stock.
(e) Mill attempts to identify capital with labor without using an embodied labor theory. It was easy for Marx to take it over and point up inconsistencies, especially surplus value as a product of labor and as exploitation. The Marxian labor theory has a closer affinity and a legitimate ancestry with the vulgar Ricardians than with Ricardo.

(3) *Wages Fund Theory*: see discussion under Senior.

The Supply Price of Capital: Not explicit in Smith or Ricardo, the notion was introduced by James Mill. People do not like to save; they are impatient to consume. Therefore, capital requires a net payment for saving. This notion was taken over by Senior, John Stuart Mill, Marshall and modern theory: the notion of subjective cost.

James Mill's dynamics was projected in the form of the stationary state of John Stuart Mill: as capital accumulated and accumulated still more, and with diminishing returns on land, the rate of profit would fall and consequently savings will totally cease, there being only a constant supply of capital with a rate of return sufficient to keep it intact.

McCulloch

Like Mill, McCulloch possessed a "pure" labor theory of value and also emphasized the wages fund branch of Ricardian wage theory, the other branch being the condition-subsistence. McCulloch felt that the subsistence level is merely a minimum level, the current equilibrium wage rate given by the relation between population and the wages fund: the provision and adequacy of the wages fund is more important than the underlying standard of living of the people. The benefits of saving all went to labor, government and union efforts being futile. Nevertheless, he favored unions, which would assure a competitive wage and offset capitalist combinations. However, the basic wage rate is outside of their scope.

His ideas are of both theoretical and ideological importance. His thinking, and that of the vulgar Ricardians, reinforced the ideas that capitalism is beneficent and interventionism is futile. It diverted attention away from the growing criticism of the economy of the period and served as a useful apologetic for the capitalists. The restraint of population, the virtues of parsimony, and the advantages of free trade were said to be necessary to increase living standards.

The Ricardians had no insignificant influence on the development of Marxian thought: the Ricardian socialists and Marx pointed to their conclusions, especially on value, and to their prestige, and argued that labor created value. Marx found in classical economics material to solidify his own analysis and adopted a value theory close to but not identical with what they had meant.

Senior

Senior carried further James Mill's notion of the cost to capital, namely, abstinence, thus solidifying the real cost theory of value; previously, profit was up in the air.

But in doing so, Senior saw incompatibility with the labor theory of value and consequently abandoned the labor theory of value and emphasized value not as embodied or created but as an exchange relation reflected in equilibrium cost in the long run – made up of labor and abstinence – still following Ricardo in eliminating land rent.

Senior confined this advanced analysis to a special case, the condition of "perfectly free competition," in which any producer could produce any product with equal facility. Competition is not so free in cases of: (a) conventional monopoly – economies of scale; (b) institutional monopoly; and (c) monopoly of land. Apropos of land, agriculture produced under diminishing returns. The unequal facility created rent and advantage over others. Such value was not given by real cost but was a quasi-monopoly price.

Monopoly for Senior turned on two elements: mobility of factors and the ability to acquire them (the distribution of property).

We may question the compatibility of real cost in regard to goods produced with no land with the idea that rent isn't part of value. Senior later saw that the notion of land as different from capital breaks down with regard to value but, with regard to distribution, still argued that land rent was monopolistic.

His ideas were taken over by John Stuart Mill: not embodiment of labor and the abandonment of the labor theory of value.

Senior's relationship to other thinkers is often characterized by the difference between cost of production and cost of reproduction, the latter, held by Senior and neoclassicism, involving not embodiment by a factor but supply price – not original cost bur current factor supply price through market forces.

Senior felt that economists should be neutral, and give not a syllable of advice. Economics was the study of the science of wealth, as defined by the professor at Oxford, with no necessary relationship to policy questions or with moral and social values – similar to physics. As a science of wealth, economics was a very partial outlook to bring to social problems.

Lecture

Senior, continued:

Monopoly in relation to cost theory of value: Since abstinence was the cost explaining the necessity for the payment of profit on capital, the cost of production theory of value, according to Senior, had two elements, wages and the profit necessary to invoke capital for production. In the main, both were psychologically viewed. His was neither an embodied nor a single cost theory of value (homogeneous labor) but one concerning the supply prices necessary to be paid: this was well received by J. S. Mill and Marshall and has carried forward to the present day.

The sale price of any commodity was the sum of labor (wages) and abstinence (profit), the real cost of the distributive shares, in the absence of monopoly. Monopoly was not neglected by Senior, the major element of which was to him land, and land rent as its "return." Under the conditions of monopoly, a commodity does not sell for the sum of labor and abstinence only, but a share goes to the landlord, there being three, not two, elements in price, of which two are cost and the other is rent. This he applied only to land, for capital could be produced by labor and capital; the rent of land was caused by the institutional structure of society that reflected on distribution. However, the relative cost of products, despite monopoly and rent, was still in accord with labor and abstinence cost, because at the margin there is no rent paid; however, later he changed his ideas on this.

Attitude toward science of economics: About the third decade of the nineteenth century, economics became self-conscious as a discipline. Senior felt it should be an abstract deductive science, deriving theorems from the concept of wealth (all goods and services scarce and exchangeable, i.e. salable). Its propositions are very broad, derived from the nature of man and things, and we simply deduce from them.

Professor Earley's Lecture Notes on Senior:

Outline of a Lecture on Senior – "the Professor"

Best known for: abstinence theory of profit; abandonment of pure labor theory – abandonment and disclaimer of embodied theories (cf. Marshall)

Other important innovations:

(1) "neutrality" of economics; economics as abstract "science of wealth";
(2) wealth and income lose their classical materialist meaning;
(3) notions on competition and monopoly.

Specific Points:

(1) scope and method;
(2) definition of wealth;
(3) competition and monopoly and real cost value theory;
(4) "cost of reproduction" and supply price;
(5) abstinence theory of profit.

(lecture on Senior)

Nassau W. Senior (1790–1864).

Professor at Oxford, 1825–1830 and again 1847–1862.

Wide interests: value of money, international distribution of the precious metals, methodology, labor problems, government policy in various fields, especially poor law and factory acts.

Outline of Political Economy, 1836 (6th edition in 1872).

Some of his lectures have been published. (See Marion Bowley, *Nassau Senior and Classical Economics*).

Best known for: (1) strictures on methodology and argument for "neutral" position of the economists; and (2) abstinence-cost theory of capital – and interest – new "real cost" theory of value, both of which were strikingly new and historically important. But equally important, though generally overlooked, is; (3) his theory of competition and monopoly.

1. *Scope and Method*

"Not a syllable of advice" from the economists. Theoretical versus practical branches.

Economics impartial as between systems of society and economy. But a positive, not a hypothetical science.

Economics based on one definition and four propositions:

Definition:

Wealth: All goods and services possessing utility and scarce. (Note inclusion of services, and exclusion of labor as a requirement.)

Propositions:

(1) Maximum wealth with minimum of sacrifice is aim of every person.
(2) Population limited only by moral or physical evil, or by fear of deficiency of wealth compared to habit.
(3) Capitalistic production can indefinitely increase powers of labor.
(4) Diminishing returns in agriculture, technique constant.

2. *Definition of Wealth*

Utility, exchangeability, limited in supply.

(a) Included services (broke with Smith et al.).
(b) Labor not required, nor cost (only scarcity).
(c) Limitation of supply "most important" because it keeps the "marginal utility" high (cf. pp. 11–12). (Supply limitation also gives "distinction," which adds to value.)

Requisites of Production: Man, "natural agents" and capital (or "abstinence"). Capital a "secondary" but very important factor.

3. *Utility Theory* (above)

4. *Competition and Monopoly and Value*

Derived from real or sacrifice cost value theory: labor and abstinence are the two cost elements. Other returns a result of "monopoly."

Very interesting. Competition is situation in which cost of production to purchasers (or potential producers of good) is the same as to actual producers. Maximum price, in general, is potential cost to consumers; minimum price is cost to producers. These equate under competition.

Competition (p. 102):
Requires complete (long run) mobility of all factors without loss of "efficiency." Equal advantages to all.
Perfect competition requires also instantaneous mobility.
Perfect knowledge also required.
In Senior's words, "equal competition, or in other words, where all persons can become producers, and that with equal advantages" (p. 102).
Competition very rare. Requires there be no natural agents, or differential advantages.

Monopolies:
Four types:

(1) Absolute sole control, without fear of rival, and where supply is fixed. (No limit on price – assumed producer would sell all (wine).)
(2) Monopolist is sole producer, but can increase his output (at reduced cost). Economies of scale bring most profitable price lower, but there is no fear of rival.
(3) Monopolist has only certain "exclusive facilities" as producer, but can increase production without rising costs or perhaps falling costs. Monopoly of invention. Price brought lower because of advantages of scale and fear of rivals.
(4) Production requires natural agents, limited in number and varying in power, subject to diminishing returns to labor and capital.

The Great Monopoly of the Land. Rent theory, intensive and extensive. Rents arise. (Explicitly abandoned sole reliance on differential principle.)

Only where no "monopoly" whatever do things sell for their "cost of production" – labor and abstinence. But relative values are according to labor and abstinence at the margin, where no rent is paid. But does not say rent does not enter into "cost of production."

Tied up theories of relative prices and theory of distribution.

Note implications of thoroughgoing extension of monopoly element. A world of monopoly: Relation to modern economic theory: (a) infinite elasticity of demand; and (b) no differential return to capital.

If there were perfect competition in Senior's sense, then both relative and absolute values would equate with "cost of production." Note Marshall's meaning.

5. *Value Theory: Senior's Cost of Production*

As against James Mill and McCulloch, the cost of "reproduction." Bygones are bygones. Not embodied cost. But, in competition, a "tendency" towards real cost, labor and abstinence.

Labor – wages:
Minimum is "necessaries," but that is unimportant.
Proximate cost – wages via wages fund.
Wages-fund theory highly refined: (a) the fund-flow, limited; and (b) size of fund dependent on productivity, etc.
Also dabbled in productivity theory.
Disutility.

Capital – abstinence:
Its productivity – carrying production through time. Division of labor. Roundaboutness.
Sought correlative to wages.
The act – "refraining" or investing (saving and waiting).
A supply-price for capital, but not thoroughgoing "cost" as Senior developed it.
In competition, cost (labor and abstinence) regulates value.
Great influence on classical theory of distribution – Mill and Marshall.
At later time, according to Bowley, Senior viewed capital and land as virtually indistinguishable. "Free capital."

Summary:

(1) Income and wealth lose their classical meaning – exchangeability. Not yet psychological, however.
(2) Attempted to disentangle competition and monopoly.
(3) Labor theory of value discarded.
(4) Scarcity of all factors "explained." (Capital for first time.)
(5) Rent concept broadened.
(6) Prototype of neo-classical structure.

Note at least two costs. Can one add dissimilars? Beside the point, unless one takes an "embodied" view – cf. Marshall.

But it was a long step in breaking down the "real cost" doctrine. It is shadowy in Marshall, and Mill quite naturally came out with only an "expense" theory.

John Stuart Mill

Mill is noted primarily for his summing up and systematizing of the things that had gone before. While they were not great, he did make some contributions both creditable and original.

First, he elaborated Senior's abstinence theory, breaking up for the first time the components of what Ricardo called the "rate of profit": differentiating the interest rate as the payment for abstinence and profit as the payment for risk and the wages of management. In this he reflects J. B. Say.

Second, in international trade theory, his principle explaining relative value through reciprocal demands, later developed by Marshall and others, plugged a hole in Ricardo's work.

Third, his recantation late in life of the wages fund doctrine was on two principal grounds: first, he saw consumption as a flow rather than a fund, and that there was no fund anterior to production (still, what causes the rate of flow?); and second, there was no determinate portion of the product "destined" to pay for labor (Senior also criticized the theory on this score).

Mill was an out and out institutionalist with regard to distribution. He saw that, whereas the forces in production are natural – the principle of diminishing returns, productivity, technique – the processes of distribution are wholly determined by institutional arrangements. This recognition on his part is tied up with his recantation of the wages-fund doctrine.

In this regard, he overlooked that distribution is not unrelated to the production of income, and neglected the necessary supply price for capital (seen by James Mill and Senior) – though the supply price of capital is in part determined by the institutional structure. Dobb feels that a reduction in the return to capital would evoke greater production. Mill was more concerned with unearned income, i.e. inherited and land income.

Stuart Mill shows clearly the influence of new ideas. In ideology, he is noted for his interventionism, "socialism," and utilitarian reformism on the basis of the greatest-good principle as he saw it. This is well known to the student.

On methodology, we will spend more time.

Mill was not willing to shift from a view similar to that of Senior on methodology, but he was not satisfied with its sufficiency. He flirted with notions derived from his studies of biology and chemistry, as well as from his study of Comte, who felt that economics was one branch of a broad social science.

In his work *Logic*, Mill sets up three types of methods: (a) the chemical or experimental, as in chemistry; (b) the geometrical or abstract, as in mathematics and physics; and (c) the physical or concrete deductive, as in the physical sciences. He would try to fashion social science, including economics, close to the last. He would treat economics similarly to mechanics: a study of the composition of forces, with deductions derived from simple premises. He is thus close to Senior.

Later in life, he was prone to the more historical and the more experimental in character. He showed the influence of the historians, Comte, and his experience with working class movements. Education and reform he felt would lead to beneficial changes in social structure. He made a great concession to the beginnings of historical economics and methodology, introducing a general social science. Mill is indicative of a transition in economic thinking, between the old Political Economy and those socially dissatisfied with the old Political Economy, especially with what became of their policy recommendations.

The Social Policy Views of Classical Political Economy:

(1) To the classical political economists, laissez-faire, as Lionel Robbins points out, was not a thorough-going laissez-faire, but a tempered one. McCulloch was pro-unionism, as we have seen, even though he felt they could have no effect on wages. Senior was a greater interventionist, in favor of the factory acts in general, although he also had strong reservations about their effect on wages. J. S. Mill and others leveled attacks on landed income and felt that the status quo was not the most desirable.

(2) As a group, they were in favor of higher wages, on two grounds: (a) high wages was a way to increase the welfare of the country, and labor constituted the largest part of the population; and (b) as Malthusians they felt that an increase in wages combined with education would create new restraints on population. They were against low wages for the sake of exports and were in favor of free trade in agricultural products so as to increase the real wage rate.

(3) To almost all of them, education was an open sesame to improvement, especially economically, and especially with regard to population proclivities and the learning of skills. All agreed with Malthus on population; education was both a necessity and a hope.

(4) All were utilitarians; economics was purposive – though to Senior it was a neutral science. The thinking of Bentham and Smith explained most of their proposals.
(5) They were not enthusiastic about industrialism. Ricardo and J. S. Mill had strong reservations on machinery, as well as Malthus on industrialism in general; they all envisioned malfunctioning of the economy. They didn't like aspects of urbanization then going on. They lacked confidence that industrialism would cure the economic ills of the country. They didn't recommend building factories and introducing machines for that purpose; instead, population control, free trade, and education. A "good" economy to them was a simple small-unit non-industrialized one. They were dubious of intervention as a remedy for the problems of the time. They were, in general, nostalgic.

They were quite different from thinkers abroad. Bastiat and others saw universal harmony. Say and Saint-Simon were the heralds of the new industrialism, urbanization and associationism. Alexander Hamilton and Henry Carey in this country had similar ideas to the last two mentioned in France. Socialist thinking was stimulated. After Ricardo, energetic economic thinking took place in Europe and America, not in England.

Lecture

THE PRECURSORS OF KARL MARX: "SOCIALISM"

Viewing the origins of socialist thought, one can see that not all its origins lay in economics, but that economics was important. Classical political economy, especially, was important, and especially for the Marxian variant.

The Pattern of Reactions to Classical Political Economy (1776 to Ricardo):

(1) The extreme right:
   (a) Manchester School: doctrinaire application of the simple principles of Classical political economy, especially regarding free trade, regulation of industry, and labor issues.
   (b) The continent: the enthusiastic acceptance and unquestioning application by such writers as Say and Bastiat, who upheld the beauties of the competitive economy and laissez-faire.

(2) Nationalism: one group reacted against Classical political economy on the grounds that it failed to consider national problems. Carey in this country; List and others in Germany. These writers provide the roots of a later economics of a more romantic sort, e.g. fascism. Inasmuch as they desired economics to be relevant and suited to a particular country in its particular stage of development, they were by no means adverse to allowing protectionism.
(3) The Historical school: Somewhat closely allied with the nationalists. Wanted an economics less abstract and less lent to abstract theorizing and more an historical science. Germany and to a lesser extent in England. A quarrel over methodology.
(4) The utilitarian reformers: Especially in England: J. S. Mill. Had no dispute over the propositions advanced by Classical political economy, but held that they called for government intervention, to prevent unearned income, secure greater equality of income, control monopolistic elements of the economy, assist in passing through transition periods, be more attentive to human needs as capitalism developed. Later, full fruit in Marshall and Pigou.
(5) The left:
    (a) A group seeing flaws in capitalism (otherwise acceptable) to be remedied: free credit, lower interest rates, danger of under-consumption. Sismondi, Malthus, Proudhon; later, Hobson, Keynes.
    (b) The collectivizers: Saint-Simon, Rodbertus, Lassalle, Blanc.

Sismondi

A historian by profession, he came to economics through his interest in the history of commercial development and commercial society. As Edmund Wilson (*To the Finland Station*) points out, he was but one of many historians so interested at the time. Like the others, he saw history more in terms of class interests and class structures and less in terms of dynasties and political and military history. In this he reflected the economists, e.g. the Physiocrats and Smith, who emphasized the economic structure of society; it also reflected the growing prominence of the economic structure with the growth of capitalism.

In 1803 he presented an uncritical review of the new society in which he accepted the propositions of the Classical school. However, as a result of his trip to England after 1815, where he saw the serious upsets after the war and became conversant with Ricardo's notions on the introduction of machinery, his *New Principles*, in 1819, reversed his position and he became critical of the received doctrine.

Sismondi's Classical Bases:

(1) Accepted the economic class structure of the Classicists (labor and capital) and, though more so than Smith, their certain amount of class struggle.
(2) Accepted the idea that capital, not want (demand), determined production and employment, i.e. capital sets labor in motion.
(3) Accepted the labor theory of value, though he didn't build on it much.
(4) Saw problems in light of distributive shares and their relative shares in light of population growth and the introduction of machinery.

Sismondi's Socialist Bases:

(1) The emphasis on class struggle.
(2) Competition not an effective regulator.
(3) Theory of capitalist crises.
(4) The necessity for social control.

Sismondi's theory of capitalist crises is essentially an under-consumptionist theory and one which is close to Ricardo's notions on machinery. Sismondi held that the revenue of one year was responsible for the employment of the following year. Capitalists were interested in the net product (in the Ricardian sense) and not in the gross product (they could move in the opposite directions). Machinery caused unemployment as the wages fund was diminished. Furthermore, there was no automatic way for employment to increase; employment could increase only if demand rose after machinery reduced employment. Since production was uncoordinated, being on the basis of individual profit prospects (increases in net product), there was a wavelike introduction of machinery with long adjustment problems as labor shifted employments. In addition, mal-distribution was responsible for failing demand. Therefore, social control, to which Ricardo was quite bland, was deemed necessary and desirable.

Sismondi's Non-socialist Bases:

(1) The slowing down of the introduction of machinery.
(2) The breaking up of large firms.
(3) The reversion to a simpler and more individualistic economy.

Sismondi's was not the collectivist solution. Rather, from the point of view of the socialists, it was reactionary. The growth of industrial society was quite amenable with their ideas and vision.

Saint-Simon

Saint-Simon's importance as a forerunner of Marx lies not in the closeness of relation of their economic analysis, but in their similar aggressive forward views.

Saint-Simon saw the entrepreneur as the key figure and would reorganize the economy to give maximum authority, power and freedom to the entrepreneurial class, especially technical and scientific people. His vision encompassed the complete reorganization of the economy.

To Saint-Simon, the remnants of the feudal regime – the *rentiers* and the bureaucrats of government – were hampering economic progress. He looked forward to a second French revolution in which the petit bourgeoisie would lose their power, and even more so the landlord, the new class of large entrepreneurs, bankers and promoters coming into their own, into the saddle.

His social theory is built on a vision of industry and the technological requirements of industry: industrial leadership, know-how, and freedom from the shackles of the old form of government as well as from interest and landed property.

What was needed is a new kind of government, built on a different class structure in which the savants (scientists, etc.) would be on top, after them the entrepreneurs, and finally the workers.

His was a notion of aristocracy not of wealth but of knowledge and also virtue.

His ideas led to an attack on the institutions of landed and money property and the freedom of the entrepreneur to manage his own affairs.

His followers, the Saint-Simonians, presented the further argument that the present economic structure of society was exploitative, and that consequently: (1) it was injurious to wealth as well as to justice; (2) wealth should go to the state upon death; and (3) a planned economy was needed.

Saint-Simon exerted vast influence in various quarters: first, on the group of projectors building up new business and industry in Western Europe; second, on certain engineers; and third, on certain groups of socialists who were impressed with the colorful criticism of capitalism, with its potentialities of increasing wealth based upon the proper organization of society, upon which they derived fancy plans for social reorganization: Blanc, Owen, Fourier. Furthermore, both Rodbertus and Marx were influenced by the notion that industry was the key social force but was merely shackled by bourgeois institutions. The vigorous dynamic qualities of the Marxian theory of capitalist development are partly due to the influence of Saint-Simon and his followers from, say, 1820 to 1840.

Marx took the ideas of: (a) the economic interpretation of history (that the economic structure is basic to historical processes); and (b) industry as the key process in society, and added other elements. Both the economic interpretation of history and the notion of primary forces were prevalent at that time.

On the relationship of the technocracy of Veblen and Saint-Simon, Veblen was more scientific and less reformist and less crackpotish, while Saint-Simon was an enthusiastic reformer. Veblen's institutional theory is based upon a theory of human behavior, while Saint-Simon has little of that. They have in common an emphasis on the importance of technology.

Saint-Simon is another good example of the disciples carrying the master's views further than he would himself, and with less quality. Saint-Simon would have no complete overthrow of the social and economic system; his followers went much further and much less carefully.

Lecture

Proudhon

Proudhon, a "utopian" socialist in a sense, was mainly a critic. Marx did not borrow from him, but reacted to him.

Proudhon's labor theory of value was vague, and he indeed did not build anything on it. Similar to statements by Locke and Smith, labor was the sole source of wealth – the basis of the critical "school." From this, or better, after this, came the assertion that "property is theft," an infringement on the true liberty of the workers; labor can't compete with those who employ them. True liberty requires a modification or circumvention of the institution of property, though not its elimination *in toto*. What he was after was not the destruction of property per se but that all should have an equal chance to have property. Senior had seen that "real cost" (including abstinence) equalled value only in the absence of monopoly, which resulted in depredation, something he didn't, but Proudhon did, harp on. Proudhon didn't draw any fundamental distinction between land and capital.

Proudhon was not a socialist: his advocacy of greater freedom and the spreading out of ownership were quite different from their program. His own "device" affects the system of exchange and would enable the workers to obtain property by borrowing, without paying interest, through his exchange bank, the judgment of the bankers determining the soundness of investments. Notes would be issued based on potential production involved in the investment; money would be free for production purposes. This money would be sound in that it was to be based on things to be produced; it would be available not only for liquidity purposes but for both circulating and fixed capital. This system,

Proudhon felt, would lead to the erasure of economic classes based on the privilege of property, by enabling all members of society to borrow money so as to acquire and use property. It would also lead to the abolition of the state, for the state's purpose was the protection of property owners. Political and economic reforms would bring about anarchy – the absence of the state due to the lack of its necessity.

Marx, in his *Poverty of Philosophy*, criticized Proudhon on several scores: (1) Proudhon saw exploitation arising in the exchange process rather than in relationships of production. (2) Proudhon's proposal of the remedy of free credit went counter to the socialist critique, namely, that true socialists attacked the institution of property directly as well as the uncoordinated character of the bourgeois economy, leaving the money and exchange system to the cranks and crackpots. It is an impossible solution, as it would lead to inflation as well as fail to eliminate such monopoly returns as rent on land, which would indeed rise as part of the inflation as well as from population, etc. growth. (3) Proudhon's solution is incompatible with the institutional structure of property. Marx concluded that Proudhon is a crackpot knowing neither economics nor political science nor history.

Proudhon was influential for his attack on the property system and for his crude use of the labor theory of value as a critique of the system of distribution based on property.

Rodbertus

Rodbertus was in the main quite close to Marx in his thinking. Here will mention only a few elements in his thinking of importance from other aspects.

Rodbertus had the idea that all returns above labor and ingenuity are rent. He thus extended the classical concept of rent to the return to capital, i.e. capital would be freely forthcoming if it were not for existing institutional arrangements. The shares of the capitalists and the landlords should go to the workers. Distribution should be on the basis of labor only. And the state should undertake some scheme of redistribution.

The concept that labor gets only part of the total product led him to hold an under-consumptionist theory of crises, namely, that the workers don't get enough to buy back the total product. Successive crises will forever worsen, because the rent share going to the capitalist and landlord will rise, the labor share will fall, because the total product will increase due to increasing productivity and the fact that a minimum of subsistence determined the wage rate. There would be a tendency for increasingly aggravated crises. This was the product of Sismondi's thinking plus Rodbertus's own idea extending the classical notion of rent.

The Ricardian Socialists

Closely connected theoretically with Marx, their literature was known to Marx, although he studied Classical political economy only after he wrote the *Manifesto*. The Ricardian Socialists were Owen, Gray, Bray, Thompson, and Hodgskin. All were utilitarian in basic social philosophy – based on Bentham and Stuart Mill – while their economic ideas were gotten from either their own thinking or Smith and Ricardo or James Mill and McCulloch. They had two facets: the labor theory of value, and a utilitarian ethic and social philosophy. Their conservative social philosophy curbed the proposals made from the more or less radical conclusions derived from their economic thinking.

With regard to the labor theory of value, they were familiar with James Mill and McCulloch, the textbooks of the time, which held the return to capital was a return to congealed labor, the profits of capital really the wages of labor. Mill and McCulloch had only endeavored to tidy up Ricardo's relative value theory, not to prove all value was created by labor.

The value of production became a function of both the labor currently spent and the payment for congealed labor worn out during the period of production. This shows that labor is exploited: labor and "congealed labor" produces more than is necessary to keep labor, i.e. a surplus. It was argued that under the free labor and property system, labor gets only its necessary minimum of subsistence, the rest, a surplus, going to the capitalists and the landlords – similar to Marx's surplus value.

Thompson: Capitalists and landlords get part of the product not because of the productivity of capital (for it is only labor) but because of the dependence of labor on capitalist and landlord for employment, i.e. the institution of property.

There is a shift, therefore, from the view of capital as a technological factor of production, increasing the productivity of labor and independently creating some value, to a property relation – to use Marx's terminology, a social category not an economic one.

This exploitation of labor was an impediment to production, as it stifles the enterprise and incentive of the workers, and also checks progress and accumulation (quite the opposite to the Classical view which held the greater the rate of profit the faster its growth). Finally, the inequality of income, because of the property system, resulted in a reduction in the happiness of the community.

Hodgskin is Marxian in his doctrines. Capital is based on property relationships, not technological productivity. Circulating capital is identified with labor. The productivity and income-producing qualities of circulating and fixed capital depended on the use of current labor, i.e. the control of labor produces surplus value. Capital itself is unproductive – similar to James Mill and McCulloch.

Furthermore, the existing forms of government are powerless inasmuch as they are controlled by the property owners. Labor must overthrow the system for only then will class distinctions disappear and the state wither, using the same terminology Marx later also used.

Later, however, his belief in individualism and ultimate harmony got the better of him and, when confronted with the choice of equality or liberty, he chose liberty with the possibility of amelioration through gradual evolution coupled with a substantial laissez-faire policy. His economic thinking led to a criticism of existing institutions but his utilitarian social philosophy plus his basic individualism made him shrink back from where tread Marx, "made of sterner stuff" and a better economist in the sense of the ability to handle material.

Lecture

HEGEL

Marx in Relation to Hegel:

Marx derived most of the peculiar features of his methodology and viewpoint from Hegel and the Hegelians – at a minimum, a substantial amount; although Schumpeter in his *History of Economic Analysis* deprecates his reliance on Hegel, Professor Hans Gerth feels there is a great dependence on Hegel even in regard to Marx's economics.

Hegel is an "absolute idealist." Hume earlier questioned the ideas of rationalism and certainty; as an empiricist and skeptic he felt that causation often was mere association and the realm of ideas was imposed on the material and was not really there. Kant put forth a dualism of two worlds, the phenomenal world that is seen and studied, and the world in itself, reality, which was not knowable. Hegel, on the other hand, was an absolute idealist, holding that the real and the ideal were one, that there is no dualism; the notion that the idea is embodied in what we find. Reality is a manifestation of an idea, of reason; reality in fact tends to so evolve as to follow the process that ideas go through in their clarification – the dialectic process of two conflicting ideas and a reconciliation of them, synthesizing into a new proposition. Ideas evolve this way and so does reality, as it is modeled on the idea. The idea is the real thing, embodied in the actual.

Society similarly evolved in this dialectic process, i.e. history on the basis of conflicting ideas. A higher and higher synthesis as society comes closer to the absolute at the end where there are no contradictions. Social science is best conceived as this dialectical process. Time thus follows logic.

In all societies, categories embody these contradictions, i.e. classes representing conflicting ideas, and this leads to social evolution. He envisions agricultural, business and universal classes, the last above particular interests, a governing class. A continuous battle exists between classes on the basis of their leading ideas; inevitably, however, all social forms, etc. are determined by the reconciling idea. Perfect society is one the principle of which has no contradiction, exemplified by early nineteenth century Prussia, an absolute but highly benevolent monarchy. Similar to notion of classless society; to Hegel, government, by philosophers, reconciled the interests of the classes, similar to Plato's guardians. Furthermore, all persons identified themselves with the interests of the state.

Bertrand Russell (*Unpopular Essays*, No. 1), an extreme empiricist, differentiates between change (inevitable) and progress (value judgment). Critical of Marx's taking over Hegel's idea that history develops in this logical way; dialectics may make sense in logic but not in history, the problem of time. According to Marx, reality has the dialectic process; ideas only the reflection thereof, an inversion of Hegel.

Professor Earley feels that Russell's criticism of the dialectic in the physical sciences is well taken. It has more application to biology; in social science, it is a vision not a well-founded method, though it has more cogency: (1) we do have class conflicts in history; (2) social evolution does reflect wars among ideologies; (3) social sciences may be ideologically grounded. In social, economic and historical affairs, the Marxian suggestion, modified Hegel with regard to material influence, has very valuable keys to understanding social change.

Marx's philosophy of history, notion of how societies evolve, union of history and abstract analysis, distinguishes him from Classical political economy – not abstract timeless economics but cutting across every social science. Since Adam Smith, economics has tended to neglect structural considerations.

Marx had a vision, a compelling one, and built much on it. His economics carried out his vision; it was not derived from the material he was talking about. As a predictive mechanism, it is therefore difficult to use. As a creative mechanism, more than anything earlier.

Lecture

Hegel on Labor, Class Conflict, and the Evolution of Society:

Hegel had the general vision that society evolves in accordance with contradictory ideas, ideologies, through the dialectical process, the final society embodying the perfect proposition, i.e. one with no contradiction.

Marcuse, in *Reason and Revolution*, advances the thesis that the concept of labor is central to Hegel's thinking, that the more productive labor is, the less freedom and the less remuneration comes its way.

To Hegel, culture has several stages. In the first, there is direct appropriation by persons for their needs – similar to Locke's "state of nature." In the second, labor is used to organize and mold the objective world, which presupposes division of labor and therefore "society" and institutions, such as the wage system, property, the state, etc. This organization of the objective world determines the social institutions. Labor is transformed into an abstraction, a generality – universal abstract labor. Dire consequences flow from this. In the first period, impersonal market forces rule; in the second, government institutes a system of justice, but doesn't interfere with property. In the final stage, the authoritarian replaces the liberal, and bridles social and economic classes. Classical Political Economy he felt was apologetics for the existing social order which social order was incapable of establishing a rational community. Thus, Hegel (in *Philosophy of Right*, para. 196) has the notion that labor is a universal entity – "quantitative abstract labor" – which is exchanged, produced; this is his unifying, organizing principle of society.

Marx's economics, possessing new elements as compared to Classical Political Economy, exhibit Hegel's influence, whether direct of indirect:

(1) The immensely greater scope of social science, all embracing; included study of morality and ideology as well; economics was the key to explaining everything social; economics wasn't a separate or autonomous social science – changing the scope of economics, it was a part of a great social science, but a key part. The problem was not to describe society but to change it – working within what was inherent in capitalism, merely speeding up the process; indeed, Marx thought it was coming very rapidly – e.g. depressions, 1848 revolution, etc.

(2) Introduction of the dialectic – the study of contradiction; quite different from the harmony of equilibrium economics. Built on historical analysis.

(3) A highly dynamic and developmental study – a study of society in process of change not of structure.
(4) Use of class structure and conflict as basic analytical method – the focus of social study.
(5) Like Classical Political Economy but also like Hegel, the assiduous use of abstraction – a high level of generality.

Marx differed from Hegel in three respects:

(1) Inversion of causal factors from idea and ideology to material elements.
(2) Empirical and inductive studies important in building his case.
(3) Revolutionary versus the status quo.

Concerning dialectical materialism, Professor Earley quoted some passages contained in the small Modern Library Edition of Marx's writings, pp. 8–11.

The mode of production is the way in which men make their living, the techniques they use in the process thereof, and it is this mode of production which determines – conditions, more accurately [this clause seems to have been added by me] – men's social relationships and the consequent stress put upon the existing society. It is a concept of economic determination but behind it is a technical determination.

It is a potentially powerful organon for organizing social studies, and we must concur with Schumpeter that it is a big step forward for economics.

It fits well into Schumpeter's thesis ("Science and Ideology") that economics comes out of a vision necessitating further empirical verification, although one may question whether it is a vision of Schumpeter's sort at all, i.e. that it is simply a perception of relationships thought important and therefore basic and to be articulated in a model, or whether it is merely a backbone of a revolutionists handbook, a step in Marx's own work and not a neutral and true analysis of Marxism. Thus it would be an ideology reflecting class conflict, a proletarian substitute for Classical Political Economy, a theory to develop and expound a class-conscious proletariat.

Professor Earley feels that Marx had his own thesis when he came to economics (the *Communist Manifesto*) and sincerely felt that he was getting at the real truth, so confident was he of his own work. Earlier economic thinking – the Physiocrats, etc. – he felt was not truth because they reflected class interests; his was the viewpoint of a classless society seeing economics in the true light – i.e. labor is the cause of all value.

The strength of Marxism, especially in the light of empirical evidence and logical argument that doesn't shake its confidence, flows from this.

Lecture

MARXIAN ECONOMICS

Marxian and Modern Value Theory Compared:

Modern equilibrium theorists, Cannan for example, criticize Marx's labor theory of value, that value is created by the expenditure of labor power, on the grounds that labor actually destroys value by creating more products, i.e. by increasing the supply of products, under the assumptions of reproducible goods and under competitive conditions. Values, according to the neoclassical school, are *relative exchange rates* and are functions of the quantities supply (plus demand), and therefore the production of additional goods, *cet. par.*, tends to decrease rather than increase their value.

The Marxian criticism of this line of reasoning is that it avoids, not only neglects, the actual creation of value.

Both bourgeois and Marxian economists are discussing different issues – they are not discussing the same issue.

The general equilibrium theorist postulates that value is price, not embodied labor, i.e. value doesn't determine price but value is rather set by a price determined per demand and supply in relation to other commodities. Furthermore, supply prices must be paid to factors to get them to produce – price is determined by both demand and supply functions.

That the two groups are discussing two different things is seen from the Marxian retort that the general equilibrium analysis doesn't analyze "real cost" of further production. To the bourgeois group, there is no absolute real cost of further production, only opportunity cost.

Marx's "socially necessary labor" comes close to equilibrium theory but is still fundamentally different: he is speaking of the average unskilled labor that is socially necessary in the production of any commodity. (According to Marx, competition among the capitalists forces prices and thus the rate of profits down, through accumulation.

Marx's Contradictions within the General View of the Capitalist Economic Process:

Using Hegelian methodology, Marx pointed out several contradictions inherent in the capitalist process of production and in capitalism generally – which are to be contrasted with that of the true, community era.

(1) Contrasts the universal production of goods with the bourgeois forms of production: the former is the production of use value – closely related to utility notions – wherein production is not of value in an exchange sense but of use value. However, bourgeois production is the production of surplus value for the benefit of the capitalists – profits, not use value, is the purpose of the capitalist productive process. The natural form of production is in accord with the needs of consumers and socially necessary labor, but bourgeois economic systems are not interested in use value but in exchange value and the interest of the process is thus in surplus value.
(2) Contrasts natural exchange and bourgeois exchange, i.e. the difference between C-M-C and M-C-M′. Natural exchange, C-M-C, is the exchange of equivalents using money as an intermediary with no surplus coming out of the process; the final "C" may have a higher subjective value than the first "C", but it is such for each exchanger, under competition, thus balancing out. However, under bourgeois exchange, M-C-M′, one exchanges or invests money for a commodity and sells it for M′ which, if the person is successful according to the system's rationale, will be larger than M – the purpose of bourgeois exchange is profit in terms of money.

Marx is clear that if it was only an exchange process, one could not get more – but it is a productive process also, and labor has the unique characteristic of being able to create value greater than its own cost, i.e. surplus value, acquired through the consummation of exchange, i.e. its realization in money form.

Notice how Marx adheres to Physiocratic theorems and conceptions: he recognized and insisted that value couldn't be created by the exchange process itself, but only in the productive process. The Physiocrats also had a thorough-going cost doctrine and the notion of the net product which is important in the process – similar to Marx's interpretation of capitalism.

(3) Contrasts two views of capital:
   (a) The technological role as an aid to labor, "an extension of social labor" not something apart from labor, which increases the productivity of labor through the indirect use of labor, and saw its importance in this respect to progress and welfare – but it doesn't create value.
   (b) The bourgeois role of capital, in which capital has the power of commanding labor, i.e. capital is really the power to command labor in the bourgeois economy; one class owns the means of production, the other only its labor power and to get employment it must sell its labor power to the capitalists allowing the capitalist, as a normal matter

> and without chicanery or monopoly, to buy a good – labor power – which will produce more value than it cost the capitalists.

Classical economists envisioned capital as a purely technological category, as bridging time between seeding and harvest, but to Marx capital was a social category under capitalism – under communism it would be only a technological category. Capital under capitalism is inexorably tied up with the class struggle and loses its significance as only a technological category.

Marx's point of view implies built-in exploitation: capital is the power to get surplus value, which by definition is created by labor.

Theory of Value:

Marx held that the only element common in all values is labor. There is an infinite variety of use values, with no common denominator. Therefore, he stated that the only thing in common is their value in terms of labor. As Veblen was quick to point out, Marx offers no direct proof of this. It is, however, backed up later (Vol. I, Ch. V) by analyses of two groups of materials. First, he analyzes the refutation of the mercantilist views by the Physiocraata and the Smithians, that value was created in the exchange process and that, therefore, a favorable balance would increase value. Early critics, Smith for example, saw it as a partial view, i.e. that you can't create value in the process of exchange, and that what one nation gained was only at the expense of another. Marx adds that changes in value can only come about in the productive process, and that only labor can create value. The Physiocrats also saw that to exchange already-created values in the marketplace doesn't create new value. Second, Marx saw that in capitalist accounting over time, the cost of a machine was fully depreciated, being spread out over the tie period of its use and that resultant value is equal to the depreciation charges, i.e. what you get out is equal to what you put in. Constant capital cannot create any more value than there is in itself, only variable capital creates value; constant capital passes on embodied value produced by labor, but no new value. Constant capital applies to both machinery and raw material.

Lecture

The Marxian Economic Analysis:

The following analysis is so ordered as to lead up to the Marxian thesis as to how the capitalist system must eventually break down.

Surplus value: Although the mercantilists and the Physiocrats had earlier identified a "surplus," Marx undertook to explain how surplus value arises in capitalism, the conditions governing its rate of rise, and the conditions inevitably leading to its disappearance.

Marx's "surplus" theory is one in terms of exchange or capitalist *value*, *not* in terms of dollars (*money*) or *goods*: it is in terms of value only. He endeavors to show how a surplus can only be explained as an aggregate for the entire economy when commodities are sold at their true value – there is no chicanery or monopoly, etc., present in his theory. Surplus in capitalism goes to the capitalists and to the hangers-on, the lenders and rentiers. This value surplus is expressed in terms of profit, with interest merely a derivative of the profit "earned," the capitalist sharing the surplus value with the lenders who furnish the money for the former to engage in production; rent is also simply a form of the surplus and is therefore not indistinguishable from profit.

The *critical* proposition made by Marx is that *only labor creates value*, and that therefore the source of the surplus is the value created by labor – built-in exploitation. But this surplus, and the exploitation flowing therefrom, arises even though all goods are bought and sold at their *true* value. This is explained by the following reasoning process. Value is labor cost. With the wage system, labor sells, in order to gain their livelihood, the commodity of labor power which the capitalists buy and which, representing labor, will produce value, which value, furthermore, is more value than the labor power costs: this is because the capitalist pay for the quantity of labor only that amount required to maintain that supply of labor – the labor cost of producing the means of subsistence, which is less than what labor produces. This seemed to be obvious at his time due to the presence of an excess over what labor used for its subsistence and by definition it is a surplus, given by the excess of total value over labor's consumption, going to the capitalists and the hangers-on. This surplus is a portion of created value and is therefore *surplus value*.

The capitalist pays "variable capital" (V), the wages bill, to the workers, which is "variable" because the quantity of value coming from it in production grows, i.e. is greater than the outlay on labor (wages). V + S is the total value produced in the period; V is what the workers get, S is surplus value, appropriated by the owners, i.e. the capitalists. Using modern national income terminology within the Marxian system, V + S is net product, the quantity of value created. According to the bourgeoisie, S is profit.

The means of production, owned by the capitalists and used by labor, together with raw materials, are (both) constant capital (C), constant, not in terms of fixed capital, but in that it doesn't vary in value, i.e. it doesn't create additional value. Gross product is, then, C + V + S. All are amounts per time, not stocks;

therefore, C represents depreciation charges plus raw material cost. For any single commodity, Marx substitutes profit (P) for S (surplus value) in the value equation, so that C + V + P is price.

Rate of Surplus Value: S/V, the rate of exploitation; emphasizes "from whence comes the surplus," i.e. from variable capital.

Rate of Profit: S/C + V, C + V representing the capital investment of the capitalist on which he must earn a return.

Simple Reproduction: C + V + S goes on without any changes in the level of constant capital, i.e. no accumulation; surplus value is realized in such a system by the capitalists taking their surplus and consuming it. There can be, however, changes in the quantity of V+S without any change in C by prolonging the working day, intensifying the utilization of labor, and by changes in technology or technique with a given quantity of constant capital, serving to increase the value produced by labor and therefore tending to raise the surplus and therefore the rate of surplus value (exploitation). Since there is sufficient purchasing power to buy the total production, this can therefore go on quite indefinitely: without net accumulation, the capitalist system would get into no serious trouble. It is only when capital accumulation is introduced that capitalism's problems begin.

Note that Marx has set up his conceptual apparatus so as to prove that surplus (profits) is exploited – for only labor produces value, and surplus comes from value produced, therefore it is out of labor and thus there is exploitation.

Accumulation – Production on Expanded Scale: The growth of constant capital results in a rise in C/V, the organic composition of capital, an increase in the quantity of capital per given quantity of labor. Why does the capitalist seek to acquire more fixed capital? There are two answers, two reasons, one sociological, one economic.

I.

Marx invokes a sociological principle with regard to capital accumulation, namely that in the capitalist production of surplus value, such production becomes an end in itself, the capitalist *geist*, growing out of the productive relationships expressed by C + V + S. Marx saw a strong impetus to save and accumulate, whereas at the same time, J. S. Mill and Senior, etc., saw an inhibition against savings. Marx felt that the capitalist lived not to consume but to increase surplus value to increase wealth to increase the power to increase surplus value – the law of capitalist accumulation: capitalism is such that accumulation is inevitable; if not, there will be trouble. The lure is surplus value, expressed as a rate of profit by the capitalist, i.e. the profitability of production. If the rate of profit should decline or disappear completely, the capitalist ideology and modes of behavior would disappear and there would be tendencies to revolution.

As capital accumulates, the organic composition of capital (C/V) rises, and if S/C + V and S are constant, then to get a given rate of profit you need to increase S/V, for only V creates value and hence surplus value (S); if not, the rate of profit will fall.

Marx takes the position that while the impetus is strong to increase the rate of surplus value (S/V), it tends to reach a plateau and, therefore, as C rises, with S/V constant, the rate of profit, S/C + V, tends to fall.

It is to be noted that the problem of realizing the surplus value brings up the question of the demand side. [In margin.]

II.

The economic reason for capital accumulation follows this analysis: Under the competitive economic structure, at least in the beginning, it is in the interest of the individual capitalist to reduce his variable outlay, his wages bill, and one of the best ways to do this and still keep the same production level is to introduce more and more machinery, i.e. constant capital, which serves to increase technical productivity (the value produced by labor). Hence, there is a strong tendency to introduce machinery, notably labor-saving machinery.

Marx was conscious of economies of scale and pointed them out, but to produce on a larger scale normally requires more constant capital relative to labor input, i.e. more machinery; therefore, with regard to both the firm and the economy, the size of the firm grows as well as capital relative to labor, and the tendency of capital is to be concentrated in larger and fewer units.

Thus, capital accumulation arises because under competition the capitalist seeks to maximize his profit and it is advantageous to use more capital and minimize his labor expense. Since, however, it is variable capital that is the source of surplus value, the capitalist can only hope to keep up his rate of profit by increasing the rate of exploitation. This can take several forms. The first is to lengthen the working day. Marx didn't the question of the optimum working time, but in general felt that in industry it was very long: (a) because the manufacturer doesn't have to keep laabor in good health, he can use and then disemploy his labor; (b) new labor is brought in from the rural and colonial areas, i.e. a growing labor force; and (c) the reserve army of labor arising from the combination of falling rate of profit, disemployment, and sharp accumulation. Hence, the capitalist had no reason to worry about keeping up worker productivity.

Lecture

An Outline of the Marxian Theory of Capitalist Dynamics:

Propositions:

(1) That profits represent exploitation and are not the payment for some necessary service or abstinence endured; rather it represents the logic of a particular institutional structure by which those with power exploits those without power – the owners of the means of production under capitalism.

This is "proved" by the embodied labor theory of value which ipso facto proves that profits appropriated by the capitalists are part of the product of labor because only labor can produce value, i.e. proved simply by definition.

(2) That for capitalism to continue as a viable economic system and therefore continue to create surplus value, the object of the system from the viewpoint of those in power, there must be progressively more and more severe exploitation of labor; and that built into the capitalist system and into capitalist behavior are the drives and mechanisms to increase this exploitation.

(3) That there are limits to the increasing severity of exploitation and that therefore the system will in fact break down.

The Increasing Severity of Exploitation: Increase in the Rate of Exploitation:

Since only labor creates value, and since the accumulation of capital creates the tendency for the organic composition of capital to rise, the long run tendency of the rate of profit is to fall, despite the increasing severity of exploitation.

$$[V \rightarrow S;\ C\uparrow \rightarrow C/V\uparrow] \rightarrow S/C + V\downarrow$$

As long as constant capital increases more than in proportion to variable capital, the rate of profits will fall unless the rate of surplus value increases appropriately and sufficiently; that is to say, the theory doesn't rest on a model in which V or C + V remain constant through time.

The Marxian law of the falling rate of profit is thus a function of the increase in the organic composition of capital and the limits imposed on the degree of exploitation of labor.

Marx does recognize that the capitalists will make every effort to increase the rate of exploitation, and lists the following ways:

(1) The lengthening of the hours of work, given the intensity and efficiency of work, since the subsistence cost, the wage cost, is about the same regardless of the hours worked.
(2) The increasing of the intensity of labor, i.e. greater value output per unit of time.
(3) The decreasing of the value of labor power: lowering the wage bill (V) through lower costs of the means of subsistence; thus, *cet. par.*, if S is constant, S/V rises.

Although Marx recognized that a general increase in productivity wouldn't increase the rate of surplus value, he did see that particular increases lowering wage cost would increase the rate of exploitation. In this he was similar to Ricardo, who saw that to keep the rate of profit up it is necessary to reduce the cost of foodstuffs and hence the wages necessary to maintain a given living standard. Ricardo, however, felt that this would only be a palliative, for it couldn't prevent diminishing returns in agriculture.

(4) The employing of women and children as well as the heads of the family.
(5) Paying labor less than the value of labor power: this is less generic to Marx's system, indeed his system is built on the assumption that labor does receive the value of its labor power; it is not a normal or common occurrence but it is a possibility, occurring:
    (a) in the theory of crises, the rate of accumulation falls, thus rendering population redundant, thereby beating wages down; i.e. in any surplus population period;
    (b) as capitalism develops, there is a tendency toward the industrial reserve army, i.e. unemployment, through displacement by accumulation and thus wages will be driven down; only in a boom will there be full employment and a "normal" wage rate;
    (c) exploiting new population sources.

But there are limits to these stratagems and still with capital accumulation the tendency of profits is to fall. Why?

(a) Imperialist aspects of the above are transitional.
(b) Workers become militant with increasing severity of exploitation, form unions and bargain for higher wages, lower hours, prevent increases in intensity, etc.
(c) Humanitarian movements other than organized labor, re: intensity, women and child labor, etc.
(d) There are maximum limits to the length and intensity of work.

Thus, the rate of exploitation tends to reach a plateau and the rate of profits falls as the organic composition of capital rises and isn't offset by increases in the rate of exploitation.

Now, then, the individual capitalist entrepreneur, faced with a falling rate of profits, will in general endeavor to increase: (a) the length; (b) the intensity; and (c) the efficiency of his labor, in other words to decrease his per-unit wage cost and to raise the rate of exploitation.

He will lengthen the hours of work and increase the intensity of labor, and also take advantage of any of the other ways by which to heighten the severity of exploitation.

But he will also substitute labor-saving machinery for labor in his quest to cut costs. Now, given the same length and intensity of labor, such efficient, i.e. labor-saving, machinery will increase productivity and therefore output per man, thereby reducing the socially necessary labor cost of each unit, i.e. the unit value of product will diminish with increasing productivity.

Now, it is said that Marx defines his unit of labor as being invariable with regard to productivity. Is this a proper criticism?

Lecture

Increases in productivity are associated not only with machines, but also with the learning of new skills (not requiring the intensity of labor to be stepped up); both lower the value of the product inasmuch as they increase the number of units of product that labor can produce in any period of time.

Marx in general held that all improvements are increases in the productivity of labor – the sole productivity factor: better division of labor, involving an increase in skills and economies of scale; the introduction of machinery was part of the process of the demand for labor and the accumulation of capital; changing motive power from that of the worker to inanimate forces.

For his analysis, labor is considered as a unit, a standardized unit; from the standpoint of the "laboring," standardized with regard to effort and therefore standardized with regard to intensity. Marshall tried the same thing, regarding a unit of disutility, whereas Marx tried in regard to a standardized productive unit.

Marx recognized that productivity increases were advantageous to the capitalists even though they decreased the value of the output. Here again Marx points out paradoxes or contradictions.

(1) Contrasts position of individual firm with that of the economy as a whole – e.g. substitution of capital for labor thereby increasing unemployment

although cutting cost below the cost of competitors. But for the entire economy in equilibrium, value equaled the socially necessary labor time, and value was equal to price; thus this was not an escape for the capitalistic economy – they were merely cutting each other's throats.

Schumpeter had an analogous but not identical concept: innovation is the source of profits; in equilibrium, no profits would be earned; as long as innovation continues, profits are maintained and the capitalist economy is viable and potentially vigorous; but, in the long run, innovation tends to be taken over by the larger firms, tends toward monopolization, and sociological influences make capitalism enfeebled and socialism will eventuate. But as long as innovation is continued, however, there are profits.

With regard to Marx and equilibrium ("normal" situation), with value equal to cost of production, in the long run, increasing labor productivity was no great help; it wouldn't keep up the rate of profit (the Classical view), i.e. it would not leave a dynamic surplus. There would be improved exploitation of labor in the transition, but following the law of value, value tended in the long run to go down to the lower cost of the new process of production.

(2) Marx saw that increases in productivity would allow increases in the "mass of value," i.e. he was not solely concentrated on the rate of profit; the capitalist he saw was interested in the mass of profits so long as the rate of profit isn't so low as to be ruinous; hence productivity increases the mass and is applicable since the capitalist drives to increase both the mass and the rate. Two methods of doing this were: (a) finding more and cheaper labor; and (b) increasing productivity.
(3) Insofar as better productivity decreases the labor cost of producing the goods entering the cost of subsistence, i.e. wage goods, it would tend to keep up the rate of profit, increase the rate of exploitation, decrease the value of labor power be decreasing its cost of production.
(4) By reducing the demand for labor and therefore increase the industrial reserve army and therefore improve the bargaining position of the capitalists vis-à-vis labor, they could decrease the wage rate or at least prevent it from rising.

With regard to periodic crises and the eventual cataclysmic crisis, Marx departs from his long run analysis regarding value and says that the determinants of the wage rate are one of supply and demand, namely the rate of accumulation and the state of employment, and as the rate of accumulation grew ever faster, increasing the demand for labor, the wage rate may rise above the value of labor power and increase the living standards of the workers and thus tend to cut down the rate of profits, blunt accumulation, and reverse the investment process – but, also, any growth in the demand for labor from rapid accumulation is perhaps nullified by the effort of the capitalists, without conspiracy, to substitute machinery for labor, i.e. employ less, not more, labor by increasing the rate of introduction of machinery the effect of which is to lower the demand for labor and keep down the wage rate and keep up the rate of exploitation and the rate of profits.

In all this Marx saw contradictions: there would be misery in the working classes and therefore militancy in their ranks, and also this doesn't help keep up the rate of profit because in the long run it was to go down; furthermore, effective demand may become deficient and give way to a crisis.

To Marx increases in the organic composition of capital were inevitable, and, when coupled with the elastic but nevertheless real limits to the rise of the rate of surplus value, the long run tendency is for the rate of profits to decline.

All the above took place in the framework of accumulation; this accumulation possesses the following attributes:

(1) It served to increase both types of capital but fixed capital in the main.
(2) It was accompanied by the concentration of capital, i.e. in larger units of enterprise rather than a multiplication of firms.
(3) Concentration per se increases the organic composition of capital of the larger scale firms, but also centralization in the modern sense; thus larger and fewer with the smaller firms being gobbled up – monopolistic industry. This all implied a more rapid rise in the organic composition of capital as well as an increased foundation for labor organizations among the concentrated workers in these large firms; also the middle class and the small entrepreneurs disappear: polarization – fundamental to Marx.

Later writers, after Marx, pointed out that the increase in size of the firms enabled them to exploit now the consumers and (in modern terms) the workers as well as get benefits from government.

In the process of accumulation, i.e. substituting constant for variable capital, Marxian dynamics contends that unemployment will increase, thus causing the industrial reserve army to grow, which will tend to keep the wage rate down and the rate of surplus value up and thus maintain the rate of profits, but only by increasing the misery of the workers.

At this point we can mention two theoretical quagmires that Marx gets into, in addition to the problem of effective demand.

(1) The problem of equivalence between value and price where there are differences in the organic composition of capital.
(2) Whether the decline of the rate of profit is compatible with the thesis of increasing pauperization or at most a maintenance of the existing standard of living: inevitably the rate of profit is to fall, because the rate of surplus value reaches some maximum, and with constant capital increasing faster than variable capital, the rate of return on both (C and V) goes down: is this incompatible with increasing productivity and immiseration of the working class: if the rate of surplus value is constant, the workers get the same share of a growing total and if the population doesn't grow out of hand, real wages must rise (Joan Robinson, on Marx, c. p. 36).

Lecture

Two Contradictions in Marx:

There are two contradictions that may be pointed out at this time in Marx's analysis. The first has to do with the relationships between prices and values when the organic composition of capital is different among industries. The second concerns the incompatibility of the falling rate of profit and the idea that the rate of exploitation (of surplus value, i.e.) reaches a plateau and the concomitant immiseration of the workers.

I. The Contradiction between Values and Prices: Böhm-Bawerk:

Marx argued that: (1) only labor currently expended produces or creates value; (2) equal amounts of labor produce equal quantities of value; (3) labor power is purchased at its value, i.e. equal quantities of labor sell for equal wages; and (4) the value produced, gross product, is V plus S, i.e. C produces no net value, and *hence the rate of surplus value tends to be equal in all lines of industry.*

Furthermore, Marx argued that: (1) the price for all commodities that have the same C plus V is the same, i.e. assuming competition, that the profit rates on C plus V tend to be equal, i.e. the *price of production* is C plus V plus S (V plus S is the *value of production*, net product) and includes, of course, depreciation, and that the rate of profit tends to be equal.

That is: (1) the rate of surplus value, S/V, tends to be equal in all lines; the rate of profit, S/C + V, tends to be equal in all lines. But: both cannot be equal in themselves because Marx assumes that the organic composition of capital, C/V, is unequal between industries, i.e. for the rate of surplus value to be equal in all lines and for the rate of profit to be equal in all lines requires that the organic composition of capital be equal in all lines.

Given two commodities, A and B:

	Commodity A	Commodity B
Production price: C + V + S	1 + 3 + 1 = 5	3 + 1 + 1 = 5
Rate of profit:	1/1 + 3 = 25%	1/1 + 3 = 25%
But, value is created by the quantity of labor, V:	3:1	1:1
	V + S = 4 is value	2 is value
	S/V = 1/3 = 33%	1/1 = 100%

Marx saw that prices were not in accord with values; his explanation was that the economy integrates all production lines, and that products with high organic compositions of capital would sell at a price greater than their value. Profit, a proportion of net value created by labor, coming out of the rate of exploitation, for the economy as a whole is spread over total capital so that the rate of profit is equal throughout, is less than the rate of surplus value, and is declining as well. All this means that the theory of value – the labor theory of value – is not fitted to explain relative values in the real world, and that his conclusion that the rate of surplus value and the rate of profit can be determined for the economy as a whole is no more than what he began with.

Lecture

II. The Immiseration Contradiction:

This second contradiction within the Marxian analytical scheme bears on the validity of his analysis with respect to its predictive qualities especially in reference to the dynamics of capitalism.

Marx said that the rate of profit had a tendency to fall as capital accumulated, for two reasons: first, because the organic composition of capital rises, and second, because the rate of exploitation approaches a maximum. From this he also concluded that at best the real wage rate would remain constant – a minimum of subsistence theory of wages in terms of the value of labor power. From this, Marx envisioned the immiseration of labor, i.e. the failure of labor to share in the product, i.e. a declining share.

But, if productivity of labor increases, as Marx saw it would, and if the workers share in the same proportion, the value of V would go up, i.e. they would have a constant share of a growing total, given an approximately constant population. Thus, the falling rate of profit is incompatible with a constant real wage: a falling rate of profits implies that the rate of exploitation is at least the same, i.e. constant, and the workers are probably better off.

> For if the rate of exploitation tends to be constant, real wages tend to rise as productivity increases. Labour receives a constant proportion of an increasing total. Marx can only demonstrate a falling tendency in profits by abandoning his argument that real wages tend to be constant (Joan Robinson, p. 36).

The explanation for this in Marx's reasoning lies in his concern with output in terms of value units in labor terms. Thus, an increasing output reduced value. His analysis was not in *real* terms: an increase in total output meant to Marx that value would diminish because labor input decreased. Thus, while his thinking is satisfactory for his own analysis, he doesn't make sense realistically.

Marxian, Classical and Orthodox Profit Theory Compared:

The orthodox theory of profit, based on marginal productivity, states that as accumulation of capital increases relative to the quantity of labor (a higher and higher capital:labor – capital per worker – ratio), the marginal productivity of capital falls relative to labor and therefore the rate of profit falls.

Marx was similar to both Classical and orthodox theory in that all three propounded reasons for expecting the rate of profit to fall within capitalism, unless innovation kept up the rate on new investment (implicit in Marx). Schumpeter, of course, added to the statement of the orthodox theory that the rate of profit could be maintained through innovation. Modern stagnationist theory flows from analysis of ineffective demand, not from the capital side.

The orthodox theory is that a fall in the marginal product, accompanied by rising real wages, causes not only a larger wage rate but also a larger share going to labor as the price of labor goes up at the margin relative to capital. But Marx declared that productivity is unique to labor, and, furthermore, Marx used a global, not a marginal, analysis.

The Marxian Theory of the Development of the Industrial Reserve Army:

Through his "industrial reserve army," Marx was able to maintain: (1) that labor wouldn't be able to share in the rising productivity; and (2) that it would put a damper on any tendency for the wage rate to rise, thus worsening labor conditions.

The industrial reserve army, in a fashion similar to Ricardo's introduction of machinery and the displacement of labor, always tends to increase. The accumulation of capital is the accumulation of *constant* capital, in a broad sense the conversion of V to C, i.e. similar to the wages fund theory, which Marx refuted. Thus, with a rapid development of capitalism, the tendency for new investment to be labor-saving takes place at a rapid pace, always bringing with it disemployment. In this, Marx didn't sufficiently see that the reduction in the wage rate would make unprofitable the substitution of constant for variable capital – relative valuation analysis. His analysis also implied some fixity of V, i.e. that it is not expandable.

This concept, that the keeping of the wage rate down so as to maintain the rate of profit, would cause mass unemployment was not worked out well in Marx's writings; furthermore, it is doubtful analytically as well.

It is not analytically clean cut, and often is inconsistent internally, although there is much plausibility to it in a fast-developing capitalism regardless of reason: the falling rate of profit, the declining rate of new investment because of it, the diminution of effective demand; and continuous technological unemployment – labor-saving capital development – is certainly not a mirage. All combine to make capitalism run with less than optimum smoothness.

The Problem of Effective Demand:

With regard to effective demand, Marx maintained an ambiguous position:

(1) In general, Marx was prone to reject the theory that the lack of purchasing power would create underemployment and cause crises; in this, he was similar to orthodoxy. Differing from Rodbertus and others, Marx argued that exploitation, i.e. the fact that labor gets only part of its product, did not mean a lack of purchasing power. This was because the essence of capitalism, as Marx envisioned it, was that the capitalists appropriate surplus value and either consume or invest it, thus effecting no diminution of purchasing power.
(2) Marx pointed out that V plus S, less than total cost by C, means income is less than gross product, i.e. by C, but that once again there would be no resultant deficiency of purchasing power: the setting aside of C means that labor is employed in the capital goods industries for purchases to replace the old, depreciated constant capital. Thus, Marx denied Major Douglas's thesis that depreciation is a debit against income.
(3) Marx had the view, similar to that of orthodoxy, that if much surplus value was saved, it did not necessarily cause any deficiency in effective demand, except with regard to savings and investment, perhaps. By assuming that savings led to investment, like the orthodox, he rejected over-saving theory as a first approximation.

Marx, however, did have several difficulties that he found with regard to effective demand; and the resultant lack of effective demand, he felt, might cause recurrent and increasingly severe crises:

(1) Analysis of disproportionality between outputs and demand of consumption and investment goods industries.
(2) The notion that disemployment of labor by labor-saving capital, plus the fact that the labor share tends to go down, would mean that the accumulation processes would inhibit capitalist growth, in fact bring about the reverse, namely crises.

Disproportionality:

In this regard, Marx generally assumed that the total V is equal to consumption goods, and that the total C is equal to producer goods.

Now, when there is *no* net accumulation out of surplus value, i.e. under simple reproduction, the only necessary requirement is to produce replacement investment goods, as well as consumer goods. If, at any time, the capitalists slacken their purchases of constant capital goods so as not to replace that which depreciated, then the division of production between investment and consumption industries is inappropriate to the demand situation, and a crisis in the capital goods industry, and thence to the economy as a whole, ensues. Thus, a failure to replace in equal value the depreciated capital causes employment and production in capital goods industries to fall and for output as a whole to fall. Marx envisioned waves of capital replacement as the important cause of the capitalist cycle, i.e. bunched – but this was not well worked out.

However, although he doesn't work it out, he does indicate that a failure of investment might cause a crisis, i.e. a recession or a depression.

Marx didn't work it out for the normal case of accumulation, where surplus value is reinvested; but it is clear that his "monster" is that changes in capital expenditure due to changing situations and expectations of the capitalists (e.g. wage movements as the demand for labor rises, etc.), are strategic and in this he is working toward a theory similar to present Keynesian and other saving and investment analyses, and the relationships between saving and investment are strategic in cycles and possibly in regard to long run secular stagnation.

Marx, to repeat, places his prime reliance for recurrent and increasingly severe crises on: (a) the falling rate of profit; and (b) the industrial reserve army.

By setting up two categories, consumption and investment, Marx grabbed hold of a modern device in cycle analysis.

But he added words that the inherent trouble is that the workers are kept down by a constant real wage rate, etc., implying that at bottom capitalist institutions and contradictions were responsible for labor not getting an increasing share.

Professor Earley stated that he had concluded that Marx's theory is similar to that of Hobson – the disproportionality between capital development and consuming power. But, with Marx, it is mixed up with his own theory to the effect that in the productive process, not in the distributive process, are the reasons that the workers do not share fully in the fruits of progress.

In general, the labor theory of value gave him a start, but it proved to be an incubus by the end, i.e. all his analysis had to be in terms of *its* categories, those of the labor theory of value.

Thus, Marx pointed out several difficulties of capitalism:

(1) The tendency of the rate of profit to fall.
(2) Technological unemployment.
(3) The failure of effective demand.
(4) The tendency toward monopolization, i.e. a smaller number of larger firms.

On the one hand, there would be a small number of monopolies and the rate of profits would fall; on the other, there would be the masses of workers, being maintained at a minimum of subsistence (usually below it) and for the most part unemployed, who therefore would become militant as they recognized the bipolarization going on. Thus, they would unionize, and hence to the "revolution," which Marx nowhere discusses in detail.

Lecture

An Appraisal of Marxian Economics and Sociology:

I. Marx's Structural Analysis of Capitalism
II. Marx's Process Analysis of Capitalism (Dynamics)
III. Marx's Social Dynamics

I. Marx's Structural Analysis of Capitalism:

This part of the Marxian schemata is determined by his point of view and the purposes for which it was derived, and in those terms it is an admirable and masterful analysis.

Basic Categories

Value: attached to labor; the real productive force and a basic non-contradictory social category.

Capital: control over labor by the property-owning class; an institutional category representing the power of the owners of the means of production over labor, employing all labor, thus giving rise to the dualism of economic categories reflecting his sociological categories.

Profit, interest and rent: surplus value; follows logically and is a key concept in his system; goes to the owners of capital because of their command over labor.

Exploitation: capital not a productive service; exploitation arises automatically out of the system as Marx characterizes it.

Marx uses these categories in analyzing problems of value, distribution, etc. From the point of view of the proletarian critique of capitalism, it is well devised and skillfully used.

It is noteworthy to recognize that Marx's sociological categories are tied in with his economic categories, the propertied versus the non-propertied.

With regard to the problems treated by Marx, namely, value, pricing of products, allocation of resources, distribution of income, etc.: (1) Marx uses too wide categories, i.e. they are not sufficiently differentiated. His differentiation between capital and labor, as remarked above, is more sociological than in terms of economic behavior: Classical political economy's classification of land, labor and capital (and later "management" or risk taking) was, it is true, partly on sociological grounds, but mainly because of the different behavior due to the particular conditions of economic supply of each "factor." It is to be noted that the Austrians later did away with this sociological basis. (2) Marx's categories do not stand up with regard to relative price. The basis for an insightful analysis of profit, interest and rent – the elements of surplus value – is absent. The labor theory of value as a quantum of value created or produced gets one into trouble in all these problems.

II. Marx's Process Analysis of Capitalism (Dynamics):

Here we can say that Marx made a greater contribution, partly because it was a new field, partly because he didn't make the same assumptions that others before and after made, and partly because he had a more realistic grasp of the nature of capitalism and how it ticks.

We can analyze this aspect of Marx by noting several elements successively:

(1) The dominant proposition in the dynamics of capitalism is the capitalist's drive, their quest for *money* profit, not being satisfied with either the mere satisfaction of utilities or with merely making a living.
(2) The quest for profit involves the purchase of labor power, a key and necessary activity, so as to make a profit, i.e. must get command of labor power.
(3) The capitalist drive plus the necessities of competition are such that the capitalist system forces reinvestment of these profits, i.e. an accumulating rather than a static society.
(4) In their quest for profits the capitalists endeavor to minimize the wage outlay that is a major cost of doing business.
(5) This leads to the growing scale of enterprise as well as to the growing concentration of enterprise – the more successful beat out the less successful – plus the tendency toward technological unemployment.
(6) This leads to increasing difficulty in the realization of surplus value (profit).

Professor Earley offered the conclusion that Marx's structural categories got him into serious trouble and thus accounts for many of his errors of prediction. For example: (a) the declining rate of profit is not necessary even as Marx pictures it, for the rate of exploitation may rise, innovation or lower interest rates may present themselves; and (b) regarding the immiseration of the proletariat, the wage rate may go up without reducing the rate of profit in a productive society. It is to be noted, however, that it is the structural categories, not so much the labor theory of value, that gets Marx into trouble here, as the labor theory of value did regarding pricing and distribution.

The crucial point is that capitalism is incapable of basic social change until the capitalist economic system is overthrown, i.e. it is always pure capitalism, even if it is not fully competitive: the profit drive, the drive to accumulate, government as the board of directors of the bourgeoisie, labor not able to exercise much of a voice in society or in government – nothing happens until things collapse, as "indeed that must with capitalism."

III. Marx's Social Dynamics:

In this field, Marx did much pioneer work; perhaps his greatest contribution lies here. Several elements that we must attribute to Marx, as their propounder and as the one responsible for their being introduced in social study, are:

(1) The economic interpretation of society systematically developed, putting people on the right track for "the economy is the center, the hub, of society and brings forth changes in society" (Professor Earley).

(2) The building of sociology on class conflicts versus class harmonies.
(3)) The treatment of the relationships between economics and politics.

Social Evolution: Marx envisions a two-class system, the antagonisms inherent between which get sharper with time due to immiseration and the industrial reserve army and, which is better recognized, the increasing bipolarization resulting in increased class consciousness.

When it breaks down as an economic system, the sociological bases for revolution in both social and economic institutions is prepared: there is in Marx great consistency regarding the final economic crisis leading to fundamental social changes. Indeed, Marx has an impressive edifice built on the two concepts of class conflict and economic determinism as the determinants of social history.

Critique: Notwithstanding the unfortunate effects of his choice of categories regarding pricing and distribution, here and elsewhere, the fundamental basis for Marx's errors in prediction was the labor theory of value. In addition, other categories, theses, and concepts were fatally defective:

(1) Marx's simplification of the economic class structure as a result of the evolution of capitalism (i.e. bipolarization) did not come about; indeed, he would have been more fortunate if he had not chosen the terms proletariat and capitalist.
(2) Marx misconceived the relations between the state and economic groups, that in effect the dominant economic groups would control the state, as their handmaiden; whereas a more realistic view is that: (1) the state has become bureaucratic and tries to reconcile rather than decide in favor of one or the opposing interests; and (2) groups gain political power not only on the basis of property but also on votes, prestige, and indeed the politician himself is something of a businessman engaged in a highly competitive business (Schumpeter).
(3) Marx misjudged the behavior of the proletariat in Britain and the U.S. as well as Germany. Labor organizations cease to behave like Marxian proletarians and engage in job and security consciousness – business unionism, not revolutionary. Perlman's thesis is quite the opposite of Lenin and Marx. Regarding Lenin, there was the emphasis on the Party as leading the workers; regarding Marx, there was the stress on the growing consciousness of the workers but there was also the recognition that there is the need to educate the workers to accelerate the pace – as seen by Marx's own efforts.

Thus, one can conclude that there are adequate substitutes for Marxian theory along most of the lines he worked at for the range of problems he dealt with.

Indeed, we have had Neoclassical monopoly and monopolistic competition theory regarding pricing, distribution and allocation; Keynes, Hicks and Harrod on cycle theory; Schumpeter on cycle theory but also, and more important, on economic development; and the institutional economists (including Schumpeter) on the relationships between economics, politics and sociology. But it must be recognized that all of these recent non-Marxians grew out of the impetus Marx gave to certain kinds of thinking neither known nor well-developed before his time and his work.

The Marxian System as a Science or an Ideology:

Capital was to Marx not a discourse in bourgeois social science but a revolutionist's handbook. With regard to the characterization as to whether social science is to be predictive or to be an engine of what one wants to happen, one can say, and it is here that Marx has had his power to last so long so strong, that Marx was not clearly in one or the other but that, in both, there are contradictory elements in his work.

Lecture

Marx held the view that previous political economy was ideologically distorted, representing the analysis of capitalism from the viewpoint of bourgeois concepts and interests; he held this to be inevitable in a class society – that its sciences, and especially its social science, reflect the interests of the dominant class.

On the other hand, Marx put his work forward as free from bourgeois shackles, viewing capitalistic society from the standpoint of a classless (on the basis of property ownership) society.

It is evident, however, that an alternative way of viewing the schemata of Marx is that it is the antithesis of bourgeois political economy, i.e. inasmuch as it is from the proletarian standpoint (the propertyless workers), it represents an equally special point of view.

The "bourgeois" concept of science is that it discovers facts, and truth, without ideological bias by being objective, controlled, and free of value judgment.

The Marxian attitude is that such a view is inherently impossible in bourgeois culture; any vision inevitably reflects class interests and conditions. Inasmuch as science grows out of the methods of production and property relationships, his point of focus – no class divisions – is therefore undistorted, the argument goes.

It is evident, however, that quite on the contrary, Marx set up his analysis from the standpoint of those interested in overthrowing the status quo, i.e. that his is the science of revolution, and *Capital*, especially of Marx's writings, is the revolutionists' handbook – not "objective."

Both *external and internal evidence* can be offered in defense of this accusation and portrayal:

External Evidence:

(1) The timing of his works: the *Manifesto*, written in 1847, published early in 1848, is a revolutionary pamphlet with the outline of the basic propositions developed later in *Capital*: class structure, labor theory of value, exploitation and its increasing severity, and the falling rate of profit. Inasmuch as his basic ideas were first put forth in this propaganda document, it is rather dubious that he had his conclusions before he studied political economy – i.e. no cognitive vision.
(2) Marx was an active revolutionary all of his life: "the problem is not to explain but to change the world"; throughout, he was anti-status quo.

Internal Evidence:

(1) In *Capital*, the way in which he followed out his argument, despite confusions, contradictions, etc., regarding the labor theory of value; declining rate of profit, steady rate of exploitation, and immiseration of the working classes

    In part, his work is due to the working out of a vision, one of how to effectuate a revolution; and, in part, to explain easily-seen aspects of capitalism (introduction of machinery, concentration of capital) carrying through but always adhering to two basic theorems from which he started as a revolutionary zealot and not an analyzer:
    (a) All values were in accord with labor.
    (b) Class conflict is solely between capital-less proletariat and monolithic class of capitalist entrepreneurs.

Nevertheless, combined with much observation, there is in Marx analytical work of a high order; furthermore, he treated aspects that were neglected by other political economists, such as industrialism, the introduction of machinery, etc. Though we have here a revolutionary vision, there is also much work of considerable value; in the main, Marx fits Schumpeter's thesis quite well. He was a capable thinker who started with a vision, defective in regard to ideology, and with a lack of knowledge, and who worked out a theory in part productive, subject to pruning and to change, yielding in the process substantial contributions to economic science.

He had revolutionary zeal; a young Hegelian not satisfied with the Prussian system as perfect.

Marx and Cycles (Crises):

The thesis of Malthus of the lack of effective demand was childish to Marx, who recognized that the capitalists' share is also purchasing power, whether it goes into consumption or investment. Hence, Marx's position is that under-consumption theories of the cycle are wrong. Indeed, the dichotomy between under-consumption and over-production is poor if not meaningless in Marxian terminology.

The capitalists' drive to accumulate means that investment is brisk; the problem, as Marx saw it, arises from two facts: (a) that in the long run the falling rate of profit will blunt accumulation and hence there will be a lack of effective demand for labor, and (b) that accumulation displacing labor would disemploy labor and lead to growing unemployment; not due to over-saving or to over-production except in the long run.

Thus, Marx's crisis theory is built upon his laws of value and the rising organic composition of capital. The thinking of John A. Hobson, on the other hand, is built upon income distribution and over-saving.

Lecture

Guest Lecturer: Professor Paul Sweezy, April 30, 1955 [the typed notes read 1956 but that appears to be in error; no other lectures are dated]

Is Marxian Economics Obsolete?

Professor Sweezy noted with disfavor the meager and poor quality of work of remodeling Marxian economics, including in the USSR. This he coupled with rigid dogmatism and fundamentalism. He quoted from Sartre to the effect that Marxism provided a frame of reference but that it was silent, not expanding and not alive. Despite these shortcomings of the state of Marxian economics today, Professor Sweezy declared that nevertheless Marxism was the only satisfactory approach to view the course of history.

On methodology, Professor Sweezy noted that the weakness of bourgeois social science was the "tyranny of conceptualization," namely, that social scientists are dominated by their models. Marxism, he declared, denies the breaking up of the real totality into social sciences: economic theory is sterile when considered independently of the political factor.

Harking back to the continuing value of Marxian economics, Professor Sweezy declared the theories of labor value and surplus value are valuable approximations showing the economic and class structure, the economic process, and can, he noted, be used as a theory of economic development satisfactorily. He stated that these theories require heroic abstraction, but this was just like any general price theory. He noted a kinship between surplus value and Ricardo's theory of profits (differential cost and the productivity of labor), and Joan Robinson's comment that there is no bourgeois theory of profit.

Lecture

Remarks on Sweezy's Lecture by Professor Earley:

Professor Sweezy considered the labor theory of value useful in connection with the exploitative character of the capitalistic economy, based upon an essential sociological conflict. The labor theory of value keeps it in focus and is devised to emphasize this point of view. The labor theory of value, remarked Professor Earley, is adequate unless the class struggle – the major element in the system – misconceived.

Professor Sweezy feels that the labor theory of value, which it cannot perhaps be applied to price, distribution or cycle problems, is applicable to problems of economic growth. With considerable ideological value, it emphasizes the rate of exploitation. Furthermore, indefinite capital accumulation leads to a top-heavy capital structure. Concerning this, Professor Earley noted that while this is an important problem, it is not unique to Marx: Smith, Ricardo, marginal productivity theory, Schumpeter and Keynes all encompass its elements.

The main stress, it was pointed out, of Professor Sweezy's lecture on "Is Marxian Economics Obsolete?" is that: (a) while very little advance has been made in the theory to date in recent years; (b) the theory does call attention to the interdependence of the social sciences. Professor Earley noted the line of questioning begun by Professor Perlman and carried on by Professor Rotwein and himself on the point of monistic causation in Marxian analysis, that the economic determination of history is perhaps too narrow and exclusive.

Lecture

THE REVOLUTION OF 1870

The period includes three groups, for present analysis:

(1) Those who emphasized the subjective theory of value and the theory of imputation – as a corollary development – as the basis for the theory of distribution – the psychological school, to use Gide and Rist's term, namely the Austrians.
(2) The system of general equilibrium – Lausanne – related to the theory of subjective value and theory of imputation but not coterminus therewith.
(3) Earlier developments in mathematical economics.

Notwithstanding the many distinctive features associated with each, they may nevertheless be identified together on four counts:

(1) Contrast with most earlier economics, especially in Great Britain, and of course with Marx; attempted to separate economic analysis more sharply from social setting and from social categories; a factor of production is no longer distinguishable by social class, i.e. the propertied and non-propertied; rather, all factors of production are identified in terms of substitutability in relation to other factors, and by certain behavior in connection with the supplies thereof – Böhm-Bawerk's distinction between natural resources and produced capital. Marx, of course, was the most extreme of the earlier group. Hence, no longer is there a vision of income distribution in accordance with classes as merely a pricing problem, but there is the separation of economic categories from their sociological setting.
(2) Turn to micro-analysis, the analysis of the behavior of individual economic units of decision – factor owner, consumer; hence utility analysis and the building up of the theory of value from individual utility analysis. Earlier, each segment, e.g. agriculture, was treated as a whole.
(3) Subjective psychological approach – especially the Austrians though also but to a lesser extent or degree the Lausanne school.
(4) Explicitly formulated analyses in static terms in the sense that they didn't deal with the long-run development of capitalism as did Ricardo, Stuart Mill, and Marx, but with the situation of a given point of time, seeking to work out equilibrium conditions for that moment given the supplies of factors of production, preferences, and technology, deferring until later dynamic analysis (processes through time, changes in data).

Why did such a revolution flower?:

(1) A natural reaction to Marx's uproar. Marx took Classical political economy – the labor theory of value – and came up with a view of society as exploitative and with a trend headed toward disaster. Indeed, with Böhm-Bawerk and Menger this was an important motivation.
(2) Their characteristics had appeared before:
    (a) The Physiocrats: induced reaction in Condillac toward a subjective theory of value, that exchange per se was also productive, that unequal values exchanged, that utility and not mere physical measure was the source of value.
    (b) J. B. Say took over Adam Smith's ideas, but changed them by emphasizing that what is produced is subjective utility, that processes of the economy are directed by demands of consumers based on

subjective factors, and hence entrepreneurs gather factors of production, valuing theme as they contribute to the sales proceeds based on consumers' values. This, though, was only in general outline and with no real development. Hence, factors of production provide productive services to the value of the product; all factors of production are demanded by entrepreneurs to produce goods valued by consumers.

(c) In England, Senior, Bailey, Longfield and others suggested the importance of subjective factors on the demand side, vis-à-vis subjective or objective factors on the supply side as determining value.

(d) In Germany, psychological factors on demand side were in orthodox texts from the beginning; but did not cut a big figure in the history of economic thought. Though he was not a subjectivist, von Thunen had the notion of factors valued by their relative value in the market. Gossen had significant ideas but was not paid any attention.

(3) Micro analysis:

(a) Previously used global categories invited closer analysis.

(b) No bourgeois counter-revolution is necessary to explain it.

(4) Static formulation:

The Ricardo-Mill predictions of the future of capitalism, derived from the labor theory of value and from distribution, were suspect as not borne out, questioned as to making predictions on such a small structure of knowledge and theorems. Result: a natural division of work and proliferation of theorizing.

Indeed, there was a new fashion of social science in the early 19th century, Comte and positivism. Say, Saint-Simon and Stuart Mill (*Logic*) were reacting to the Hegelianism and historicism in social thinking growing up in Germany, seeking a more objective formulation of examination of social phenomena, not underlying ideas, values and trends; don't go below phenomena, exorcise ideology from social science, otherwise it is not scientific as are the physical sciences.

Comte, nevertheless, had his own historical law, the three stages in the development of all philosophic thought:

(a) The theological: irrational, revelations
(b) The metaphysical: abstract entities, essences, substances; e.g. labor theory of value.
(c) The positive: see facts "in their empirical certainty" with all their interconnections.

Such an approach attracted Stuart Mill and Say (later editions): get a structure of society at a given point of time and know it thoroughly and then proceed to study processes:

(a) Social statics: laws of coexistence of variables
(b) Social dynamics: laws of succession of variables; a progressive improving tendency; continuity.

The course of history is a natural process, governed by natural laws, identifiable by studying social statics.

Eliminate value judgments (metaphysical) and go slow.

Also, there is definite order and perhaps harmony in the social structure, as in celestial mechanics; identifiable with the notion of harmony of interests and maxims of laissez faire, though not necessarily, however. This may be contrasted with Marx and his dialectics.

Positivism was a reaction to the use of Hegelianism by reformers, socialists, etc.

Nevertheless, Comte himself was not innocuous to problems.

This was Comte's contribution: study the thing at a point of time, not what it is becoming. Especially attractive to Lausanne; to Austrians, somewhat.

The Classical system, on the other hand, was not what it might be in regard to the realism of its postulates or its fruitfulness, nor its theorems: psychological aspects were neglected, as was the demand side, and there was no unifying principle. Furthermore, it hadn't handled monopoly or allocation of resources with reference to value and distribution in which fields there was thus much pioneer work to be done – and Marx showed the danger of leaving it unreformed.

(5) Another cause of the flowering of the Revolution of 1870 was the natural inventiveness of man, e.g. Jevons.

As a result, it may be said that this new course of political economy, now economics, leads to still waters, to the examination of trivia, not very suitable for reformers, fitting in well with the academic environment.

Lecture

We will continue to discuss the central theoretical characteristics of these groups from the methodological standpoint, doctrines, and their place in the history of economic doctrines.

(1) They each had, in common, a systematic micro-analytical approach, as well as, though less universally, a fairly explicit static approach or formulation. Their problem was formulated as one of valuation: the formation of values, starting from those of the individual and building up to an analysis of values of items in the economy as a whole, under varying market conditions

but in general a world of almost perfect competition and perfect or near-perfect knowledge.

They started with the individual valuing consumption goods on the basis of subjective desires, preferences, needs, wants: this starting point gives unity to the group, a greater unity than had existed before. Rather than diverse strands of doctrine about rent, wages, etc., all were wrapped up into one theoretical problem.

Value thus had its origin in subjective factors and not in technological conditions.

Pareto etc. rebelled against this later without taking up a counter-position, extracting the subjective element from the functions dealt with, using only the functions themselves.

Thus, the important subjective factors were found on the demand side: from the demand for consumer goods comes the basis for the values of factors – derived from their value contributions to consumer products.

(2) In direct contrast to Smith, Ricardo, and Marx, they rejected *real cost* as the determinant of value or of distributive shares, and substituted an *opportunity cost* concept – a basic change in the theoretical structure.

In the work of Wieser we find this clearly worked out. Cost goods are contrasted with free goods (non-scarce) and monopoly goods (specific to one particular use, i.e. no important alternative use), cost goods, having alternative uses, having a "cost" in the sense of the foregone use in other lines by virtue of using it in any one particular line – foregone opportunity is the relative cost. Not only must the goods have alternative uses but they must be regularly and continuously produced and under perfectly static competitive conditions.

Even here he saw that the foregone alternative reflects utility and hence there is still (again) no essential real cost: Values are not in accordance with any "labor" or "pain" cost, but with *marginal utility*. Thus, they appear as working out an "economics of exchange" in which valuation is seen as a problem of exchange, incorporating problems of production (combining factors so as to maximize value, minimize foregone utility) and distribution.

This type of reasoning led to the marginal productivity theory of distribution in which the marginal products of the factors of production are determined by their value contribution to the product, influenced by their scarcity and not any inherent productivity or cost. This fit in well with their static framework. They assumed a given factor supply. The only thing involved is to allocate factors among their alternative uses.

Another contribution is their analysis of imputation that, while not a sufficient theory of distribution and of valuation, was a facet of factor choice and pricing. The price system is thus a unified whole.

Their opportunity cost doctrine is valuable in the theory of allocation. Furthermore, they provided an indispensable element for the theory of allocation that hitherto had been missing, namely, demand analysis.

They made an important contribution to the theory of welfare economics, emphasizing the allocation of resources. They saw for the first time the thing to be maximized – consumer welfare.

Another contribution is the immense sharpening of marginalism as an analytical tool through their imputation analysis and opportunity cost analysis. Marginalism was thus applied to the consumer, to the behavior of the firm, and to factor combinations.

They revealed clearly and emphasized the interdependence of all elements in a static economic system – especially the Lausanne school, but also Jevons and the Austrians.

THE VIENNESE GROUP: MENGER, BÖHM-BAWERK, WIESER

Perhaps their most special characteristic is their interest in conceptualization as such – the derivation of proper concepts – not quite in line with positivism.

Hence they raised the question: What is "value," i.e. the correct concept, an entity – a relationship and not a quantity. Thus, they set up the case for the subjective theory of value and endeavored to refute both the Classicists and Marx.

The weakness of Marx was his emphasis not on value as a relationship but as an embodied quantity.

Value must exist prior to exchange, not found just in the market. Value expresses the relation between an individual and his environment, and is a function of the degree of his dependence on the particular thing valued. Thus, as did Menger, they saw a system of valuations brought to market: a schedule of values for different products.

Jevons demonstrated his marginal utility relationship, derived for each product individually from the utility hypothesis: the downward sloping marginal utility curve.

Menger and Böhm-Bawerk, following Dawson, recognized the utilities but denied that they are derivable independently, inasmuch as they express interrelationships between different commodities (complementary goods, e.g.), in accordance with some overall consumption plan. But, they agreed, utility does have a cardinal measure.

Hence, theirs is a psychological theory: the value concept is psychological – utility increments – not just price (system) economics.

In the principle of utility is the real cause of value, scarcity given by nature, plus the insatiable desire for satisfaction. This was carried by imputation to the valuing of factors of production.

Thus,

(1) there is the explicit introduction of rationality, and with it the basic elements of Robbinsian economics;
(2) the proposition that utility is cardinal;
(3) opportunity costs traced back to foregone utilities, not just opportunities;
(4) all this was worked out without much mathematics.

Another characteristic, something Böhm-Bawerk treated very clearly in regard to capital and interest, is the distinction between *original and produced factors of production*. Land and labor were original in the sense that they are in existence and not analyzed on economic grounds. Land and labor are used to produce intermediate goods (capital goods) which are then used to produce consumption goods. All imputation goes back to the original factors of production over the long run. He didn't see mutual interdependence here; he saw causal relationships only, and had therefore a narrow view of the problems of economics.

All value productivity is trade back to the original factors; if a capital good has value because it is scarce and contributes to the value process, then the resources producing it have value imputed to them. Produced factors of production can have a net value product only because of psychological over-valuation of present goods – contrary to the exploitation theory of interest as a rate of profit, as well as to the technical productivity theory and the abstinence theory. Rather it is a function of perspective, of the length of the production period; an *agio* theory. This net value product is not imputed back to the original factors because they have to be used over the long, roundabout process, and are the most discounted of all. Still, therefore, basically psychological:

(1) Impatience with regard to the future.
(2) Better prospects for provision of future goods; high value, therefore, on present goods.
(3) Technical superiority of present goods – can be used in roundabout productive process.

Lecture

Böhm-Bawerk's Theory of Interest:
Characteristics: Roundabout process of production is a function of time. Final consumer goods are present consumer goods. Roundabout processes are

technically more productive. Discount of value of ultimate factors and intermediate goods due to: (a) impatience; (b) expectation of being better off in the future; (c) present goods enable one to carry through roundabout processes using the more efficient methods, i.e. not entirely an *agio* theory (time discount) but that roundabout processes are more efficient. Hence the value of labor is also discounted as against present consumer goods: labor must work in short periods not roundabout – the reason why labor does not get the full value of the product (products are future goods): gets him back close to notion of capital as a wages fund, as circulating capital.

With respect to the efficiency, i.e. superiority, of the use of capital over the longer roundabout processes of production, Böhm-Bawerk saw decreasing returns to the use of capital, i.e. he saw some increase in technical productivity with an increase in the period of production but with diminishing returns.

Equilibrium, as we will now see, is a function of the rate of interest, the supply of capital, and the length of the period of production: the marginal productivity of capital is a function of the length of the period of production, with diminishing returns to roundabout processes of increasing duration. The supply of the factors of production is assumed to be constant, so that the marginal yield and the rate of interest are equal at the margin.

Böhm-Bawerk did recognize that an increase in saving would lower the rate of interest by extending the production period.

The wage rate is determined by the rate of time discount appropriate to the length of the production period.

Schumpeter has this same Austrian notion that the value of consumer goods is imputed back to the original factors of production: his theory of the stationary state (circular flow) is one without innovation and net investment, and is one in which the interest rate is equal to zero. He thus questions Böhm-Bawerk's argument for discounting.

Böhm-Bawerk corrected the Marxian theory of exploitation; the labor theory of value is itself defective. Schumpeter has observed, however, that the exploitation notion still remains: those without property, as a result of the institutional structure of society, have no control over their production period, need to consumer, and are therefore at a disadvantage. All must either suffer or enjoy the time discount, depending upon their ownership or non-ownership of property. Professor Earley noted that this has more technical propriety on the subject than the labor theory of value.

Nevertheless, Böhm-Bawerk's theory possessed an ideological quality. It lent readily the feeling that things were as they must be, "in the cards," and reflect human nature (discounting the future; rosy expectations of future provision and wants). Yet it reflects the technological requirements of roundabout production, and therefore holds for a socialist economy as well. Labor even then would not receive the total product.

J. M. Keynes, in his chapter on "sundry observations on capital," has some remarks on Böhm-Bawerk's theory, especially in criticism. Böhm-Bawerk's theory was never widely accepted or held. Criticism includes: (a) no *numeraire*; (b) present versus future goods dichotomy; and (c) use of production period.

Fetter and Irving Fisher tried to point up an inconsistency within Böhm-Bawerk's arguments for interest, but, Professor Earley stated, there does not seem to be any.

General Contributions of the Austrians and the Other Groups:

(1) Theory of value:

At the time, as with Ricardo, etc., earlier and with some if not many today, the theory of value occupied the central place of economic thought and analysis.

The Classical theory was one of labor cost and had for our purposes two cases:

(a) Constant costs as a function of the rate goods were produced.
(b) Ricardo: increasing costs as a function of diminishing returns in an important sector, agriculture.

With regard to *constant costs*, if such are assumed, Austrian demand theory has *no influence on value*; demand theory is not necessary given the constant cost conditions. However, in as much as without it there is no possible determination of points, it does give the analytical framework for producing 0A and not OB on diagram (1). [Diagram (1) with two downward sloping (demand) curves crossing from above a horizontal (constant cost) line, the points of intersection having corresponding points on the horizontal axis of OA and OB, respectively. Contrasted with diagram (2) with two downward sloping curves crossing a vertical line.]

Böhm-Bawerk and Jevons placed their emphasis on what we now call the marginal rate of substitution for determining value, with the implicit assumption that the quantity of products were given. Here, then, the effect is not on allocation but on price, i.e. on value (diagram 2).

If the factors of production are homogeneous, i.e. perfectly substitutable, then we have a theory of allocation and not of price or value. Thus, we see the contribution made thereby to the theory of allocation.

(2) Theory of distribution:

Here we have two important contributions:

(a) Theory of imputation.
(b) If the supplies of factors are constant, and if through imputation we can derive the demand for factors, and hence determine factor prices, we get a theory of value of the factors of production – on the strategic assumption that the supply of factors is constant. Here we have the marginal productivity approach; their principle of distribution is based on factor pricing – important but not complete.

If we combine the upward sloping Ricardian supply curve with the downward sloping Austrian demand curve, we arrive at what is essentially Alfred Marshall's scissor analysis, although Marshall went further with it and analyzed constant, increasing and decreasing cost situations.

(3) Keen realization of economic processes as a result of their stress on the interdependence of all prices, especially by Walras: demand for any product is a function not only of the utility thereof but also of the price, etc., of other goods and hence also of their supplies.

J. B. Clark

A very representative example of the non-mathematical economists of this group.

Clark built on Austrian foundations but he also felt that their theory was not sufficient and searched for a theory of wages, interest and profit (returns to factors) that would be applicable to a dynamic society. The theory of the Austrians, and that of the Lausanne group, is quite static, even more so than Alfred Marshall's.

Clark was thinking at a time when the structure of industry was undergoing vast and profound changes; when large-scale industry was becoming important; when the trust problem was arising; when there was much social unrest, e.g. labor problems.

Clark was very much of a positivist, in this similar to Walras. He wanted to build up first a theory of statics and then go to that of dynamics; any study of the process of the economy was predicated on the study of the structure of the economy at some point in time. He believed that economists should undertake the method of heroic abstraction.

Clark's model was that of a perfectly competitive economy, with given factors of production, technology and tastes; from this he worked out the laws of distribution as the foundation of basic social-economic statics.

Clark envisioned but two returns, wages and rent, to which the law of variable proportions applied. [Two structurally identical diagrams, each with an inverted U-shaped cost curve intersecting a vertical line during the former's downward range; from the point of intersection a horizontal line is drawn perpendicular to the vertical axis. On (1) the resulting rectangle is labeled "W" and the area above the line within the curve, "R", and the reverse on (2).]

In the first diagram, under competition, labor is paid at its marginal productivity, the total product being divided up into wages and rent. Rent to Clark was not just a land rent, but included as "rents" that which is imputed to any given capital good, e.g. machinery. Interest was then on the capital fund, which in total was equal to the supply of capital, i.e. the rents to capital is interest on the capital fund.

Now, then, as in the second diagram, we can turn the situation around, and instead of applying labor to land, we can apply land to labor, with labor getting the residual, i.e. still the same curve of variable proportions, but with the portrayed share the reverse.

Clark then had a generalized rent theory of factor payments, in substance quite similar to that of quasi-rent of Marshall, though the two concepts played different functional roles.

Lecture

J. B. Clark analyzed first of all a "static system," in which he assumed given technology, supplies of factors of production, population, tastes, identical cost structures, and competition (including knowledge and factor mobility regarding different uses) from which he derived the conditions necessary to equalize factor returns and costs in all lines.

It is to be noted, however, that he did not posit any atomistic structure of firms, nor perfect foresight; more about this in a moment.

From this he derived his theory of distribution – a generalized theory of rent – by a multiple dosing analysis; each factor of production receives its return at the margin, its "specific productivity" according to Clark, the sum of which factor payments would add up to the total product (i.e. no profit), though he did not go too deep into this problem. The marginal productivity principle therefore holds throughout and there are no profits.

Clark elaborated not a theory of competition per se, but a theory of statics, which served as the basis for his dynamic analysis, namely, the processes by which the economy adopted itself to change, and the effects of monopolistic conditions, then becoming very apparent, by comparison with competitive conditions, etc.

Profits come about, according to Bates Clark, as a result of change; and therefore the process of capitalist adaptation was one of adapting to profits resulting from change. This led to greater attention being given to expectations, questions of foresight, and Frank Knight's theory of profit (uncertainty, or the inability to foresee rather than change per se).

With regard to competition and monopoly, Bates Clark held that static competition doesn't require indefinitely large numbers of competitors, that you could have small numbers and get a horizontal demand curve. Of importance, however, was that the number was large enough that attempts to act in concert would be ineffective.

Although he recognized that with the more probably differential cost structures running throughout industry profits would not be erased, he held as a static norm that the lowest cost at any time would be the one to which prices would tend to gravitate as a result of imitation in the adoption of more efficient methods and equipment.

The dynamic aspect concerns the altering of cost through innovations as a continual process. Hence, one obtains the competitive result even without large numbers (or a perfectly horizontal demand curve). This line of reasoning is similar, then, to that of Schumpeter's competition between potential monopolists. And here, too, we have the beginnings of contemporary price analysis – Chamberlin, Schumpeter, the "new competition" – derived from the application of the static state.

The Lausanne School and Schumpeter

Their notable accomplishment, general or complete equilibrium, is marked by the assumption of a static state, namely, constant supply of capital, constant technological and given technical coefficients of production (constant factor combinations), money as a mere nu*meraire*, general knowledge of all variables. From this was derived an equilibrium in which every firm and every factor owner was in equilibrium and the entire economy was in equilibrium, that is, the equilibrium of all segments must be complete if that of the whole is also to be complete.

We may thus note the absence of innovation, no change in the supply of capital, and prices treated as parameters.

This brief summary of the Lausanne School is presented because Schumpeter was very impressed with this epitome of the pure theory of the static variety; indeed, his own theorizing is a combination of it plus Marx and Böhm-Bawerk's theory of imputation.

Lecture

Joseph Alois Schumpeter

Outline:

(1) His vision and his origins;
(2) His static model;
(3) His dynamic model (theory of cycles);
(4) Appraisal of his methodology;
(5) His sociology.

Schumpeter, together with J. M. Keynes, are the eminent theorists of the generation. As to inventiveness, Schumpeter ranks alongside Smith, Ricardo, Marshall and Keynes; and, similar to Marx, his range of interests and work was wide.

Schumpeter was: independent, a perfectionist, a prima donna, the entrepreneurial type in science (bent on devising a new system, one improved over the older ones).

Building upon his wide range of thinking, he attempted to construct a unified structure in which to fit the specialties of his analysis.

(1) The Schumpeterian Vision: Elements

Schumpeter's concept of a "vision" (cf. "Science and Ideology," in *Essays*) is essentially a process of advancing knowledge and science. The first step is a cognitive action, gotten by observing things and seeing a picture of what makes the system what it is – the perception of a set of related phenomena. Although prescientific, it is conditioned to some small extent by one's previous scientific work and training, i.e. a small scientific element. The next step is that of model building, operating on the material preferred by the vision, in a deductive manner. This is later subjected to tests by verification.

Schumpeter's own vision has its own scientific element, from his training. Schumpeter, by 1908 (*Das Wesen*), was well acquainted with the received doctrines and models – at an early age. Most influential were:

(a) The Austrian-Lausanne groups: Böhm-Bawerk was his teacher in Vienna; he knew Wieser; other students there were Marxist (Bauer, Hilferding); and the two great controversies were raging over Marx and with the historical school.
(b) The Marxian system: independent study, the controversy.
(c) J. B. Clark: less significant but important; 1899, *Distribution of Wealth*.

The Austrian but also and more important the Lausannian (especially Walras) technique is the prototype of Schumpeter's model in the technical sense (the static model). This had four features:

(a) The close approximation, in both Walras and the Austrians, to perfect competition regarding the mobility of factors, as well as "knowledge" and atomism.

(b) Equilibrium was general; all quantities and prices are interdependent; rigorous universal equilibrium for all units of decision and processes. For Smith, Ricardo and Stuart Mill, general equilibrium was of supply and demand, in which industries were in equilibrium, not each and every firm. Also Marshall.
(c) Timelessness (instantaneous). However, the slight treatment of the process of getting to equilibrium is contrasted with the vast work Schumpeter did in this respect. For them, though, all processes work simultaneously and are synchronized, with no lags or leads.
(d) All productive factors are in fixed supply for the system as a whole, not as schedules but as given amounts invariable to prices; also constant technology, preferences, and a given institutional order (free contract, perfect competition); also costs were subsumed under opportunity-cost analysis.

In Böhm-Bawerk and Leon Walras, Schumpeter found even more. In Böhm-Bawerk the point was brought home that capital is a derivative factor; that land and labor are the ultimate factors back to which goes all imputation. Capital isn't productive of *value*—future goods are discounted which gives rise thereto. Capital stands apart from other factors and its imputed returns must therefore be explained on different principles than the value of consumption goods.

Schumpeter reacted against Böhm-Bawerk's theory of capital and interest, from which criticism he derived his own theory of interest. Criticisms of Böhm-Bawerk's theory of interest:

(a) In a stationary system, where the supplies of productive factors are given, there is no growth (net investment), no changes in processes, and thus no uncertainty: interest can arise only if there are changes in the circular flow – precluded in a static state. That is, there is no systematic preference for present goods – expect the same thing through time.
(b) Regarding provision and want: no uncertainty and with a constant age distribution and opposite attitudes, they all balance out.
(c) Regarding technical superiority: only where you have adaptation of a more roundabout process of production, i.e. more productive, superior (not necessarily, and rarely, less important, a longer period), is there some advantage for control of present goods and willingness therefore to pay an *agio*: hence, no technical superiority in a stationary state. Technical superiority is incompatible with a circular flow system – all roundaboutness is already carried out. "More roundabout," to Schumpeter, is an innovation, not an increase in the time period.

Interest is only payable permanently out of profits. In the static economy with perfect competition there are no profits, similar to J. B. Clark, and hence neither interest nor profits can exist; hence there is needed an alternative explanation for the phenomenon of interest – which amounts to the necessity for a change of model – the static economic model is not suitable for analyzing the interest problem.

An innovation comes from action initiated by entrepreneurs; hence, Schumpeter analyzes the entrepreneurial credit economy, using J. B. Say's model in which the entrepreneurial function is differentiated from that of supplying capital. Note: In the stationary state, the entrepreneur has no function, as his sole function is tied up entirely with innovation.

Interest is a derivative of the innovating process and is a payment for the present position of capital.

Lecture

Guest Lecture: Professor Bronfenbrenner: Mathematical Economics

"*Precursors*": Among the early economists to indulge in the mathematical technique of theorizing were, in eighteenth-century Italy, several of the mercantilists and also several of the anti-mercantilists. Second, there is Marx, especially in connection with his reproduction schemes in Volume Two of *Capital*. Finally, among the precursors we may include W. S. Jeveons, whose work preceded thot of the others about whom we are about to speak by ten years, but which (due in part to its style) was neglected.

We may note in passing three other "types" which involved mathematical economics: first, those who translated from the literary to the mathematical form the works of others, e.g. Whewell, who translated Ricardo into mathematics; second, those who were concerned with the elaboration of "special cases", such as Edgeworth, who also contributed to economics the "indifference curve"; and third, those who went "hog wild on wild ideas."

A. A. Cournot:

The first major mathematical economist was Cournot who, in 1838, published his *Mathematical Principles of the Theory of Wealth*. Cournot's noteworthiness stems from the following accomplishments:

(a) Introduced for the first time the demand function.
(b) Introduced the concept of elasticity of demand.

(c) Stressed the need to investigate the elasticity and inelasticity of different commodities.
(d) As a positivist economist, he concentrated on price, and not value.
(e) Although he lived in a world of Classical economics, which regarded any imperfection in competition as something which would vanish (except for state-chartered monopolies), he presents the first treatment of imperfect competition as if it were here "to stay".
(f) Work on the incidence of taxation.

Cournot was neglected for some half-century because he was a heretic in the field of international trade, inasmuch as he endeavored to work out a mathematical proof of the superiority of protection – failing, Professor Bronfenbrenner pointed out "as far as he knew", in his failure to differentiate between real and money income.

The Lausanne School: Leon Walras:

The greatest contribution of the Lausanne School is its great contribution subsumed under the name "principle of mutual interdependence," which we may take as an answer to the criticism of Davenport that all economics was circular reasoning.

Where the number of equations is less than the number of unknowns, then there is circular reasoning. But when the number of equations is equal to the number of unknowns, there is mutual interdependence (where the number of equations is greater than the number of unknowns, the case is "over-determinate" though not insolvable). [Two diagrams, each with y on vertical and x on horizontal axis. In the first diagram, have rising curve labeled F(x); in the second, have falling curve labeled F(y) and rising curve labeled F(x).

Leon Walras:

Leon Walras, who in 1874 published his *Elements of Pure Economics*, presented in full-blown formulation the mutual interdependence analysis of the Lausanne School. Indeed, he is the founder of the Lausanne School and, with Menger and Jevons, is the founder of the marginal utility school.

For Walras, value theory is based on utility, marginal utility called by Walras *rarete*, or rarity, and it was assumed by him that it was measurable (in his system of general interdependence it is obvious that individual marginal utility is one of the factors that are quantified). Utility, then, was measurable as well as the only source of value. There were fixed coefficients of production, fixed stocks of the productive factors; all cost elements were thus secondary, something he had in common with the Austrians.

Walras was the precursor of Wicksell on interest and monetary theory. He had the notion of the *encaisse desiree*, or desired cash balance – a liquidity preference notion – and made the determination of the interest rate a matter of money.

He also had the idea of a *numeraire* – one commodity similar in every respect to every other commodity except that it had fixed price – not, therefore, an abstract unit of account – and this was a condition of equilibrium.

Walras was also interested, quite early it is to be noted, in welfare economics: his approach was that of a regime of pure competition maximizing welfare.

He was likewise concerned over the problem of stability: the question about the difficulty of individual products achieving equilibrium when they are complementarily related with other commodities, the instances of interrelationships between commodities. His solution was *tatonnement*, a process of moving from one to the other, a process more significant, in Professor Bronfenbrenner's estimation, than Edgeworth's recontracting scheme.

Finally, Walras was a social reformer in many respects; one example concerns his favoring bimetallism: he favored the state fixing their ratio, which he felt could be set within wide limits.

Vilfredo Pareto:

In Vilfredo Pareto, a better mathematician than the cumbersome Walras, we have three noteworthy elements:

(a) He employs Edgeworth's indifference curve as the basis of his value theory. However, he uses two postulates, which, although he thought avoided the question of measurability, it has been shown by O. Lange to imply that the total is measurable: that individuals can differentiate total utility and marginal utility of a higher sort from a lower sort.
(b) He used variable production coefficients, as against Walras' fixed ones, in his production theory, and in so doing fitted in a marginal productivity theory, in which "Paretian rent" was based on the special case of constant coefficients.
(c) He went in heavily for empirical study, i.e. his "law of income distribution."

Gustav Cassel:

The simplifier of the Lausanne school; although he did a poor job, his work is marked by:

(a) Fixed coefficients of production.
(b) Like Cournot, he started with demand and supply without an explanation thereof, a theory of price and not of value.
(c) Has no numeraire and hence needs equation of exchange for determinacy – a false dichotomy of price and monetary theory.
(d) Interest rate related to length of life.
(e) Regarding business cycles, a relative gold supply theory, with the supply of gold increasing about 3% per year on the average, with a lower percentage than that bringing depression, and vice versa, inflationary boom.
(f) Regarding foreign exchange, purchasing power parity theory.

Finally there is the American, Irving Fisher, who based his work on two Germans, Auspitz and Lieben.

In general, they were nineteenth-century liberals, envisioning: (a) a self-adjusting laissez faire; (b) pure competition; and (c) that this was the best of all possible worlds, although Cournot, as to international trade, and Walras, as to his activities as a social reformer, were of heterodox views in some respects.

With regard to the Lausannian theory of exchange, excluding here all consideration of production:

There is one price fixed, the *numeraire*, and the unknowns include all utilities and n-1 prices.

The system is based upon the assumption of the principle of equalization at the margin of marginal utilities, including that of money income as well as for all goods, for all individuals.

The supply is equal to the demand, and the quantity of total goods is invariant in regard to exchange – merely reshuffling.

The total value of goods possessed by any individual doesn't change in exchange (invariance of values); the benefits derived are in the form of increased utility, not value.

One good exchanged must have its price fixed – mathematically necessary (degrees-of-freedom argument).

Later developments:

It is obvious that all the endeavors of the above mathematical economists were *microeconomic* in character. Hence, foremost among the later developments was the extension of mathematical economic analysis to macroeconomic problems. Other advances and developments include: the extension of analysis to imperfect competition, the tying up of statistics with mathematical conceptualizing in econometrics, the application to problems of planning and programming with regard to both firms and governments, and finally to dynamic problems.

Although Cournot was the first to consider demand and supply as a function of price, Fleeeming-Jenkin first used demand and supply curves.

Lecture

Schumpeter, continued:

Schumpeter, then, was quite critical of Böhm-Bawerk's interest theory, asserting that in a circular flow economy the rate of interest would be zero.

Schumpeter's criticism maintained that even in a stationary-flow economy (no net capital accumulation, no change in population, technique, innovation or tastes), the yield of capital tends toward zero – all value being imputed to land and labor with the entrepreneurial function having been routinized; what with certainty, there could be no net capital yield.

Professor Earley noted that there could be in fact no certainty of the results of any particular transaction even if there were no changes in tastes. And as far as a routinized or habitualized decision-making function, habit is not characteristic of entrepreneurial behavior.

Secondly, Schumpeter noted that man's limited life requires an interest payment for capital (Cassel) as well as uncertainty regarding the length of life.

Thirdly, certainty is a degree of monopoly by the owner of capital, especially when tied up with enterprise.

Finally, the question arises, why would anyone renew depreciated capital in the absence of an interest payment?

Thus, according to Schumpeter, profit and interest both disappear in a stationary economy *because both are a function of innovation.*

Schumpeter stresses that the short-run yield of capital is *not* long-run marginal productivity; and that interest theory is a dynamic analysis in a world of risk and uncertainty; and, of course, he emphasizes the role of banks.

The Three Strands of Schumpeter's Analysis A:

(a) Austrian-Lausanne
(b) J. B. Clark
(c) Marxian

Walras: General equilibrium is established through money-expenditure flows, a balanced and repetitive circular flow; this formed the model for Schumpeter's circular-flow analysis. The essential economic process is a circulation of money expenditure carrying production along with it.

Clark: Clark differentiated between "static" (unchanged economic processes) and "dynamics" (the introduction of change). This line of reasoning suggested a method to analyze a system in movement in comparison to the analysis of a stationary system.

Marx: Marx, Professor Earley noted, "gave Schumpeter the challenge": it was Marx who envisioned the evolutionary processes of economic and social systems, a theory of capitalist development. Furthermore, the economic interpretation of society is an important element in Schumpeter's analysis. However, certain elements in Marx's analysis were unsatisfactory to Schumpeter: they conflicted with his Austrian theory of value and imputation and they didn't appear to explain the facts about the turn of the century (c. 1900): the rate of profit wasn't decreasing and the standard of living was rising; and, finally, he was "unsatisfied" with it ideologically (which language Professor Earley called an understatement). Nevertheless, Marx, in being refuted by Böhm-Bawerk in his static analysis, had not been thoroughly refuted in hiss dynamics, the theory of capitalist evolution.

Professor Earley noted that, in contradiction to Schumpeter's own delineation of the "vision," his own "vision" was a function of his training rather than a precognitive vision.

In characterizing economic analysis as consisting of statics, dynamics and history, Schumpeter injected dynamics and historical or secular structures into economic analysis.

Noting the cumulative and suggestive character of knowledge and theory, Professor Earley stated that Schumpeter's perception was based on his scientific training rather than on some creative cognitive vision. The entrepreneurial theory of science is a projection of Schumpeter's own personality: it came out of his armchair thought system itself, and out of his empirical study and verification, as well as out of some social problems.

Professor Earley noted that inasmuch as Schumpeter stuck to his original model, failing to introduce new theoretical elements, he ran into difficulties that came up from time to time. He contrasted Schumpeter to Alfred Marshall, who was eclectic, pointing to many models, not articulating a particular one.

Lecture

There were, therefore, to repeat in essence, three facets to Schumpeter's "vision":

(a) The scientific component: the theory he learned as a student, the then-dominant theory, his intellectual legacy – more important than his interpretation of "vision" would imply.

(b) The empirical element: the views of a well-informed and bright person aware of history and his contemporary environment.
(c) The sociological component: hinted at in the present discussion but to receive more elaborate treatment later.

The Empirical Element:

(a) The rising standard of living of the late nineteenth century, despite great population growth, caused him to question the Classical propositions, noting that diminishing returns were not operative.
(b) Great economic instability.
(c) New developments in technology, types of product, new products, markets, forms of enterprise: competition between the old and the new through innovation.
(d) As Marx predicted, capitalist evolution accompanied by tremendous increase in the size of the firm such that "A. Smith's" and Ricardo's model was disappearing in significance and application.
(e) Revolution in economic forms, the revolutionizing of technical agriculture in Western Europe, etc., not performed by any *rentier* type (Marx's money-bags) but by new people with little money, new firms arising: by the bourgeoisie and not the *rentiers* or old firms, by new firms and new entrepreneurs, financed by banks. Hence, it was the entrepreneur, the banks and innovation that were the keys to increasing productivity.
(f) The innovators were financed by banks of issue, and not just investment banks.

The older models of Quesnay, Smith, Ricardo, Marx, etc., were too stationary, too highly competitive with regard to atomism, and were not designed to meet change and development.

Schumpeter was attracted by the Marxian model, not by its theory of value or by its sociology, but by its economic interpretation of history, its treatment of the economy as a revolutionary system, and the highlighting of the growth of large firms.

As mentioned earlier, Professor Earley noted Schumpeter's recognition that Marxian theory was built of a faulty theory of value, neglecting the fundamental process of imputation, as well as disagreeing with its sociology. He also noted that its predictions of increasing misery and the reduction if not the elimination of the rate of profit were not borne out. Schumpeter preferred rather to build a new model on the bones of the old.

Schumpeter showed the old models to be defective in several ways:

(a) In explaining certain phenomena: change, economic development.
(b) In explaining the facts of recent history.
(c) In interpreting certain constant phenomena, or basic concepts: value theory and the theories of rent and of wages were, fundamentally, handled properly in Walras' and J. B. Clark's framework; but profit and interest were poorly conceptualized and the notion of capital was objected to: it was either the wages fund, a stock of consumer goods or by extension that plus given types of fixed capital; accumulation was saving through increasing the wages fund or increasing the quantity of fixed capital; the function of credit and its relation to the economic system was poorly seen (a monetary flow seen in Walras by Schumpeter); the concept of management or entrepreneurship had been developed but slightly by Say and Stuart Mill and was still not appropriate for the theory of economic development.

Innovation to Schumpeter was indigenous to the economy and not exogenous, from outside, an economic category and not a scientific one outside the realm of economic analysis, one to be incorporated in the general model as a factor leading to development.

"Development" involved for Schumpeter a fundamental changing of what we call today the production functions, i.e. in the methods, products, and forms of enterprise.

"Growth" involves increases in population and capital in a stationary economy.

"Change" has many causes, such as invention, discoveries of new resources, etc. For J. B. Clark, however, change came from the outside to be adapted to.

The *prime mover* to Schumpeter was the entrepreneur or manager, who is conceived as an innovator as distinct from a risk taker. Earlier analysts saw in the entrepreneur both risk taker and manager, as well as innovator, but, Schumpeter saw, the innovator can hire both of these.

The entrepreneurial function, however, had certain difficulties facing it:

(a) The lack of knowledge outside of mere experience and habit and routine – the need for imagination and superior knowledge.
(b) The psyche of most men makes them reluctant to do anything new, and thinking in new ways is difficult to most.
(c) The resistance of the social environment to deviating conduct and by groups whose cooperation is needed, including consumers in relation to new products, as well as labor.

Leadership, or the function of innovatorship, was a necessary function though not a rank, nor was the innovator necessarily at the top of the social structure; in one sense, a theory of an elite, Professor Earley remarked.

Features of Schumpeter's model: a system of *monetary flows*, from Quesnay and Walras, *organizing the original factors of production*, labor and land, in a *circular flow, through competitive markets* (competition will exist without an atomistic structure because of the competition of entrepreneurs in new products, etc.; in this he was the father of monopolistic competition) and the *entrepreneur as the agent of change*.

From Walras he received the notion of a general stationary equilibrium and the notion of circulation (monetary transactions); and from Bates Clark, competition "to a high degree" but workable competition rather than a larger number of firms.

Process of development: Begins with the entrepreneur who by definition owns no resources but needs the capital with which to develop innovations, namely, money, the way to get resources (factors), which he gets at the bank; capital is defined as "the lever by which the entrepreneur subjects to his control the concrete goods which he needs, nothing but a means of diverting the factors of production to new uses, or of dictating a new direction to production" (*Theory of Economic Development*, p. 116). This is thus an institutional concept in contrast to the old technological concept. Here Schumpeter is similar to Marx, to whom capital was the lever to control labor power to create surplus value; to Schumpeter, to get factors of production to make innovation to raise living standards.

It is to be noted that he assumes an already existing condition of full employment of productive resources; hence, they are not "free"; rather, the innovator goes to the bank which manufactures money and receives the lever to create new money; note that the banks expect interest. This injection of new money – the power to attract factors – upsets total equilibrium: more money, bidding of factors away from present uses, using them in new ways.

The assumption is made by Schumpeter that there is a tendency of the economy to return to a position of universal or complete equilibrium. First, then, among the contours of the process of return is the notion of a cycle, which immediately arises: economic development takes the form of a cycle, i.e. a cycle is a form of economic development and economic development is the cause of cycles. In addition, he noted the irregular movement due to the rarity of the innovative function and that the important ones come in spasms, swarms or clusters.

Lecture

To Schumpeter, the origin of the business cycle was the same as the process of economic development: innovation causes an undulating movement for special reasons:

(a) Resources are fully employed in equilibrium from which the model starts; innovations are disturbing as they call for the transfer of resources to new uses and compete with their use in existing employments.
(b) Entrepreneurship is relatively rare; new firms are a discontinuous phenomenon; the process is not merely adaptive but disturbing.
(c) Innovations occur in swarms; disturbances created by any important innovation, while possibly stimulating others, are on the whole seen as disturbing; occur at upswing.

The consequences of innovation: Inflation due to an increase in the demand for factors, which in full employment causes borrowing to increase the quantity of money so as to result in a price rise. The price rise tends to induce profits to other prices by the introduction of quasi-innovations made possible by the basic innovation. A secondary wave comes near the top of the expansion by new initiating or by expanding existing firms. Technological and financial repercussions wear the process out—loans paid back out of profits: "auto-deflation." Output expands only at and after the peak, before high profits. Cumulates downward; invention taking place; recovery coming after the liquidation of weak firms, over-tightening of market, favorable price-cost relationships.

Had three-cycle schema: Kondratieff, Juglar and Kitchin.

Based on the three assumptions of: (a) full employment; (b) profit equilibrium; and (c) atomistic competition. We may also note two characteristics: (a) tendency toward equilibrium; and (b) that conditions of equilibrium are most conducive to the upswing, i.e. to innovation.

Evaluation:

Schumpeter was criticized on several scores:

(a) That the case for swarms is not a strong one.
(b) That the imitating process is too long to cause shorter cycles.
(c) That innovation in the short run may decrease profits for similar products, etc., and for those who do not innovate.

(d) That equilibrium conditions are so favorable to innovation, that innovation should, it is said in criticism, be higher in periods of high production and at the bottom.

Schumpeter's analysis flows from his basic full employment assumption and from his notion of complete equilibrium as a starting point. It is a defective point of view as regards business fluctuations – over-emphasis on monetary factors and auto-inflation. Neglect of multiplier principle. Very adamant that trouble was not caused by over-saving; didn't go as far as Hayek, thought, that lack of saving cut the boom short. Nor was there under-consumption through over-saving. Merely petering out of the effects of innovations. Professor Earley noted that Hobson, Keynes and Marx did more regarding saving and investment, and Schumpeter could have used some of their analysis, but he didn't say anything about saving that was detrimental.

To Schumpeter, economic waves (cycles) were due to economic development necessarily and because economic development inherently causes them. In a stationary economy there would be no cycles, not by definition but by equilibrium and adaptation. Professor Earley noted what seemed to him to be a misconception of technological (broadly defined) improvements; we can have steady advance without them coming in swarms. Furthermore, economic development and cycles can result from different causes. But, to note in conclusion, for Schumpeter, swarms and fully employment allow the cycle. Still he lent considerable insight, although his contribution is to the theory of economic development and not to that of business cycles.

Lecture

Guest Lecture, by H. M. Robertson, University of Cape Town

Marshall's tradition:

Attacked for certain amount of blindness in his mistreatment of William Stanley Jevons. Jevons' work only recently seen as path breaking. Read his Introduction to *Principles of Political Economy*, important. Final utility approach through demand, using differential calculus. To Marshall, not entirely original; Marshall already teaching similar things: the mathematical approach to small changes; from von Thunen and Gossen. Marshall regarded anti-Ricardo revolution as in part unjust to Ricardo and that it would lead to sterility in economic thinking.

Criticism of Ricardo:

(a) Neglected utility and concentrated on cost (equated to labor cost).
   (i) Ricardo: possession of utility a prerequisite to value. Cost approach, because fitted in with what he wanted to do. Utility theory in chapters on taxation, man's "conventional scale of expenditures,' and different objects of expenditure. Land rent involves a sort of marginal analysis.
(b) Concept of what economics is about.
   (i) Marshall: Smith's approach, problem of economics was that of progress and per capita distribution of wealth of nation; important elements are: (a) production of greatest amount of material wealth; and (b) its distribution.

Approach of Jevons and the Austrians seemed to lead to another problem: all that economics is concerned with is the allocation of scarce resources. Marshall came into economics with ideas and background of reform. Progress through study of economics. Concern over allocation of resources at various margins made study of doubtful usefulness, cramped the scope of economics, a narrow scope.

Jevons and the Austrians saw in theory of value the cornerstone of economic study; Marshall agreed.

Approach study of value solely through demand, based theory of demand on subjective evaluations of utility of goods to individuals making up the market. Total of collective utilities compose a translation into market price.

Cut out [?] traditional idea that must be a balance between demand and supply, between dollar price and cost, between like utilities and real cost.

Smith: invariable standard: labor command theory, as real cost: toil and trouble of acquiring it. Bold assumption that equal quantities would be equal at different times. Question-begging but an attempt to reckon real cost.

Marginal utility school: all costs are merely costs of displaced alternatives through different allocations. All costs due to fact can't use resources in two uses at same time, function scarcity of factors of production, but it depends on fact that factors of production have alternative uses. Asserted that although factors of production appear to be perfectly elastic as between uses, in last resort they are scarce and therefore final factors of production must have a scarcity value derived from fact that they are limited whereas possible alternative uses are not.

Neglects any analysis of supply or cost. Factors of production available for use because called into being by productive process undertaken with view to employment and profitability.

Marshall's criticism of unrealistic nature of this analysis based on fundamental factor of labor: i.e. children are not a function of a demand for children, children are not an economic good, though did admit connections.

If real costs are involved (toil), saw supply of capital different from supply of labor (intensity and quality of work).

In short run, Jevons correct; factors of production are limited, and have allocation problem. But economics isn't concerned merely with such, but with progress of society.

Marshall's method largely that of Jevons but more developed. Jevons felt he had key to new theory of distribution but only presented a revamping of old categories before his early death. Marshall went further, to marginal rate of substitution.

Movement away from Marshall on basis that this analysis only dealt with partial equilibrium, i.e. for a single good or for a single firm, neglecting competing uses, many competing means of employing resources, that a demand for one good, A, is meaningless: the demand for A is different if the price of good B is very different – the germ of the modern indifference approach (distribution of factors of production among more than one good with scarcity of factors of production).

But Marshall had developed his concept of elasticity carefully limited to small changes in price, insisting that it is only when small changes in price are involved that one can use such methods of analysis.

Economics an organized body of knowledge with real practical utility and for purposes of analysis in a field in which human element looms so large. Will get better and more usable by using rough, approximate tools of analysis rather than by attempting refinements to replace realities of real society by artificial concepts suited for an econometric model.

John Maynard Keynes: practical man of affairs. Convinced Marshallian in late 1920s. See J. A. Hobson's "real surplus." See Marshall before Gold and Silver Committee and industry and trade committee [?]. See *Memorials of Alfred Marshall*. 1880s: saw tornado might be salutary in depression to provide employment.

Keynes: Tongue in cheek when criticized Marshallian tradition because it was confused with treasury doctrine that pump priming was impossible: state spending merely denied private spending. Exaggerated departure from Marshallian tradition to impress disassociation from attitude about doing nothing about it.

Lecture

Schumpeter's Economic Sociology:

Schumpeter, like Marx, went all out to build an economics incorporating sociology, i.e. the evolution of capitalism and its end product.

The inspiration for Schumpeter's sociology and socio-economic dynamics of capitalism came from Marx. Although Böhm-Bawerk et al. had refuted well the Marxian statics and theory of exploitation, he was impressed by the Marxian dynamics as an important branch of economics and yielding insight into how capitalism develops, something neglected by Böhm-Bawerk; in particular, large-scale production, concentration of capital, immiseration, crises.

So, similarly, Schumpeter concludes that capitalist development is uneven, cyclical, and associated with large-scale enterprise; but, contrary to Marx, it is wholly on the meliorative side, with improvement and not exploitation.

Schumpeter's "Imperialism and Social Classes" is an answer to the theory of classes and to Bauer aand Hilferding's theory of imperialism.

He notes the benign social effects of capitalism: the maximization of progress and welfare without basic social (economic) conflicts; the class structure is not one of capital and labor but such description is more apt in terms of small and large business units – horizontal structuring.

Capitalism by its very efficiency creates education and leisure as well as gives rise to a much greater rationality. But in so doing, it leads to the decadence of the entrepreneur and of the bourgeoisie. Innovation becomes institutionalized in large concerns, and intellectuals and politicians take over during a gradual process resulting in socialism. While this is close in essence to the ideas of Pareto, Professor Earley pointed out, Schumpeter has more stability, more class structure, and more optimism.

On the matter of class structure, Schumpeter's basic social classes are not economic classes, i.e. not based on property and income differences. There is no inherent conflict between any such classes. Indeed, the capitalist process creates a middle class. Rather, for Schumpeter, there is a dichotomy between the leaders and creators, and the rest of the people.

Leadership qualities are basically biological, and in Schumpeter's opinion, also hereditary. However, he also notes the considerable mobility between classes. Furthermore, stability requires a hierarchy, not just an isolated elite at the top, with each level performing different functions. The elite needs also a strong will to power; they will maintain a structure corresponding to their own particular creativity.

With the progress of capitalism, the bourgeoisie at the top comes to lack: (a) a genuinely recognized social function (because of institutionalized innovation and capital provision); (b) they lose their status and prestige, they don't stand out, rather they are submerged in the bureaucracy of modern business; and (c) they lose their power drive, élan and creativity. Therefore they become of little economic and social importance, and the politicians and intellectuals become of greater importance – they win out due to the former's lack of a will to resist and lack of support.

Thus, economic advance undermines the bourgeois basis of life.

Social analysis is not one indivisible whole; rather, the economic force is the most autonomous and most forceful. The economy Schumpeter recognized is the backbone of society and under modern capitalism progress is rapid while the non-economic forces are stable. There thus arises a differential rate of development, but inasmuch as the non-economic are the more stable, they are the inevitably stronger. The opposite of Karl Marx here, Schumpeter is similar in reasoning to Selig Perlman and John R. Commons: the cultural (non-economic) forces are therefore dominant.

On this point, we may further compare Marx and Schumpeter:

(a) Methodological purge: different methodology for each (economic and non-economic) despite relationships; the non-economic do not emanate from the economic for Schumpeter.
(b) The economic interpretation of history is less complete in Schumpeter than in Marx. It is not economic determinism in the strict sense (not to say that it is so in Marx).
(c) The impact of cultural forces is the most important for social evolution. Similar to J. M. Keynes, Schumpeter sees economic problems being solved by the evolution of capitalism.

Notwithstanding Professor Earley's earlier remarks, he noted that there was a good case for the initial vision concept for Schumpeter himself, based on the consistency, etc. among his different books written at different times.

The view of Schumpeter of the leaders and their role in society is akin to his view of the entrepreneur as innovator, as a thing apart, and as the real moving force in economic development. Once the entrepreneur loses his function to perform, capital as a social structure must change to socialism.

Lecture

ALFRED MARSHALL

Instead of building grandiose models, Marshall built an apparatus with which to deal with particular problems. There is no grand idea of how the economy looked much less of to where it was evolving. Marshall built his economics a bit at a time; hence his greatest contribution is methodological, rather than a grand model.

Schumpeter admired Marshall greatly, noting his advances in the machinery of economics.

One of his great contributions is that of time analysis, and his differentiation of the short and the long run. While this may have been stimulated by the Jevonian analysis, it may also have been due to his consciousness of pluralism in the problems of economic analysis.

Hence in Marshall we have no one model, rather a tentative handling of problems; a pluralism.

Nevertheless, Marshall had a characteristic *point of view*:

Sociological: Society was a highly stable organism, with continuity, with only gradual change, with no one group standing out in economic importance (although he tends to give importance to the entrepreneurs, defined somewhat more broadly than does Schumpeter). The economy isn't stable; rather, cycles are accidental though perhaps inevitable (recurrent).

Psychological: The characteristics of man are neatly summed up in the phrase "deep and steady motives." Man has the desire for satisfactions, both high and low. The Benthamite notion of maximizing net subjective income is also present in Marshall's thinking. The strongest force is the economic, the desire for material satisfaction. He also notes the strong resistance to the provision of the factors of production; hence the important role of costs: the marginal disutility of work and waiting and to bear uncertainty. The economic problem then is to overcome this resistance, and not one of mere allocation.

Ideological: He was a Victorian reformer, feeling that the economy tends to melioration, and that it is the function of economic science to aid such movement.

Long-run goals are the basic framework of his analysis. His pluralism in his apparatus is due to the impact of Jevons and the Austrians – has to deal with both short and long periods. He developed new concepts and partial models that are still valuable today, although his long-run emphasis on cost is not considered by most to be important today. On the other hand, his hints and suggestions on technique are the most remembered. Still, his basic framework is ours today.

Note his *Principles*, page 366, for a discussion of his approach, on the subjects of the time element as a limiting factor in analysis, the use of *ceteris paribus*, and the stationary state and its use.

JOHN MAYNARD KEYNES

(1) His broad model and concept of the capitalist economy.
(2) His methodology.
(3) His ideology.

(1) Keynes' Model and Concept of the Capitalist Economy:

Reacting against the view that the economy was fundamentally caused by real forces, he took the realistic view emphasizing the particular institutional structures of capitalism. Here he noted three things:

(a) That it was an entrepreneurial economy in which the entrepreneur, especially in his capacity as an investor, plays a key role, i.e. they are not passive in any sense. Production is geared to a market for profit; all decisions regarding consumption and production are not strictly coordinated. In this, Keynes shed his forbears in Say, Marx (M-C-M′, not C-M-C), and Schumpeter.
(b) That it was a monetary economy, that is to say, money has its own value, it is not just a neutral medium of exchange or numeraire. Money is a bridge between the present and the future in a world of uncertainty. This view yields, among other characteristics, the feature that monetary conditions dominate capital holdings – money is the active element. In this, Keynes had as his forebears Walras, Schumpeter, Veblen and Mitchell, though, of course, he was undoubtedly not influenced by the latter ones.
(c) That the economy is dominated by the state of consumption expenditures, that consumption is the determinant of investment and of business activity. The demand for factors of production is positively correlated with consumption, not negatively as was held earlier such that a reduction in the demand for consumption was held to be conducive to investment (doubtful as to Walras). In Keynes, we have a sharp break (with Marx it was only ultimately so and not proximately). Schumpeter, on the other hand, sees the innovators as creating their own demand as well as new methods and the savings permitting the investment. Here Keynes has as his forebears Sismondi, Malthus, and Hobson, all rank heretics.

As a result, his is a much different model than any in the orthodox tradition.

(2) Keynes' Methodology:

On the matter of the problems for general economic theory to investigate, earlier theory centered around the allocation of resources and the distribution of the resultant products. In the *General Theory*, Keynes is interested in the level of output and employment, full employment in particular. Also interested in this same problem were the mercantilists, Smith, Marx and Schumpeter, even Marshall, as well as the ever-increasing number of cycle theorists.

In comparison with the others, Keynes' theory is one of the general level of output. In this, consumption behavior is given more importance whereas in Classical cycle theory (J. S. Mill, Marshall, Robertson, Pigou and Schumpeter) the theoretical framework was modeled after long-run equilibrium tendencies.

The *Keynesian Revolution* is mainly the abandonment of long-run equilibrium norms as a methodological device; not of the equilibrium method itself, but its application to short-period conditions, which, for Keynes, took the form of the Marshallian short run with capital fixed in both quantity and allocation and with given firm size. It is the theory of employment and the aggregate level of output in the Marshallian short run. Nevertheless, Marshall's influence on partial analysis with emphasis on short-run problems is important but not dominant in understanding Keynes.

Three limitations to Keynes's methodological approach:

(a) No explicit application to price, distribution and allocation problems, which are necessary to get full explanation of the determination of the level of income.
(b) No application to secular problems; he, of course, was not so interested, although he did note possible stagnation.
(c) Little attention given to the actual processes by which equilibrium comes about – very static, assuming a constant propensity to consume and a constant technique. Comparable in character to that of Ricardo, it is a theoretical structure to cover particular problems.

(3) Keynes' Ideology:

Is Keynes revolutionary? Schumpeter, in "Science and Ideology," advances the thesis that Keynes: (a) was ideologically revolutionary; and (b) had an early vision which was articulated into his model.

Schumpeter notes Keynes' attack is on the virtue of thrift, a cardinal bourgeois virtue and a cardinal foundation of capitalism. Over-saving is seen to cause possible collapse or general stagnation, as saving increases and investment opportunities decline.

Professor Earley offered the conclusion that Schumpeter's thesis is a profound (radical) misstatement of Keynes' earlier position, that rather it reflects Schumpeter's notion that all economists behave like he himself did. In the *Economic Consequences of the Peace*, different dangers were seen than in the *General Theory*. There was the Malthusian bogey, that Europe had too high a population on an intricate economic organization, that the reformation of frontiers and the dismemberment of [word indecipherable] and the crippling of Germany would make it impossible to feed the accumulated population and future population growth. Hence it was not overproduction but too high population and consequent poverty that worried Keynes.

Furthermore, he noted that capitalism was made palatable to the masses by the savings of the rich turned into investment and so raising living standards; savings, therefore, were a savior of capitalism, which had a fragile economic and psychological underpinning. This latter was a function of social stability, whether people were careless with their money due to war inflation, a more unequal distribution of income and conspicuous consumption, with inadequate capital for the economy to persist.

Lecture

In his *Economic Consequences of the Peace*, Keynes' views were essentially different from those appearing later in the *General Theory*; in the former, under-saving was emphasized (see pp. 18–19).

In his *Tract on Monetary Reform*, Keynes called attention to three economic classes: (a) the investing class (savers); (b) the business class (makes the active investment, employs labor); and (c) the earning class (the employees). The investment system is the dominant characteristic of advanced capitalisms, with investment done by others than the savers (see page 8, where he notes the dichotomy of management divorced from ownership). Here the problem is changes in money values, i.e. of inflation and deflation, with greater fear of the latter, inhibiting enterprise and employment. Here Keynes advocated nationalized policy making, with central bank policy foremost, including the fixing of bank rates: unemployment versus the disappointment of the *rentier*. Thus, his emphasis is on monetary reform, as the tile indicates, and on policies to solve problems.

In *The End of Laissez Faire* (1926; see pp. 32ff), he notes the incomplete hypothesis of laissez faire and calls for the management of the standard of value (stability), population control (quantitative and qualitative), and coordinating saving and investment.

In his *Treatise on Money*, Keynes examined the causes of changes in the quantity of money, using the class analysis presented in the *Tract*. Here he sees the disequilibrium between saving and investment as the fundamental cause of instability, and grafted on Marshallian ideas of equilibrium, normal profit, and optimum output. Investment greater than saving meant that profits were abnormally high, which led to a *profit inflation*, which implied that the demand for factors of production would rise, thus leading to an *income inflation*, bringing about a changed level of monetary prices. Thus, he sees saving and investment balanced by profit or loss, the new equilibrium level of prices a function of the level of employment; hence we note his moving into the theory of employment.

The interest rate he saw as disruptive, inasmuch as it doesn't react to changes in saving and investment: (a) Changes in saving and investment change profit or loss to correct any existing discrepancy, not changing the interest rate. (b) Bearishness and bullishness in regard to securities (liquidity preference) enter in also.

Once again, monetary management is emphasized, and deflation is hinted as the more important problem.

The *General Theory* evidences differences in his theoretical approach. In both the *Tract* and the *Treatise* Keynes emphasized disequilibria in an unregulated capitalism, a short run analysis. In the *General Theory*, however, he adopts the equilibrium system of the Classicists, stressing the fundamental determinants of employment and income, and not instabilities. He likewise departs from the concept of normal profits (Marshallian long-run analysis). He adopts new fundamental relationships using marginal and equilibrium principles but with different determinants and applied to different problems – a return to conventional analysis but in a different framework. It is also a general work, at a high level of abstraction.

The problem in the *General Theory* is that of the tendency to *over-saving* and of the failure of the rate of investment. This was due, at least in part, to the facts around him: the long depression in Great Britain during the 1920s and 1930s, and the world-wide one in the 1930s. He felt that the economic problems of greater production and efficiency was of less importance than were non-economic problems.

He thus follows Marshall's idea of building up apparatus to handle various problems, not a model: theory is to Keynes an apparatus to help in clear thinking.

Social Philosophy: Keynes felt that capitalist society is unstable but not unsound; that it can be controlled; that notwithstanding its fragile economic and social balance there was no basic class conflict; that men are rational, educatable and reasonable and therefore can determine and solve problems; that reasonable competent economic management could overcome the instability; and that the economic problem was a passing problem and really wasn't very much of a problem. In "The Economic Possibilities of Our Grandchildren" (1930), he noted the over-emphasis on Benthamism and the similar over-emphasis on economic motivation (See *My Early Beliefs*, p. 253, Meridian Edition).